THE LOW BLACK SCHOONER: YACHT

America

1851—1945

A new history of
the yacht *America*
based on the exhibit held at
Mystic Seaport Museum
November 1986 through March 1987
cosponsored by the New York Yacht Club.

Essay written by
JOHN ROUSMANIERE
Yacht Historian

Captions written by
B.A.G. FULLER
Curator, Mystic Seaport Museum

STUART PARNES
Associate Curator for Exhibits
Mystic Seaport Museum

MYSTIC SEAPORT MUSEUM STORES
Mystic, Connecticut 06355

Photo Credits: Mystic Seaport Museum Photography Laboratory, Mary Anne Stets
Design: Marie-Louise Scull
Composition: Mim-G Studios, Inc., West Mystic, Connecticut 06388
Printed in Hong Kong by the South China Printing Company
Copyright ©1986 Mystic Seaport Museum Stores, Inc., Mystic, Connecticut 06355
All rights reserved
ISBN 0-939510-04-9

Contents

1.1 When *America* crossed the finish line at Cowes ahead of the British fleet on 22 August 1851, she sailed into yachting history. Artists on both sides of the Atlantic seized upon her as a symbol of American skill and achievement, even if they weren't too sure what she looked like.

Foreword

Several years ago, Mystic Seaport Museum was lucky enough to acquire the finest rigging drawing of the "low black schooner" *America* that anyone had seen. After study, it appeared to be unpublished and unknown to yachting historians. Even the foremost authority on *America*'s era, William P. Stephens, whose papers are an important part of the Seaport's Archives of American Yachting and Boating, had never seen the plan. Further research led us to the New York Yacht Club, where the librarian showed us yet another lines plan and a sail plan that were also unknown to Stephens.

With these discoveries came the idea for this book and exhibit: publishing and displaying the three drawings together, all the while wondering if they might have decorated the office of George Steers himself in the fall of 1851, as he savored his schooner's triumph and looked forward to further successes.

Three plans—no matter how interesting—do not an exhibit make. A fourth was added to the group when Colin E. Ratsey donated to the Museum the original sail plan drawn in England in 1852. Then a colleague from Sweden told us of another unpublished source of drawings there.

With the cooperation of the Historical Committee of the New York Yacht Club, we were able to transform this group of source materials into a comprehensive exhibit. We combined the Seaport's own collection with the Yacht Club's, to draw together as many illustrations, prints, paintings, and photographs of *America* as possible. To these were added rare images from other museums and private collections, to provide as complete an iconography as possible.

It was, finally, this year's keen interest in America's Cup racing, fueled by the loss to *Australia II*, that provided the occasion to tell the story of the world's most famous yacht, and put into print a complete biography of *America*.

This volume is a team effort: besides the authors, thanks go to

Andrew W. German, editor; Mimmi and Lynn Scull for design and typography; Mary Anne Stets, photography; Robert B. MacKay, Chairman of the New York Yacht Club's Historical Committee; Sohei Hohri, Librarian, New York Yacht Club; and Thomas Aageson, President, Mystic Seaport Museum Stores, whose belief in the exhibit made the book possible.

B.A.G. Fuller
Curator

1 Preparing for the Adventure

America was born of the industrial revolution; without it, there would have been no reason whatsoever for her to have been built, much less to have been sailed across the Atlantic and raced around the Isle of Wight against the fleet of the Royal Yacht Squadron. Like the industrial revolution itself, her story begins in England.

In the spring of 1848, while visiting a farmer friend in Sussex, Prince Albert, consort to Queen Victoria, discovered that his host knew little about modern scientific agricultural equipment and techniques and was consequently losing so much money that he was on the verge of selling the farm. Albert bought some equipment for the farm, which was soon back in the black, and went on to look at other farms. Most of them suffered from the same problem. With the practicality and internationalism that marked his career (in an era that was otherwise dedicated to theories and super-patriotism), he decided to sponsor an international exhibition of farm equipment much like the trade fairs that he remembered from his boyhood in Germany. As he planned the fair, Albert, who was widely considered to be a passionless cipher dominated by his wife, displayed an energy and breadth of vision that first surprised and then converted many of his critics.

Before long, Albert had transformed his original goal into something far more grand — the Great Exhibition of 1851, where science, industry, and art, the three handmaidens of progress, would meet. At the banquet announcing the Exhibition, Prince Albert placed the fair in historical context. "We are living," he said, "at a period of most wonderful transition, which tends rapidly to accomplish that great end, to which, indeed, all history points — the realization of the unity of mankind." To mark this watershed, the Exhibition would provide a picture of humankind's status to date and be "a new starting point from which all nations will be able to direct their further exertions."

Inventors and manufacturers from around the world clamored for space to show off their products in an enormous new glass hall called the Crystal Palace. When the Exhibition opened on 1 May 1851, the crowds of royalty and commoners packing the palace gaped at the collection that included Indian pearls, American farm machinery, Prussian firearms, Swiss lace, English knives, a telegraph, photographic equipment, and a crowd of paintings and statues. A big attraction was the audience itself. Women and men of many races came from all around the world to attend. Queen Victoria frequently joined her husband to inspect the exhibits, and when the ancient Duke of Wellington and Marquis of Anglesey — the conquerers at the Battle of Waterloo in 1815 — tottered arm in arm through the Crystal Palace, all could see how far Britain had progressed from the long-ago days when she lay insecure in the shadow of Napoleon Bonaparte.

On the same day that Queen Victoria opened the Exhibition, 3000 miles to the west the *New York Herald* reported in its "Marine Intelligence" column: "Mr. W.H. Brown, foot of Twelfth Street, has finished his yacht for the World's Fair, and will test on Friday her powers of sailing in a match with Mr. Stevens' yacht *Maria*." This yacht was *America*, and William H. Brown had built her on the speculation that she would beat the fastest yacht around and then be purchased by a syndicate of New York Yacht Club members, who would take her to England for the Great Exhibition.

1.2 The Crystal Palace, London, site of Prince Albert's Great Exhibition of 1851 where science, industry, and art, the three handmaidens of progress, would meet.

2

To understand the builder's confidence, we should understand the builder. Of the many shipyards shouldering each other along the mile of East River shore front running from Thirteenth Street south to South Street, one of the half-dozen most successful was William H. Brown's. To say this was to put him among the elite of the world's shipwrights. Midway through the century, Brown and other builders — including Isaac Webb and Brown & Bell — were thriving partly because of their well-equipped shops and skilled craftsmen, and partly because of the boom in the city's maritime economy. Between 1845 and 1850, there was a doubling of both tonnage of goods imported into the port and tonnage of ships built there. In 1855, according to state census, there were thirty-one shipbuilders in Manhattan and Brooklyn, with 2313 employees and $3,538,000 in finished products. In *The Rise of New York Port*, marine historian Robert G. Albion estimated that in 1855, between the shipyards, riggers, sailmakers, and other marine craftsmen, there were ninety-six companies dependent on ship construction on both sides of the East River.

Compared with their Boston and Down East competitors, the New York yards suffered from two disadvantages: the relatively high cost of labor (in boom times, workers were paid $2.50 a day for working from dawn to sunset), and their distance from forests. Both drove up the price of a New York-built pilot boat or packet, but the builders neutralized this problem and even turned it into an advantage by specializing in strong, well-finished vessels. The East River yards were "the standard for nearly all ports in the commercial world," wrote the influential naval architect John W. Griffiths in 1851.

1.3 In the summer of 1851, the publishers of *Gleason's Pictorial Drawing Room Companion* took pride in America and *America*, printing: "We predict the day is not very remote, when this species of maritime craft, constructed by Yankee energy and talent, shall fully rival those of any other nation in the world, and even, as in other exhibitions of naval architecture, surpass them."

3

1.4   This rare and spectacular tribute to American genius (as presented at the
Great Exhibition of 1851) features the *America* under full sail, surrounded by
other notable achievements of national skill and industry. This lithograph was not
printed in black and white and then hand colored, as Currier's prints were done. It
was printed in color, by a very complicated procedure known as "chromolithography",
and is believed to be the first American print of its kind.

William Brown had started out building canal boats to service the Erie Canal, which, as the primary transportation route to the west, was a major source of New York port's prosperity. By 1850, he had moved on to bigger vessels, including pilot boats, Hudson River steamboats, and ocean-going steam-driven paddlewheelers for the Collins Line. In that year alone he built seven of the fifty-five ships launched in New York. Three were paddlewheelers that he launched within an hour and one-half on a single day, 28 January, before a crowd of spectators estimated at twenty thousand. One of these steamers, the 216-foot *New World*, went down the ways with her steam up, and powered herself away from his wharf within half an hour. An investor as well as shipbuilder, Brown owned shares of the vessels that his yard built. He profited: in 1855, his name appeared on a list of people having fortunes of $100,000 or more.

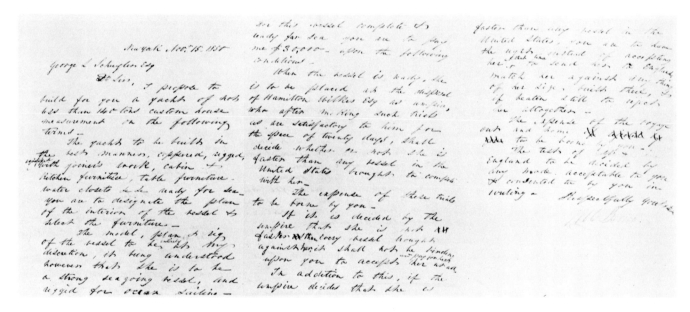

Brown, then, was no fly-by-night operator; neither was he a cautious craftsman. He built good ships, and he liked to gamble on their success. So it is safe to guess that nobody had been surprised when he agreed to build an expensive racing yacht on speculation. In an agreement dated 15 November 1850, Brown proposed to George Schuyler, a prominent New York Yacht Club member who represented a syndicate, that he build a yacht, "The model, plan, and rig of the vessel to be entirely at my discretion, it being understood, however, that she is to be a strong seagoing vessel, and rigged for ocean sailing." The price would be $30,000, but if sailing trials determined that the new boat was not faster "than any vessel in the United States brought to compete with her," Schuyler was under no obligation to accept her. If she beat any American vessel, yet was beaten in England by a boat of her size, Brown was obligated to take her back without payment. In a response on the same day, Schuyler accepted the offer. "The price is high," he wrote, "but in consideration of the liberal and sportsmanlike character of the whole offer, test of speed, etc., we have concluded that such a proposal must not be declined."

1.5 In this letter of 15 November 1850, shipbuilder William Brown agreed to build "a strong seagoing vessel, and rigged for ocean sailing" for George Schuyler and the other members of the N.Y.Y.C.'s first syndicate.

With an agreed upon launching date of 1 April 1851, construction began on the vessel at Brown's shipyard, at the East River at the foot of 12th Street (where Avenue D and 12th Street now intersect). Probably due to a hard winter, work proceeded more slowly than projected, and a codicil was added to the contract calling for launching by 1 May and covering two legal loose ends: Brown was to be responsible for any damage incurred during the trials, and the syndicate was to cover the expenses of taking the yacht to England.

Which party initiated the relationship is not clear. All that is known about the background of the 15 November agreement is that an English merchant had written to a New York friend to suggest that a vessel be sent as a representative of U.S. shipbuilding skill to Prince Albert's Great Exhibition. Apparently, this letter, which has been lost (not even the nineteeth-century yachting historians saw it), was shown around in New York shipping and financial circles. It eventually ended up in the hands of George Schuyler and his friend John Cox Stevens, Commodore of the New York Yacht Club. Whether on their own initiative or pushed by William Brown or an intermediary, they assembled a syndicate composed of themselves and four others.

Two of the six, John Cox and Edwin A. Stevens, were from one of the more remarkable families in U.S. history. Their grandfather was a member of the Continental Congress, and their father, John Stevens, was a Revolutionary War colonel turned entrepreneur and inventor of steam engines and boats. Working from his mansion on the bluffs of Hoboken, New Jersey, overlooking the Hudson River and Manhattan Island, the colonel and his sons developed the first steam ferry to cross the Hudson but, confronted by Robert Fulton's monopoly on Hudson River steamship navigation, moved on to other, highly profitable areas. When one of their boats, *Phoenix*, was sent to service at Philadelphia in 1809, she was the first steamer to go offshore.

1.6 The building of the new schooner at Brown's Shipyard on the East River was news in London months before she was launched — the engraving appeared in the *Illustrated London News* on 15 March 1851.

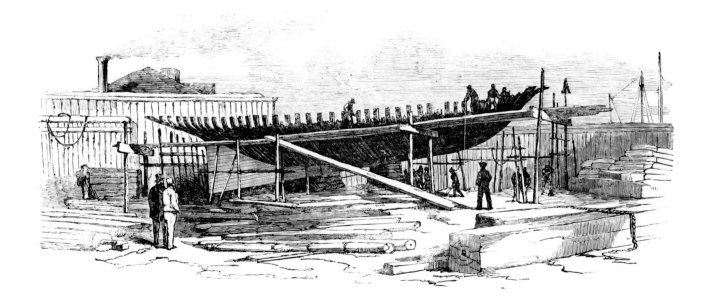

1.7 John Cox Stevens (1785-1857), railroad and steamship promoter, man about town, and sportsman extraordinaire, was a founder of the N.Y.Y.C., its first Commodore, and head of the *America* syndicate.

In 1804, at the age of nineteen, John Cox Stevens steered the first propeller-driven boat. Soon after, he built an early American sailing yacht, *Diver*, in which he raced fishing and ferry boats up and down New York Harbor for bets. As an adult, he was a railroad and steamship line promoter and man about town — "a mighty good fellow and a most hospitable host," Philip Hone, a Mayor of New York, once said of him.

An avid sportsman, Stevens was elected the first commodore of the New York Yacht Club when it was founded aboard his yacht *Gimcrack* in 1844. While not the first American yacht club (clubs in Boston and Detroit preceeded it), the N.Y.Y.C. became the keystone in the arch of American yachting, and especially yacht racing, as the pastime developed into an organized sport in the mid- to late-nineteenth century. Its first clubhouse was located on the Stevens family property at Hoboken, and is now at the Mystic Seaport Museum. To John also goes the credit for designing, and pressuring the Congress to approve, the first U.S. yacht ensign, which allowed pleasure boats to enter ports without paying commercial duties.

His brothers were equally competitive. Edwin, a financier and railroad promoter, was elected the yacht club's third commodore. Robert was more technically competent — he designed the 97-foot sloop *Maria* for his two brothers, drew the lines of several Stevens steamships, and invented the T-shaped railroad track and a bomb that could be shot from a cannon. The brothers collaborated on the designs of their yachts, usually trying them out in model-testing on nearby streams. Their extravagances were legendary. Before a horse race in 1823, the three brothers bet all their cash, their diamond stick pins, and their gold watches on their horse Eclipse in a match with the southern champion Sir Harry. Eclipse won by a nose, and John later became president of the prestigious Jockey Club. It was estimated that they spent a total of $100,000 on experiments and alterations involving *Maria* in the twenty-two years that she was in the family. Edwin spent approximately $1 million on an ironclad gunship, called the Stevens Battery, that was never completed, and at his death he left $650,000 to found the Stevens Institute of Technology on the family property in Hoboken. For many years models of America's Cup defenders were tested in a towing tank at the institute.

The other four syndicate members were not lacking in status or cash. Two were related to the founding father Alexander Hamilton: James Hamilton, a son and a former U.S. Secretary of State; and George L. Schuyler, twice James Hamilton's son-in-law (after his first wife died, he married her sister), a grandson of a Revolutionary War general, an heir to one of the great colonial fortunes, a historian, and a developer of steamship lines. Filling out the group were N.Y.Y.C. Vice-Commodore Hamilton Wilkes, son of the President of the Bank of New York, and

1.8 The first clubhouse of the N.Y.Y.C. was located on the Stevens family property at Elysian Fields in Hoboken, New Jersey. The one-room Gothic Revival cottage was probably designed by New York architect Alexander J. Davis, who also designed J.C. Stevens's New York townhouse — "Stevens Palace." The clubhouse was used by the N.Y.Y.C. until 1868, when the club moved to larger quarters on Staten Island. At the time of this photograph, it was the home of the New Jersey Yacht Club. It is now preserved at Mystic Seaport Museum.

8

John K. Beekman Finlay, a sportsman from upstate New York who knew little about sailing but joined the syndicate out of friendship for the others. Wilkes was asked to referee the trials and oversee the yacht's construction (so assiduous was his attendance at the yard during the cold winter that he became consumptive and died in 1852). Schuyler, the youngest member at thirty-nine, was appointed to represent the syndicate in negotiations with Brown. Both of the 15 November letters are in Schuyler's handwriting. Perhaps this was because William Brown had no option other than to accept the syndicate's terms, but maybe Brown relied on Schuyler to put his own proposal into legal language.

Both sides were incurring sizeable risks — the syndicate a hefty fee (the equivalent of well over a quarter of a million dollars today) if the yacht was fast, and Brown the expense of building her if she proved slow. Yet both sides had reason to have confidence in the finished product, for they were both betting on a man who was almost certainly the main figure in the relationship, though not mentioned in the letters of agreement. This was George Steers, superintendent of the mold loft at Brown's yard, who was in charge of the design of every vessel built there.

Although only thirty-one, George Steers was one of the rising marine architects in New York. Schooled by his immigrant shipwright father, he

1.9   George Steers (1820-1856) was only 31 years old in 1850, but he was already an experienced naval architect. His pilot boats were among the speediest and most seaworthy sailing craft of their day. What's more, he had previously designed several yachts for J.C. Stevens and his colleagues at the N.Y.Y.C.

had built his first boat when he was ten, but his older brother James destroyed it to save George from drowning. At the age of sixteen, he built the quick sloop *Martin Van Buren*, and two years later he constructed a fast rowboat, which he had the wisdom to baptize *John Cox Stevens*. Stevens looked him up and eventually commissioned Steers to build the schooner *Gimcrack*, on board which the New York Yacht Club was formed.

By 1850, Steers was best known for his pilot schooners, designed to carry harbor pilots out into the ocean to meet incoming ships. These vessels had to be fast, as the pilots competed with each other, and they had to be seaworthy, as they were frequently out in appalling weather. Steers designed his first pilot boat in 1840, when he was twenty-one. His best known — *Mary Taylor*, named after a popular singer, and the *Moses H. Grinnell* — came out of Brown's yard in 1849 and 1850, respectively.

There were striking differences between these later boats and the ones that Steers designed before 1848. Not only were these two vessels faster and more seakindly then their competitors, but they had an entirely different look. Until 1848, Steers, like most shipbuilders, had produced boats with a shape that was called "cod's head and mackerel tail," having a bluff bow, the widest beam about one-third of the way back, and a fine underbody running aft to a narrow stern. The idea was that, since the

1.10 This is a George Steers "family portrait" featuring three of his most famous designs—the schooner yacht *America* (1851), the steamship *Adriatic* (1856) of the Collins Line, and the steam frigate U.S.S. *Niagara* (1855), which was used to lay the first transatlantic telegraph cable.

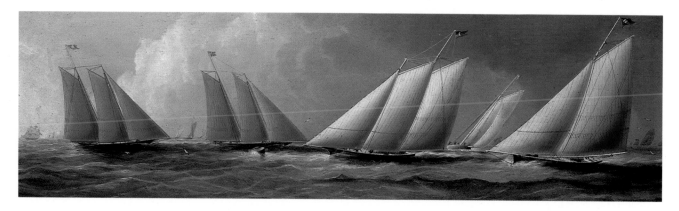

shape of the underbody aft most affected a boat's speed, a long, fine stern would more than compensate for the added resistance of the full bow. As the *Taylor*, the *Grinnell*, and *America* demonstrated, Steers had radically changed his thinking. The maximum beam on these vessels was about one-half way back from the bow, which was fine if not actually hollow, or concave. The after sections remained fine as well, but since they flared out quickly to the relatively wide beam amidships, they presented considerable power when they were heeled (*America*'s stability was further increased by a healthy amount of ballast in her bilge).

In the mid- to late-'forties, Steers was a partner in a shipyard in the Williamsburgh section of Brooklyn, but in 1849 he came across the East River to work for William Brown. Perhaps his own yard had not succeeded, or some legal troubles with his old partner prevented his turning out vessels under his own name. In any case, after two highly successful years with Brown, in the autumn of 1851 he left Brown to form a partnership with his brother James, who was twelve years older. He went on to build the extreme clipper *Sunny South*, the steam frigate *Niagara*, and the notable ocean steamship *Adriatic* before his untimely death at age thirty-six. By that time, everybody who could make a semi-honest claim to having a hand in *America*'s production was proclaiming sole responsibility for her design, and Brown and his descendents were no exceptions.

There are several arguments in Steers's favor, the first of which is the fact that the only yachts that Brown ever built — *America* and the successful *Sylvie*, which went up side by side — were produced in the years when Steers worked for him. Second, given George Steers's close relationship with the Stevenses, it is extremely unlikely that the agreement between the syndicate and Brown would have been signed, much less initiated, had not Steers been Brown's in-house designer and been given major responsibility for the vessel. Quite possibly, Steers or his brother James, who served as a kind of father-protector over his gifted younger sibling, may actually have suggested the project to one or both of the parties. Finally comes the best evidence of all: after he returned from England in 1851, John Cox Stevens wrote the *New York Herald*, "I will take this occasion to repeat — what I have over and over again stated, both in England and this country — that the model and construction of the yacht *America* were due, and due alone, to Mr. George Steers."

1.11 Five of the earliest members of the N.Y.Y.C. race one another around the mark in this painting by J.E. Buttersworth. The scene was painted in oils on a panel for the interior of the schooner yacht *Sybil*, which is shown leading *Ultra*, *Una*, *Cornelia*, and *Spray* in a race about 1850.

11

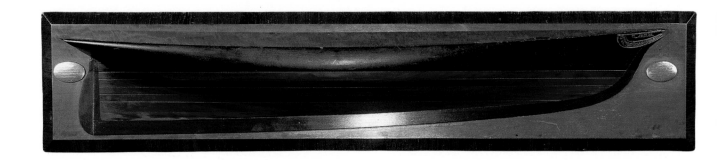

1.12 Like most U.S. marine architects before the 1880s,
George Steers shaped the hull of a new vessel by carving a half model,
from which he took off measurements for mold making.
It is believed that he carved this model of *America* to send to Queen Victoria,
but his premature death in 1856 prevented him from presenting it.

Nevertheless, this does not mean that Steers was working in a vacuum, and that (to turn Isaac Newton's famous disclaimer around) there were no giants on whose shoulders he could stand. *America*'s most notable feature was the combination of sharp, wedge-shaped bow tapering very gradually to her widest point about halfway back from the stem, and another subtle taper back to a broad, rounded transom. Because this concept seemed new, and because *America* was so dramatically successful, it has often been suggested that George Steers either invented the hollow bow out of whole cloth or stole the idea from somebody else. What is the truth?

First of all, George Steers did not invent this shape. The idea has been circulating on both sides of the Atlantic for quite a while, but in very different forms and contexts. In England, in about 1835, a naval architect named John Scott Russell began propounding an idea that he called "the wave line principle." According to his theory, the hull shape that makes the least resistance to the water has the beam about halfway back and a bow with hollow waterlines (the cross-sections taken from the stem to the rudder). Russell argued that every boat should have the same shape, which was precisely determined mathematically: the forebody under water should have the sweeping concave shape of a curve of versed sines, and the afterbody under water should have the bulbous shape of a trochoid curve. It was that simple.

It was also wrong, not in its result but in its argument (the yachting journalist and historian W.P. Stephens compared Russell to "a man who, by long search, discovers a fine house but is unable to locate the entrance"). The theory's mistakes were not determined until the 1880s, well after Russell had laid it out in excruciating detail in three tombstone-sized volumes weighing over 50 pounds each, under the collective titles, *The Modern System of Naval Architecture*, published in 1865. One of his many

1.13 Very little is known about the men who actually built the *America* for William Brown and George Steers. However, at least one, an Azorean carpenter named Franciscas Garcia Da Silva, was presented a silver cup by Commodore Stevens, as a token of the syndicate's gratitude.

examples of the value of his theory was *America*, which he described as "a pure wave-line vessel." Long ignored by his fellow countrymen, whose vehement commitment to the bluff-bowed yacht was encouraged by the prevailing British measurement and racing handicap rules, which made certain features of his ideal shape expensive, Russell proudly took credit for this American product and gloated in the memory of her triumph.

Was Russell correct? Was *America*, in effect, designed by an Englishman? It is inconceivable that George Steers or anybody else interested in ship design in New York in the 'forties was ignorant of the wave line principle. It was the most significant, if not the only mathematical approach to shaping hulls, and for a designer to be unfamiliar with it would have been a sign of technical illiteracy. It was referred to as common knowledge in a popular manual on ship and yacht design published in 1850 (with subsequent editions in 1852 and 1853), John W. Griffiths's *Treatise on Marine and Naval Architecture, or Theory and Practice Blended in Ship Building*.

Yet this is no proof that John Scott Russell fathered *America*. As Griffiths pointed out in his book, the general shape that Russell defended on theoretical grounds had been used in many U.S.-built boats for the simple reason that experience and experiments led to the conclusion that it *worked*. His best example was George Steers himself, whose work Griffiths lauded. The *Mary Taylor* and her successors, Griffiths said, demonstrated not only the value of a fine bow, which decreased resistance, but also the vital importance of moderate, symmetrical proportions. The two men probably were friends, and perhaps Griffiths was speaking for Steers. Steers once said that "for a vessel to sail easily, steadily, and rapidly, the displacement of water must be nearly uniform along her lines." Not surprisingly, the curve of displacement found on some plans of *America* is a perfectly fair arc. On another occasion, using the language of genius (which always finds a way to describe a difficult concept in a simple analogy), Steers described the subtle taper from amidships to bow and stern in one of his designs as "just like the well-formed leg of a woman," which, he went on to say, was his inspiration.

Unfortunately, none of this explains why Steers changed his approach so radically about 1848. Before, he designed cod's head and mackerel tail boats — good ones, but clearly boats with bluff bows and skinny sterns. After, he turned everything around and designed boats with skinny bows and wide sterns. Steers left no explanations before he died in a carriage accident in 1856, but we may guess that although Russell's theory and Griffiths's faith in experimentation may have encouraged him to change his concepts so radically, some other stimulus played a more important role.

Steers was almost certainly influenced by the Baltimore clippers and other fine-ended vessels that led to the great clipper ships of the late 'forties and early 'fifties. Another very likely influence — one that sailing readers might at first find a bit distasteful — was the design of steamboats. Although the sharp bow was a relatively new idea in sailboat design, it was nothing new in steamers. Judging from drawings, the Stevens family's

1809 100-foot sidewheeler *Phoenix* had a long, fine bow, a broad stern, and her widest point near or perhaps even abaft amidships. Likewise, in a collection of plans of ships built by the firm of Isaac Webb and his son William, most of the steamboats built before 1850 had profiles and waterlines very similar to those of the *Mary Taylor* and *America*. And in John Griffiths's *Treatise*, first published in 1850, the example used to demonstrate a system of computing displacement has lines that are like the schooner yacht's lines — the only difference being in the cross-section, which reveals Griffiths's vessel to be a flat-bottom ocean-going steamer. For support for the last proposition, we turn to Howard I. Chapelle, whose books on ship design are standard texts. In *The Search for Speed under Sail*, Chapelle pointed out that well before Russell came up with the wave line theory, sharp-bowed and even hollow-bowed steamers had been built, and some had been successfully converted to sail. "It was therefore logical," Chapelle concluded, "that the very long, sharp bow and the round counter stern of American steamers be copied in the clippers." Would it have been any less logical if they had been an influence on smaller sailing vessels as well — and even in a yacht?

Although there has always been plenty of agreement about *America*'s general shape and proportions, her exact shape and dimensions have been a matter of dispute. Like almost all U.S. marine architects before the 1880s, Steers started with a carved half model from which he took off lines and enlarged them to full scale on the lofting floor, making adjustments where he thought proper. The original half model disappeared; Steers made another as a gift for Queen Victoria, but he died before he could present it. The model is now in the Mariners' Museum collection. Because the yacht excited intense interest among serious sailors, shipbuilders, and naval architects, lines were taken off her hull many times. Mr. Sohei Hohri, the librarian at the New York Yacht Club, has tracked down at least sixteen published sets of lines, and there must be many more. The earliest known lines are a set, presumably taken off the model, that John Griffiths published in the third edition of his *Treatise* in 1852. Another, found in British Admiralty records, was taken off the yacht herself at the Portsmouth Dockyard in 1851 and 1852 and published in Howard Chapelle's *The History of American Sailing Ships*.

Another early set of lines that can be considered authentic was drawn by Nelson Spratt, a New York draftsman who may have worked for or with George Steers. Some historians have suggested that they were taken off the original model, but since they show lines both inside and outside the planking, it is at least as likely that they were taken off the mold loft floor, where Steers scaled the model offsets up to full size. More than some other lines, the Spratt drawings emphasize how *America*'s bow flared out to the deck in order to provide the necessary buoyancy when she heeled or plowed into a head sea, yet allowed sharp waterlines for an easily driven hull in smooth water and light air. In his commentaries on *America*, John Scott Russell always stressed the importance of this flare with some envy, since English tonnage rules penalized it heavily.

1.14 Fully rigged model of yacht *America*.

Even *America*'s dimensions are in dispute. There are plenty of them, and some differ considerably. A contemporary set was published in an extensive article on *America* in the 21 June 1851, issue of the *New York Herald*:

length on deck: 95 feet
length of keel: 80 feet
beam amidships: 23 feet
draft: 11 feet
measured displacement: 180 tons (actually 170 50/95 tons)
bowsprit length: 32 feet (17 feet outboard).

America was constructed of a composite of woods, including 3-inch white oak planking; yellow pine decks, clamps, and deck beams; mahogany coamings; and white oak bulwarks 14 inches high. The frames were made of white oak, locust, cedar, chestnut, and hackmatack. Like those of large steamships and first-class sailing ships, her frames were braced by diagonal iron straps. In her deep bilge she carried 61 tons of ballast, two-thirds of it stored between the timbers around the step of the mainmast. Almost certainly it was iron, as internal lead ballast did not appear in yachts until the 'seventies. Copper-fastened throughout, she

15

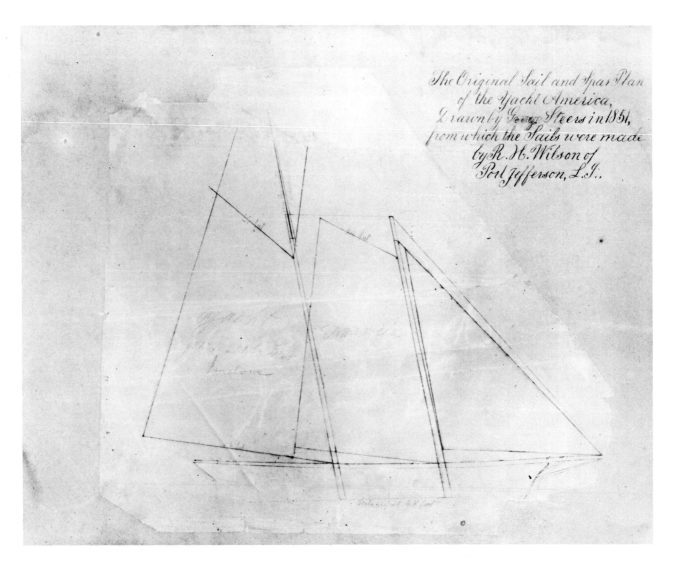

The Original Sail and Spar Plan
of the Yacht America,
Drawn by George Steers in 1851,
from which the Sails were made
by R. H. Wilson of
Port Jefferson, L.I..

1.15 Sail plan of *America,*
a pencil drawing by
George Steers, 1851.

had copper sheathing on the bottom and waterline to prevent fouling.
When she was launched, her topsides were painted lead gray; they were
repainted black after she reached France and before she headed to
England. Her interior was simple but comfortable, with accommodations
for fifteen crew forward, two private cabins, and a large saloon sleeping
six. Aft were the sail bins and another private cabin. On deck, the most
notable aspect of her appearance was the large circular cockpit, 30 feet in
circumference and surrounding a long tiller. Like the pilot boats that inspired her, she had a break in her deck forward of the mainmast, giving
her a slightly raised quarterdeck.

Aloft she carried 5263 square feet of cotton duck sailcloth, which
stretched considerably less than the flax used in British sails; this duck
was woven at a mill called Colt's Factory, in Paterson, New Jersey. The
sails themselves were cut at the loft of Rubin H. Wilson, who made the
sails for most of New York's racing yachts. Steers made a rough sketch of
the sail plan on heavy brown paper, and eighty years later it was still in
the possession of Wilson's son, Robert N. Wilson, an awning maker in
Port Jefferson, New York. In a letter to the Stevens Institute of

Technology in 1932, Wilson said that although Steers drew a gaff topsail to fit over the mainsail, it was not made. The only three sails that *America* carried in New York were a large boomed mainsail, a boomless foresail, and a single boomless jib (the boomed jib shown in most paintings was not installed until after she reached England, and the boom broke about halfway through the race around the Isle of Wight).

One noticeable feature was the extreme rake of her masts, which was typical of pilot boats. This allowed the masts to be stepped fairly far forward, permitting a large mainsail while keeping the vessel in balance. According to a rigging plan drawn by John F. Shearman in October 1851, the rake was 2 3/4 inches per foot of mast. The Shearman plan also provides information about ballasting and construction — for example, the rope headstay was 10 inches in diameter (wire stays did not come into general use until the 1870s).

And so *America* was born of two gambles — one by a prince betting that his country would benefit from an infusion of foreign goods, the other between a shipbuilder and a group of wealthy sportsmen wagering that a brilliant young naval architect could make a winner by marrying some ideas, old and new, to each other. When the yacht hit the water on 3 May 1851, the risk must have seemed enormous.

1.16 The American eagle, whose 9-foot wingspread decorated *America*'s stern in 1851, was removed when the yacht was repaired near London in 1858. Years later, it was found adorning the entrance of the "Eagle" Pub on the Isle of Wight, and obtained by the Royal Yacht Squadron for its clubhouse. It was returned to the N.Y.Y.C. in 1912.

1.17 Although *America* was not to return home for more than a decade,
American artists were quick to paint her portrait following the August victory.
Here, James Bard portrays her in triumphant splendor,
flying a homeward bound pennant.

The 2 Sparrowhawk among the Skylarks

One of the legends about *America* is that she was invincible, yet the trials against the Stevens brothers' centerboard sloop *Maria* showed that William H. Brown had not made good on his promise to produce the quickest vessel in the United States. This should have surprised nobody. Brown had clearly stated in the agreement that among his goals were enough strength and seaworthiness to cross an ocean, and *Maria*, a fragile racing machine that existed solely for competing in protected waters, had neither. Her wide, shallow hull was dwarfed by a 7890-square-foot sail plan (some 2500 feet larger than *America*'s), and her 95-foot main boom was only 2 feet shorter than her deck. She required a fifty-five-man crew, several of whom were needed to wrestle with a massive 12-foot tiller to keep her more or less on course.

On 14, 15, and 16 May, the two boats and another yacht named *Cornelia* sailed against each other in a good variety of conditions in New York Bay and on the ocean off Sandy Hook, New Jersey. *America* had typical new-boat problems: she quickly proved tender, so 8 tons of ballast were taken aboard at the end of the first day; and she retired on the third day with a sprung foremast and broken main gaff. By then a general trend was clear. To quote George Schuyler, in a letter to the *New York Courier & Enquirer* on 17 May, "As far as the trials went, the *Maria* proved herself faster than *America* — but so nearly are they matched that the builders of the *America* feel confident that with new spars of proper dimensions, and by some alterations of sails, etc., that a different result may be anticipated." John Cox Stevens, in his own letters to New York newspapers, stressed that *America* was slower, but added that the schooner was surely the better sea-going vessel. The purpose of all this publicity, with its mixed message, became clear on 24 May, when Schuyler offered William Brown a take it or leave it proposition: the syndicate would accept her at a discount price of $20,000. Brown had no alternative but to accept that offer. No doubt he still made a profit.

On 21 June, *America* headed east. She sailed under a shortened rig, flying sails borrowed from the George Steers-designed pilot boat *Mary Taylor*, which at 66 feet overall was about two-thirds the yacht's size. For running in the ocean, she also carried a yard and squaresail. Her captain was Mystic, Connecticut, native Richard Brown (no relation of William H. Brown), a New York pilot and part-owner of the *Mary Taylor*. Under Brown sailed eight professional sailors. Aboard as guests were George Steers, his older brother James, and James's seventeen-year-old son George.

Judging from the log kept by James Steers, the passage was mostly dreary. Not only did he endure steady rain and a five-day calm, but he constantly nursed his brother and son, who both suffered from endless stomach distress probably brought on by seasickness. To make matters worse, the designer was depressed. "If George was not so homesick," James complained on 6 July, "we would enjoy ourselves much better." Three days later, James broke into the ship's rum supply, ostensibly because his brother had a stomach ache, but more likely to find a way to cheer him up. As gifted a naval architect as George Steers was, he was no sailor.

Yet the boat's performance must have cheered the brothers. Sailing near ships of all kinds in the crowded North Atlantic, *America* faced a test of speed more reasonable than the one she had failed against the radical *Maria*. She passed with high marks. James noted on 25 June: "Everything set, and the way we passed everything we saw was enough to surprise everybody on board." On 27 June: "She is the best sea boat that ever went out of the Hook. The way we have passed everything we have seen must be witnessed to be believed." On 1 July: she goes over waves "like a Portuguese Man-of-War, taking over little or no water on deck." On 8 July: she "passed a large ship with everything set . . . like leaving a dock." The pilot who was picked up off the Isles of Scilly was amazed that *America* could go so fast while making so little fuss through the water.

At 8:30 on the morning of 11 July, *America* hove-to off the French coast after averaging 6.6 knots on a run of twenty days, six hours. In Le Havre, she was hauled out in a French government drydock, scrubbed down, and repainted — black with a gold stripe over her gray topsides, gold on her trailboards and the magnificent eagle on her transom, and white on her bulwarks, booms, gaffs, and topmasts. The racing sails were bent on, and the interior furniture, which had been secured for the passage, put back in place. The simple cooking and eating gear that sufficed for the ocean passage was laid away and replaced with French-made utensils, and many bottles of French wine were brought aboard to join some choice selections that John Cox Stevens had already hidden in secret lockers.

Waiting in France to board *America* were John Cox and Edwin Stevens, who had taken a steamer across. George Schulyer was unable to come due to business commitments in New York; John K. Beekman Finlay, who had no interest in sailing, also remained in the U.S.; and Hamilton Wilkes was fighting bad health in a small village in the French interior. Besides the Stevenses, the only syndicate member to follow the boat to Europe was James Hamilton, who was smarting from a lecture by Horace Greeley, the New York newspaper editor, who warned him in Paris: "The eyes of the world are on you. You will be beaten, and the country will be abused." To Hamilton's protests that it was too late to turn back, Greeley responded, "Well, if you go and are beaten, you had better not return to your country."

2.2 Francis H. Schell, art director of *Frank Leslie's Illustrated Newspaper*, minced no words when he inscribed on the reverse of this painting "Commodore John C. Stephens famous sloop yacht *Maria*, which the *America* was designed to beat and failed in."

On 30 July, *America*, now with the Stevens brothers aboard, set out across the English Channel to make the Royal Yacht Squadron's anchorage off the village of Cowes, on the Isle of Wight. After rounding the east end of the island during the night, she sailed up the Spithead estuary toward Cowes until, at about 6:00 A.M., she was forced by calm and contrary tidal current to anchor in fog off Queen Victoria's and Prince Albert's summer house at Osborne, about 6 miles east of Cowes. As the fog burned off, England had its first look at the vessel whose imminent arrival and vaguely dangerous characteristics had been threateningly rumored for weeks. At noon the tide turned favorable, a light westerly kissed the water, and one of the fastest English racing cutters, *Lavrock*, sailed out from Cowes and approached the anchored visitor. *America* weighed anchor, and the two yachts sailed closed-hauled toward Cowes in company.

In answer to the inevitable question, there are two somewhat contradictory accounts. One is a straightforward news article in the 3 August issue of *Bell's Life in London*, a sporting and social weekly. *Lavrock* "held her own," the anonymous reporter wrote, yet "it would be premature to offer an opinion of the relative merits of either" since *Lavrock* was towing her longboat. In the other account, presented two months later at a banquet held in New York's Astor House to honor the syndicate, John Cox Stevens dramatically turned this skirmish into a major battle. At the commencement of what he called "this eventful trial," *America* followed 200 yards astern of the cutter. On board the schooner "for the first five minutes not a sound was heard, save perhaps, the beating of our anxious hearts or the slight ripple of the water upon our sword-like stem. . . . The men were motionless as statues, with their eager eyes fastened upon the *Lavrock* with a fixedness and intensity that seemed almost unnatural." Finally, "It could not, and did not, last long. We worked quickly and surely to windward of her wake. The crisis was past, and some dozen of deep-drawn sighs proved that the agony was over." In his story, Stevens apologized for *America*'s cruising condition ("We were loaded with extra sails, with beef and pork, and bread enough for an East India voyage . . ."), yet somehow neglected to mention *Lavrock*'s longboat.

2.3 *America*'s performance on her transatlantic voyage and on the open waters of the English Channel proved her to be "the best seas boat that ever went out of the Hook."

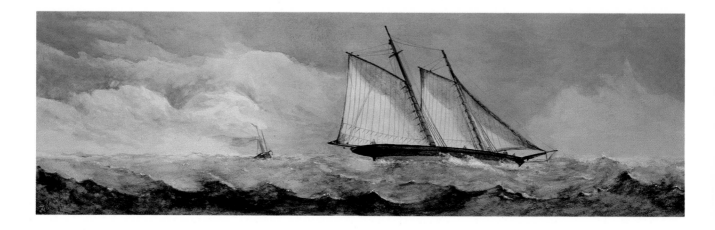

While this breathless narrative was no doubt embellished by the reporters and editors who took it down and published it in the New York newspapers, there is no disputing the fact of Stevens's agonizing, which he described as only "one-hundredth part of the responsibility" and "one-hundredth part of the fear" that he had felt when his horse Eclipse briefly appeared to be losing to Sir Harry in the great intersectional match race of 1823. Beneath the veneer of amiable sportsmanship that gilded his project lay a tough core of patriotic aggression, for his and his club's prestige depended solely on *America*'s performance against English yachts. In short, the yacht's purpose was clearly announced in the nationalistic name that the syndicate had chosen for her.

Coupled with some other news and impressions, this pick-up match had an effect that was exactly contrary to what Stevens desired, which was to encourage English yachtsmen to sail against him in high-stakes matches. Even before she dropped anchor in the roadstead off Cowes, *America* was a feared boat among betting yachtsmen, for *Bell's Life* had already reported that the pilot who guided her into Le Havre thought her "a wonder." When she arrived, her no-nonsense appearance convinced the hosts that there was something to worry about. She was different from their yachts, with her low freeboard, sharp bow, wide beam amidships, and full stern. Her rig — the typical pilot boat sail plan — seemed absurdly simple, with its two steeply raked masts bare of topsails, a boomless foresail, and a single boomless jib. The mainsail was lashed the length of the boom, and it and all her sails were cotton and cut flat. Many English racers, on the other hand, were cutters carrying an enormous mainsail, a big topsail, and two or more jibs (one of them set "flying," or on a boom) on a plumb mast. English mainsails were set loose-footed,

2.4 The British cutters and schooners of the day —like *Mirage, Xarifa, Mosquito, Bianca,* and *Pearl*—featured complex rigs flying huge, loose-footed mainsails and two or more jibs.

23

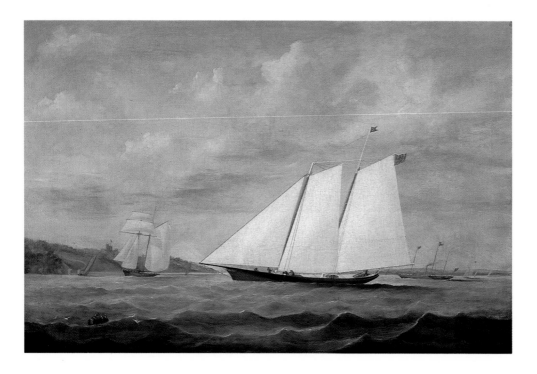

secured only at the tack and clew. Unlike the Yankee's sails, the English sails were made of flax, which stretched so badly in any sort of wind that the crews were kept busy wetting sails — or throwing water on them to shrink them back to a proper shape.

"Piratical" was one term that was often applied to her looks; another was "strictly racing craft," since her accommodations seemed skimpy; a third was "clipper yacht," for she had somewhat the same look about her as the fine-bowed clipper ships that U.S. shipyards were turning out. Otherwise, if *America* looked familiar, it was in only one way: her forward waterlines were hollowed out like those on the handful of yachts designed to the controversial wave-line theory of John Scott Russell. At times, she was even referred to as a wave-line design. Yet there were differences, the most important of which was that George Steers had made her wider, and had placed the widest beam aft of where Russell put it. Under the English "tonnage" or measurement rule, a wide 'midships section incurred a severe penalty. Some numbers tell the story: *America* was rated at 170 tons in New York and 208 tons in England. Since any time allowance would have been based on her English tonnage, it was fortunate for the New York Yacht Club syndicate that the race around the Isle of Wight was sailed without handicap.

Within half an hour after she dropped anchor at Cowes, several officers and senior members of the Royal Yacht Squadron, England's most prestigious yacht club, came aboard to pay their respects and offer hospitality. One of them was the eighty-three-year-old Marquis of Anglesey, an active member of the R.Y.S. since its founding in 1815. He took one look at *America* and declared, "If she is right, then all of us are wrong." On another day, he leaned over her transom to try to spy the propeller that, he was certain, was the key to her success, and would have fallen overboard had not John Cox Stevens grabbed the pegleg acquired after his own leg was shot off at the Battle of Waterloo. When Anglesey saw that she had a steeply raked stem and a relatively vertical sternpost — exactly the opposite of the English underwater profile — he mourned that all his life he had been sailing backwards.

Back in February, the Earl of Wilton, the Squadron's Commodore, had written to invite Stevens and his friends to be the club's guests. While generous, this invitation from the head of England's foremost yacht club to his opposite number said nothing about races. In his response on 26 March, Stevens seemed to ride over this obstacle by assuming that Wilton had simply forgotten about competition. He genially predicted that his yacht would get "a sound thrashing" once she reached England. Stevens's fishing expedition did not come up with a match, and on 2 August, he wrote Wilton to ask for help in arranging a race between *America* and English schooners. The fact that this challenge for a schooners-only race came only two days after the encounter with the cutter *Lavrock* suggests that *America* had not done quite as well in that improvised match as Stevens would later remember in his speech. Stevens set as a condition that the race be held in the English Channel in a breeze stronger than 6 knots. Built as she was for an ocean voyage, *America* carried a relatively small rig even by English standards, and Stevens wanted some wind. (As we shall see, her great triumph was in exactly the conditions that Stevens most feared.)

Six days later, Wilton responded that there was too little time to gather a schooner fleet, and went on to invite Stevens to compete in a race on 13 August, with one class for cutters and another for schooners. The prize would be a cup and £50. These stakes must have seemed insufficiently dramatic for Stevens, who had come over looking for more lucrative prizes, and he responded with a challenge "against any cutter, schooner, or vessel of any other rig of the Royal Yacht Squadron" for stakes "not to exceed 10,000 guineas." When James Steers called this bet "a staggerer," he was understating the matter, for this sum was the equivalent of $54,000.

Having made clear where his priorities lay, Stevens did not enter the 13 August race, preferring rather to await a challenge. But a competitive person needs a stimulant. *America* had been sitting in Cowes for almost two weeks without a race — in fact without even hoisting her sails other than on an easy daysail down Spithead. So Stevens started her out after the fleet when it was about 3 miles ahead, passed the yachts after only one hour, thirty-eight minutes, then quit the course. Showing off like that did not help Stevens's cause.

Among the yachts most often mentioned as a suitable defender of English honor was *Alarm*, Joseph Weld's long-time champion cutter of about *America*'s size. There were predictions of a match between them for $5000, but it never took place. With a great deal of headshaking, people muttered that it was too bad that, since an accidental sinking, *Alarm* was not the boat she once was.

ROYAL YACHT SQUADRON
REGATTA,
1851.

ON MONDAY, AUGUST 18th,
HER MAJESTY'S CUP,

By Large Class Cutters of the R.Y.S. (105 Tons and above.) If three enter before Midnight, August 1st, if not, it will be open to R.Y.S. Cutters from 50 and under 100 Tons, to close at Midnight, Saturday, August 9th.

TUESDAY, AUGUST 19th,
THE R.Y.S. ANNUAL DINNER.

WEDNESDAY, AUGUST 20th,
HIS ROYAL HIGHNESS
PRINCE ALBERT'S CUP,

By Large Class R.Y.S. Schooners (140 Tons and above.) If three enter before Midnight, August 1st, if not, it will be open to the Small Class R.Y.S. Schooners (under 140 Tons,) to close at Midnight, Saturday, August 9th.

THURSDAY, AUGUST 21st,
THE
R.Y.S. ANNUAL BALL.

A Subscription Cup— By Yachts of any R.Y. Clubs not exceeding 30 Tons. Start at Eleven

FRIDAY, AUGUST 22nd,
THE R.Y.S. £100 CUP,

Open to Yachts belonging to the Clubs of all Nations, to close at Midnight, August 16th.
No Time allowed for Tonnage.
Three Vessels must enter and start for each Prize, or no Race.

FIREWORKS
At 9, P.M., August 22nd.

JOHN BATES,
SECRETARY.

W. W. YELF, PRINTER TO THE R.Y.S, NEWPORT, I.W.

2.6   The race "open to yachts belonging to clubs of all nations" was just one of several events planned for the Royal Yacht Squadron's Annual Regatta of 1851.

English yachtsmen's refusal to pick up Stevens's gauntlet had by now become an international *cause célèbre*, just as U.S.-manufactured farm tools had become the talk of Prince Albert's Great Exhibition. "If the Americans do excite a smile, it is by their pretensions," the *London Times* had sniffed in early July, referring to some odd-looking plows and reapers, which were quickly proved in tests to be more efficient than any English equipment. A *Times* correspondent asked why, if John Bull had learned so much about farming from his new-world Brother Jonathan, he could not sail against *America*. The reaction of English yachtsmen, the writer continued, was like "the agitation which the appearance of a sparrow-hawk on the horizon creates among a flock of woodpigeons or skylarks. . . . The effect produced by her appearance off West Cowes among the yachtsmen seems to have been completely paralyzing." In New York, the *Herald* was delighted to run on its front page a snippet from an English paper reporting that English professional sailors were "in great dudgeon at the Yankee being allowed 'to crow over the gentlemen,' and if the match is not made, yachtsmen will not be very popular, at all events, about Cowes, Ryde, and Portsmouth."

The challenge was finally accepted by Robert Stephenson, a railroad engineer who, back in 1830, had been one of the first to see merit in Robert Stevens's T-shaped railroad track and who, in turn, had sold the Stevenses the famous early locomotive "John Bull." Stephenson owned *Titania*, one of the few yachts designed by John Scott Russell. Slightly smaller than *America*, she had shown no great speed and so was given little chance of winning the £100 stakes. The race would be held on 28 August.

Disappointed that the only match that could be arranged was with a friend obviously trying to ease an embarrassing situation, John Cox Stevens finally admitted defeat and entered *America* in a 53-mile R.Y.S. fleet race to be held on Friday, 22 August. Unwelcomed as it was by *America*'s camp, this was the best that they could do unless they wanted to return to New York after only a single match against an admittedly slow competitor.

This event had been on the schedule since 9 May, when the Squadron's members, at a general meeting, voted to hold a race around the Isle of Wight, with no time allowance and with entry "open to yachts belonging to the clubs of all nations." The prize would be a cup with a value of £100. Sailed around the standard long course, this would be the last race held during the Squadon's five-day annual regatta, which was a swirl of social activities — the club's annual dinner was held on Tuesday, its ball on Thursday, and the week would end with fireworks at 9:00 P.M. on Friday — intermixed with three races. On Monday, the Squadron's cutters competed for a trophy presented by Queen Victoria, on Wednesday the club's large schooners raced for a cup given by Prince Albert, and on Friday came the open race.

The prize was an "ordinary trophy" — a keeper prize and not a perpetual trophy on which winners' names are engraved. A typical piece of gaudy, bulbous Victorian silver, it weighed 134 ounces, stood 27 inches high, and measured 36 inches around the bulge and 24 inches around the base. Although referred to as a cup, it is a bottomless ewer. (This was rediscovered in 1983 when some sentimental New York Yacht Club members, in a lugubrious farewell ceremony before the trophy was taken from the club to Newport, Rhode Island, to be presented to the Australian winners, poured champagne into it and saw the wine sluice out onto the club floor.)

This trophy has been called by many names. In 1857, the syndicate referred to it as "the cup won by the *America*" when they presented it to the New York Yacht Club. Until well into the 1880s, it was sometimes called "the *America* Cup," but more often it was known as "The Queen's Cup," a name that reflected a self-serving and inaccurate announcement by John Cox Stevens that Queen Victoria had presented the trophy. The more recent name, "the America's Cup," lacks the italics that specify the connection with the vessel; this has misled many people into believing that the trophy has some sort of official relationship with the United States.

In the official announcement before the race, it was called "the Royal Yacht Squadron £100 Cup." Informally it was known as "the Squadron Cup" or "the Hundred Guinea Cup" (a guinea being slightly more than an English pound). Historians have long interpreted the financial ingredient in the name as a reference to the price charged by its London manufacturer, Robert Garrard. Rather, the amount mentioned was a cash prize that accompanied the trophy. In an article summarizing the 1856 yachting season in the 9 November 1856 issue of *Bell's Life*, William Cooper (who used the pen name "Vanderdecken") wrote, "The great race was, as it always is, that for the Squadron Cup, or rather for a prize

2.7 This portrait of *America* by T.S. Robins clearly shows the additional jib boom, which was added in England and carried briefly, until it broke, during the 22 August race.

28

of 100 guineas, subscribed to by members of the R.Y.S." Since a guinea was 13 shillings, 1 shilling more than a pound, and since a pound was worth $5, the cash prize was the equivalent of $541. In 1851 and most other years, it was awarded on the basis of winner-take-all.

Interestingly, when the R.Y.S. scheduled the race for "yachts belonging to the clubs of all nations," a U.S. yacht club was probably not foremost in its mind. The Squadron's attention was attracted to the three-year-old Imperial Yacht Club of St. Petersburg, in Russia, whose members had been granted special permission by Czar Nicholas I to cruise to England in a fleet of two dozen yachts in order to take in the Great Exhibition. The British Commissioners on Customs had granted special privileges to Russian yachtsmen entering the country (these privileges would be extended to U.S. yachtsmen in the fall of 1851). However, *America* was the only non-British yacht in the 1851 race.

America and her people were treated more than fairly by their hosts. The Yankees had no trouble getting equipment. Somebody talked John Cox Stevens into rigging a flying jib, and, although Captain Brown was opposed to the idea, the boom and a new jib were made. George Steers succeeded in getting them for free by betting on the race, the stakes being their price. In addition, a gaff topsail was made.

At Stevens's request, the Squadron granted an exception to English sailing rules by allowing crews to "boom-out" sails — wing them out with poles when sailing before the wind. Because of the steep rake of *America*'s masts, her sails would not hold themselves out without aid. The spinnaker had yet to be invented, and yachts needed all the projected area they could produce. The best-known print of *America* at the finish of the race, copied by such artists as Fitz-Hugh Lane, shows her with her jib and foresail boomed-out.

2.8 "The *America*, winning the match at Cowes for the Club Cup. Open to Yachts of all Classes and Nations, August 12nd, 1851. From the original sketch taken on the spot by Oswald W. Brierly."

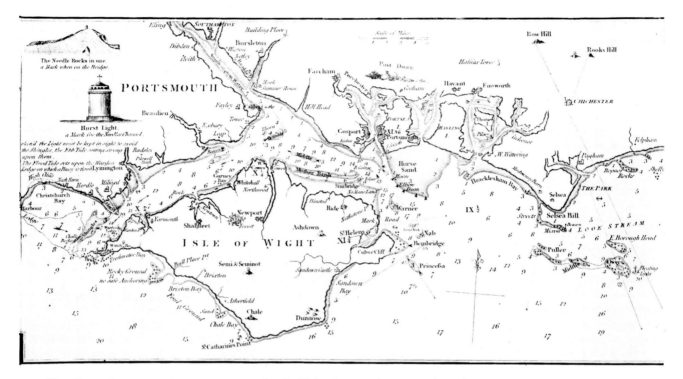

To allow the visitors to compete, the R.Y.S. dropped its usual prohibition of boats owned by syndicates, which were considered too businesslike for true sport. (Earlier, the neighboring Royal Victoria Yacht Club had barred *America* from a race by refusing to waive a similar rule.)

An English pilot named Robert Underwood was located by the U.S. Consul in Southampton and hired by the syndicate to help navigate around the challenging course, which a yachting writer described as "notoriously one of the most unfair to strangers that can be selected," with its fast-moving currents and many shoals. After the visitors were warned not to trust any English pilot, even one hired by their own embassy, a Royal Navy admiral in the mainland port of Portsmouth wrote Stevens that he would immediately provide a reliable replacement if Underwood did not work out (Underwood quickly won the trust of Stevens and Dick Brown). The same admiral later provided quick and free repairs after *America* ran aground and damaged her keel before the match with *Titania*. As final proof of English hospitality, an English schooner named *Surprise* loaned Dick Brown some sailors to fill out his crew.

There were twenty-one men aboard *America* for the race, with thirteen professionals, the pilot, a representative of the Royal Yacht Squadron, the two Stevens brothers, James Hamilton, and three guests. The U.S. Minister, or ambassador, Abbott Lawrence planned to sail, but arrived in Cowes too late. The only Steers on board for the race was James's fifteen-year-old son Henry.

George and James Steers had left Cowes for New York a couple of days before the race. Tensions had arisen between them and John Cox Stevens, who treated them as hired hands and who especially annoyed James Steers by making a personal inventory of his wine and rum supply, into which Steers frequently and surreptitiously dipped. "He is a damned

2.9 The 53-mile course clockwise around the Isle of Wight was referred to at the time as "notoriously one of the most unfair to strangers that can be selected."

old hog, bristles and all," complained James in his diary. Still, if personal bitterness and distrust were the only reasons for the Steerses' departure, then it is hard to understand why James allowed his son to remain behind or why Stevens was as surprised as he was when they told him that they were leaving. There are other likely explanations: they had been away from home and work for two months; George was prone to homesickness; and there was important business in New York. On the wings of *America*'s reputation, George had decided to leave William Brown's yard and go into business with his brother. While they could contribute little in the Squadron Cup race, they could gain substantially by being at home when the news of her triumph — and that is what everybody expected for 22 August — reached the maritime community in New York by steamship.

2.10 George Steers, creator of the *America*, left England a few days before the R.Y.S. race in August. Perhaps he wanted to be back in New York in time to profit from any news of victory. He was obviously happy to endorse Brown & Severin's new print of 'his' yacht: "Gentlemen, I consider your print of the 'Yacht *America*' correct in every detail and a very beautiful Picture — Truly Yours, George Steers, Builder."

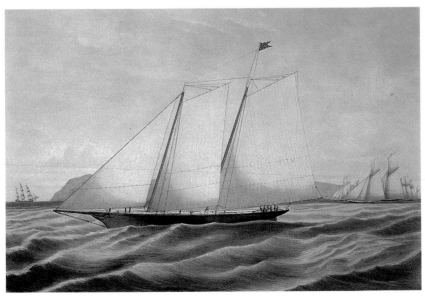

2.11 "The New York Schooner Yacht *America* Commodore J.C. Stevens in the Grand Yacht Race of All Nations Around the Isle of Wight, The 22nd of August 1851."

Cutter *Freak*　　　　　　　　　　　　　　　　　　　**Cutter *Bachante***

Schooner *America*

Although only six British yachts were entered by the deadline of 16 August, another eleven owners were cajoled or shamed into signing up. Three entries, including *Titania*, did not appear, so a total of fifteen yachts—seven schooners and eight cutters — anchored in their appointed places on the starting line before thousands of observers who crowded along the Cowes shore and the rails of the one hundred-odd spectator yachts and passenger steamers. Actually, there were two starting lines, one for cutters and another, 300 yards to the west, for schooners. This double line stretched out from Cowes Castle, the sixteenth-century fortress, built on the west shore of the mouth of the Medina River, where the Marquis of Anglesey lived and where, after his death, the R.Y.S. would establish its headquarters in 1857. Stevens had warned Wilton that *America* probably would not start "should there be little or no wind." While those conditions predominated after breakfast, a light rain and overcast sky hinted at something more than the soft westerly wafting down the Solent, the estuary stretching from Cowes to the chalk rocks called the Needles, at the west end of the diamond-shaped island.

2.12 James E. Buttersworth travelled to England in 1851 to "cover" the Royal Yacht Squadron regatta. He did a series of drawings there, 17 of which have been preserved by the Dauntless Club of Essex, Connecticut. In pencil, chalk, and gouache, Buttersworth has captured the *America* and her British counterparts with remarkable vitality and detail. The immediacy of these views today, after more than 130 years, is a tribute to the superb draftsmanship of the artist.

Cutter *Freak*

Schooner *Beatrice*

At the preparatory gun at 9:55, foresails were raised; at the starting gun five minutes later, mainsails were raised and anchors weighed. *America* was the last to get off because the westerly wind and strong east-bound current conspired to make her overrun her anchor; to get the rode clear, her crew had to douse the sails. Once straightened out with the anchor on deck, she set out after her fourteen competitors, now running before the wind in a grand parade through the massive fleet of spectator craft. *America* brought a new breeze up on the fleet, dodged around a larger rival who tried to block her, and after half an hour succeeded in working up into second place. She was then victimized in the same way; other boats brought the wind up until, at Noman's Land buoy, after nine miles and one hour of sailing, she was fifth. Yet the nine boats in the lead pack were separated by only three minutes, fifteen seconds.

2.13 A total of 15 yachts, seven schooners and eight cutters, started the race of 22 August:

Volante	48 tons
Arrow	84 tons
Alarm	193 tons
Mona	82 tons
Bacchante	80 tons
Freak	60 tons
Eclipse	50 tons
Aurora	47 tons
Beatrix	161 tons
Wyvern	205 tons
Ione	75 tons
Constance	218 tons
Gipsey Queen	160 tons
Brilliant	392 tons
America	170 tons

2.14 "Pride, The Schooner Yacht *Wyvern* R.Y.S. 205 Tons."

The leader at Noman's and for awhile thereafter was the narrow, fine-lined cutter *Volante*, the second smallest entry. Her length on deck was only 69 feet 6 inches, but on a low-speed run before the wind in light air, length is nowhere near as important as a low-resistance shape. *America* also enjoyed these conditions. When she sailed upright, her bottom's high deadrise angle lifted her wide after sections and topsides clear of the water so that she, too, presented an easily-driven shape to the water. More than a century later, in 1967, a model of *America* was tested in the Davidson Laboratory towing tank, at the Stevens Institute of Technology. When Pierre DeSaix of the laboratory compared her with several modern yachts of comparable waterline lengths, she was found to have the least resistance in light-air conditions.

If she could hold her own on a run, she was untouchable on a reach, when she heeled and her greater length and powerful quarters went to work. At Noman's buoy the boats came up about 20 degrees, and the wind increased until there were a few white caps (which in those shallow waters might indicate 10 to 12 knots). The schooner's crew had already lowered the jib, and now they doused her small gaff-topsail to leave her under mainsail, foresail, and a forestaysail. Off she flew, and a spectator steamer was barely able to keep up. A *Times* reporter who was on that steamer later wrote, "While the cutters were thrashing through the water, sending the spray over their bows, and the schooners were wet up to the foot of the foremast, the *America* was as dry as bone."

America rapidly reached away from *Volante* and the other boats, and had a big lead at 11:47, when, with her jib now set and her forestaysail handed, she tacked for the first time on the beat around the back side of the island. The usual course on this race was around the Nab Light

2.15 The cutter *Volante*, second smallest boat in the race, led the field at the first mark.

Vessel, which was anchored 5 miles off the shore to guide shipping clear of shoals. However, the race instructions that were given to Stevens said nothing about rounding the lightship, and under pilot Underwood's guidance *America* hugged the black and white buoys marking the outskirts of the shallow water about 1 1/2 miles to the west of the vessel. The four yachts that did round the ship, either out of habit or because they had been given different instructions, lost that 1 1/2 miles, or about ten minutes. (After the race, one of these yachts protested *America*, but the protest was disallowed.)

America worked her way up the shore line, tacking sixteen times in four hours — sometimes as frequently as every ten minutes — in order to avoid the worst of the foul current. The *Times* reporter noted that while her sails were remarkably flat and her motion was particularly easy, her tacks were inconsistent, taking as long as a minute or as short as thirty seconds. Perhaps Dick Brown was experimenting with different styles of tacking.

She pulled away dramatically until the wind lightened and the smaller boats began to gain. Then the topsail was set, and she stretched her lead again. But at 12:58, while trimming the jib sheet, her crew ground too hard on the windlass and, to Dick Brown's loudly expressed joy, broke the jib boom. Brown brought her head to wind and luffed for fifteen minutes while the crew made repairs. What was done is unclear; most likely, the crew handed the damaged jib and set the U.S.-made jib.

The slow beat to windward ended after 15 miles at about 3:45, when *America* bore off around St. Catherine Point for a 12-mile reach to the Needles. When she rounded at 5:50, the *Times* reporter estimated that

2.16 *America* slowly beat her way 15 miles to windward up the shoreline from Nab Light to St. Catherine Point, leaving her closest rival 7 1/2 miles back.

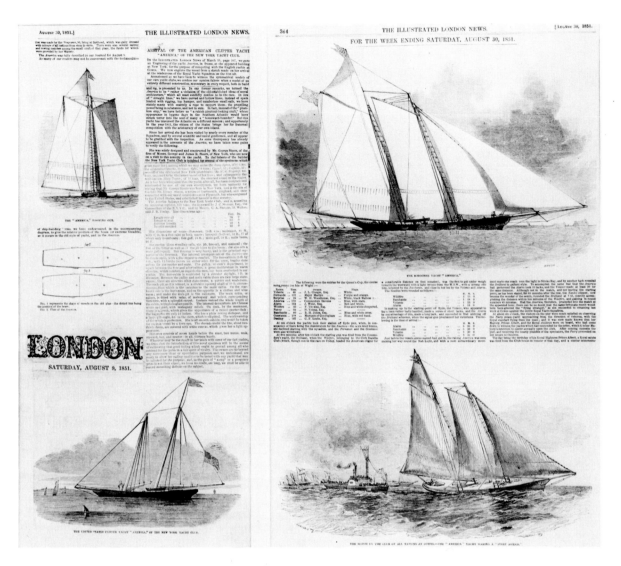

the second-place *Aurora* — the smallest entry in the race — was 7 1/2 miles back, and the third-place *Freak* was 1 mile behind her. By this time, several crews had become so discouraged that they withdrew. Three boats had to drop out for other reasons: one ran aground; another, Joseph Weld's *Alarm*, accompanied the first boat home after she was pulled off; and a third, *Volante*, which had been fighting *Aurora* and *Freak* for second place, lost her jib boom when she was rammed by *Freak*.

They had little chance to catch *America*. She was an amazingly good performer when going to windward in winds lighter than about 10 knots — which was what prevailed during most of the beat in the Squadron Cup race. The Davidson Laboratory tank tests showed that in light air she made 3.8 degrees of leeway, only slightly greater than the 3.2 degrees made by a 1967-vintage Twelve Meter.

A few minutes after 6:00, as she ran slowly toward the finish in light air, *America* passed the royal yacht *Victoria and Albert*, and John Cox Stevens and his crew had the pleasure of dipping their flags and doffing their hats to Queen Victoria, Prince Albert, and the Prince of Wales. The next day, the royal couple paid an admiring, and much admired, visit to

2.17 From the *Illustrated London News* 6 August and 30 August 1851.

2.18 *America* held her own on a run, but she was untouchable on a reach.

2.19 As *America* drifted past the royal yacht *Victoria & Albert*, her crew dipped their colors, with pleasure and pride, as the first to finish.

the visiting schooner and her crew. Queen Victoria also plays a part in the best known of the myths concerning the *America* adventure, for it is said that when she asked which yacht was second, a seaman aboard the royal yacht responded somberly, "Madam, there is no second." This tale is a version of an account in the long *Times* narrative, in which people waiting in yachts off Cowes ask, "Is the *America* first?" The answer comes: "Yes." Then, "What's second?" Comes the reply, "Nothing."

Actually, there probably *was* a second. Some time after guns went off at 8:37 to announce *America*'s slow finish — she took almost three hours to cover the last 12 miles — another yacht crossed the line off the West Cowes Castle. Since she appeared in the dark, amidst the excitement over the schooner's triumph, and near or at the beginning of the scheduled fireworks display, her time was not taken with care. The interval was given variously as eight, twenty-one, and twenty-four minutes. Most observers identified her as *Aurora*, although one newspaper claimed she was a non-racing boat coming back from a daysail.

If she was *Aurora*, and if the estimate that she had been 7 1/2 miles back when *America* rounded the Needles was correct, she had gained some 6 miles in only three hours. This is not unlikely. She could easily have made up half the distance while reaching toward the Needles, when she would have been sailing as much as 3 knots faster than the Yankee schooner, which was drifting along on the slow run home. After making the turn, she could have brought up some puffs of wind, just as *America* had at the start nine or more hours earlier. If the race had been sailed with handicaps, as the smallest entrant she would have handily beaten *America* on time allowance. Somehow, however, this "what if" scenario — with its suggestion that *America* was conquerable — seems as irrelevant today as it did on that extraordinary August night long ago.

3 Honored in Glory

America was entered to sail against the Squadron fleet once again in the Queen's Cup race, on 25 August, but as the "6-knot breeze" that John Cox Stevens set as his lower limit was not blowing, she did not start. However, when the wind increased about an hour after the gun, she weighed anchor and eventually caught the entire fleet. The next day, she lost 30 feet of deadwood on her false keel when she ran aground on a shoal in the Solent. After a day in the Portsmouth Navy drydock — where the English crowded around to get their first, startled look at her underbody — she returned to Cowes to race *Titania*, on the twenty-eighth.

As one of the first yachts built with an iron hull and wave-line shape (which *America*'s success had instantly raised to respectability), *Titania* was favored to win by some English yachtsmen. They prayed for strong wind, probably on the assumption that a boat as fast in light air as *America* could hardly be competitive in a blow. Their hopes were first rewarded by a gale from the north and then shattered by *America*'s performance. At the end of the 20-mile run under squaresails from the Nab Light Vessel to a vessel stationed in the Channel, *America* led by four minutes, twelve seconds — a small margin considering that *Titania*, measured at 100 tons, was much the smaller boat. Somewhere on that leg the jaws on *America*'s main gaff carried away, yet on the hard 20-mile beat back to the Nab, she sprinted off to win by fifty-two minutes, completely outperforming her tender, wildly pitching rival. *America*, wrote a *Bell's Life* reporter, was "perfectly upright and slipping gracefully through it. On the contrary, the *Titania* 'bowed,' or rather dipped her nose into it. . . . The *Titania* wetted her sails, but all efforts even to recover her former position appeared useless."

The public reacted to the visitor's all-around speed with awe. "That boat of yours is a wonderful creature," an Englishman confided to an American. "She beats us going large or to windward, and when the breeze died the other day [in the Squadron Cup race], she actually *out-drifted* us." For the next few months, English newspapers and sporting journals ran long, technical essays about the whys and wherefores of her success.

Some writers argued that the key was her flat cotton sails. A Royal Navy captain, who had observed her from off her weather bow, declared that "it became a question among us whether that vessel had any mainsail set or not." Still, most authorities gave major credit to the shape of the hull, although they could not agree on its parentage. Some claimed she was an English creation, either because George Steers's father was a Devonshire man or because she was a wave-line vessel. John Scott Russell himself exploited the coincidence between his ideas and *America*'s sharp bow with the declaration that "America reaped a crop of glory; England reaped a crop of wisdom. It was worth the loss of a race to gain so much." A few self-styled experts saw something more exotic in her lines. After an old India hand argued that she looked amazingly like fishing boats he had seen in Bombay, somebody else answered that if any Asian vessels had the same characteristics, they could be found in Singapore. All of these claims, the possible as well as the impossible, were quickly countered by writers who had seen or been aboard a New York pilot schooner. Regardless of the origin of the hollow bow, English shipyards were soon hard at work "*America*izing" yachts. One vessel's bow was lengthened by 12 feet (this trend was not isolated to England, for back in New York *Maria*'s length would be increased from 97 to approximately 120 feet.)

Underlying these disputes was a conviction that *America* was bad news for the Empire. "We have had 'Britannia Rules the Waves' over our door for a long time," mourned one Englishman, "but I think we must now take down the sign." *Punch* parodied this attitude in a "Serenade for John Bull":

> Lullaby, Johnny, upon the tree-top;
> When thy ships fail, the Navy will drop;
> When thy fleets yield, thy glory will fall,
> And down comes Johnny, and Commerce and all!

In the United States, these omens were repeated with greater cheer. Upon hearing the news of the Squadron Cup race while addressing the Massachusetts House of Representatives, Daniel Webster burst out, "Like Jupiter among the gods, America is first and there is no second!" A more realistic appraisal was offered by George Templeton Strong, a New York lawyer, who complained in his diary, "Newspapers crowing over the victory of Stevens's yacht, which has beaten everything in the British seas. Quite creditable to Yankee shipbuilding, certainly, but not worth the intolerable, vainglorious vaporings that make every newspaper I take up now ridiculous. One would think yachtbuilding were the end of man's existence on earth."

After the winners were toasted at a formal dinner at the Royal Yacht Squadron, they sat back to figure out what to do next. Before the Squadron Cup race, a R.Y.S. member named W.H. Woodhouse had

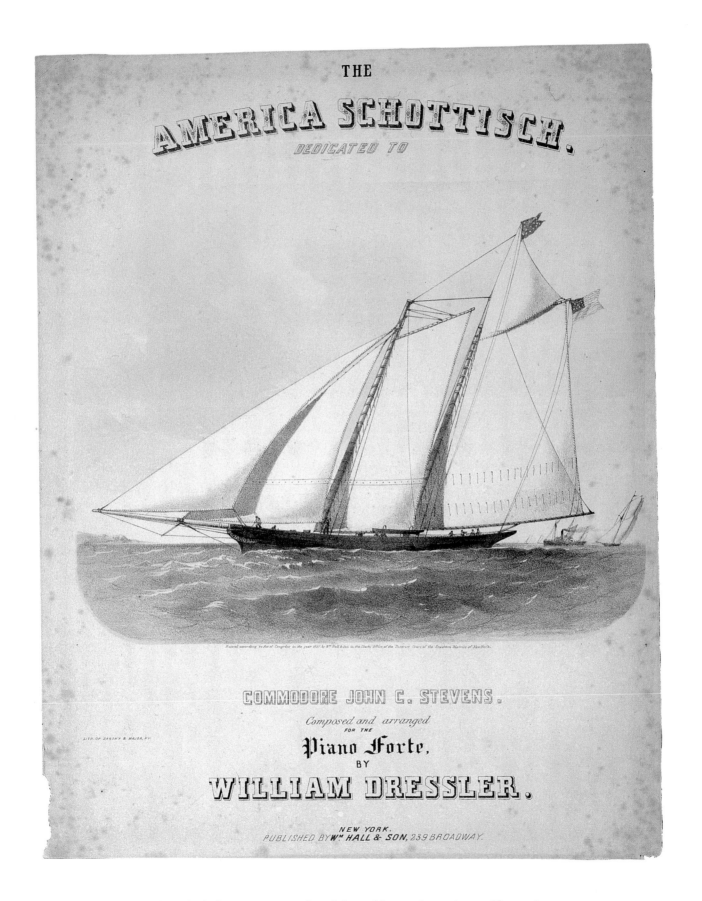

3.1 *America*'s fame was not only celebrated by marine painters. Her praises were also set to music, as in this work by William Dressler of New York.

challenged Stevens to a 250-mile race around the Eddystone Light and return in October, with stakes of £200. Stevens helpfully suggested that Woodhouse's *Gondola* first sail along during the *Titania* match. If Woodhouse then thought his yacht competitive, *America* would race at five to one odds, with Stevens putting up £1000. Nothing more was heard from Woodhouse, who apparently did not require a trial sail to conclude that his 76-ton cutter was no match for the schooner. Another challenge that did not come off has the stuff of legend about it. In a speech given many years later, Henry Steers (who was a boy of fifteen in 1851) recalled that some Cowes shipbuilders offered to build a challenger in ninety days and sail for stakes of £500. Stevens, he continued, made a counteroffer of £25,000. That match, too, never occurred.

No doubt disappointed in their receipts — the total of the announced stakes of the two races *America* had sailed was only five percent of her purchase price — the syndicate took advantage of the rising market in the schooner's reputation and let it be known that they would sell the schooner at the right price. Although some said that Prince Albert was interested, a good offer had not appeared by 29 August, when in a letter to his daughter Mary, in Hoboken, Edwin Stevens reported that they intended to sail to London in order to visit the Great Exhibition. Those plans were short-lived. On the next day, with a Captain Lyons serving as a middle-man, the syndicate agreed to sell *America* for £5000, or $25,000, to a 39-year-old army captain called John de Blaquiere. Add to that sum the $1000 known to have been won in the two races (undoubtedly there were private bets), and the gross receipts were $26,000. Subtract costs—$20,000 purchase price and an estimated $3750 for the voyage and racing expenses — and the syndicate netted a profit of $2250. Under a strict accounting, this profit would have been wiped out by the value of two dozen bottles of fifty-year-old wine that, after the yacht's launching, had been placed in a secret locker and then forgotten until Stevens returned to New York. He wrote to de Blaquiere to tell him how to find the treasure trove, which he made a gift.

Collecting their price and promising to return soon in another yacht, the Stevenses and Hamilton left England to go home to a grand reception. The only flaw was temporary forgetfulness on the part of the Commodore as to the contribution of George Steers; this was soon settled by Stevens's clear insistance that Steers was the designer in fact, if not of record.

While Stevens did not return to England, he did borrow the Royal Yacht Squadron's idea of "a race for the clubs of all nations." On 4 February 1853, the New York Yacht Club (of which he remained commodore until 1855) voted a $500 prize for the winner of a race scheduled for 13 October, "open to yachts of all nations, provided one foreign yacht be entered for the race." The *New York Herald* grandiosely described it as a "challenge to the world and the rest of mankind," and suggested that the English and Russian press pay special attention. The race was not held, but the idea was repeated in 1857 when, a few months after the death of John Cox Stevens, the survivors of the *America* syndicate presented the

Royal Yacht Squadron Hundred Guinea Cup, which they had been passing around among themselves, to the N.Y.Y.C. The deed of gift specified that it be a prize "open to be sailed for by yacht clubs of all foreign countries." As the deed of gift bears the names of Stevens and Hamilton Wilkes, who died in 1852, we can suppose that the idea for this international race was discussed soon after the schooner's triumphs in England. (For some reason, James Hamilton's name is not on the deed.)

The year 1851 was not a happy one for John de Blaquiere, *America*'s new owner. His wife had died in February, and in November his father, an army general, shot himself rather than face ugly death by smallpox, making John the fourth Baron de Blaquiere of Ardkill (the family, of French Huguenot extraction, derived its title and wealth from estates and tax collections in Ireland). With a crew of twelve, the new Lord de Blaquiere sailed off on a seven and one-half month, 8000-mile cruise to Greece that involved more than a fair share of nasty weather during seventy-two days under way. To the surprise of yachtsmen who had thought *America* an unseaworthy racing machine, the schooner survived very nicely. In a letter to *Bell's Life* soon after his return in July 1852, her owner praised her "admirable behavior under very trying circumstances of wind and weather" and hoped that "our English yachts may in due time emulate, if not surpass, the speed and docility of their Transatlantic sister." Some U.S. newspapers were pleased to print these words as well as a letter from an American named John Winthrop, who after a visit aboard *America* at Leghorn, Italy, reported that the only alteration to her was the addition of stanchions and life lines on top of her low bulwarks.

3.2 **The London print publishers wasted no time in updating their *America* editions. Barely a week after Stevens accepted John de Blaquiere's offer of £5000 for the schooner, Ackermann & Co. produced this lithograph of "America, 170 tons, formerly the property of Commodore J.C. Stevens . . ."**

Soon after her return to England, *America* sailed in another "hundred guinea cup" race, this time for the Queen's Cup, sailed around the Isle of Wight but sponsored by the Royal Victoria Yacht Club. Her skipper was Robert Underwood, the pilot in the 1851 race. Flying her by now well-worn sails, she took the lead but was passed by two smaller cutters on the run to the finish and ended up third, only one minute, fifty seconds behind the winner. She was moved up a place after the second-place boat was disqualified for fouling the winner, *Arrow*, whose bow had been considerably lengthened and sharpened after the 1851 race. This was big news, and the headline over the report of this race ran, "Defeat of the *America*."

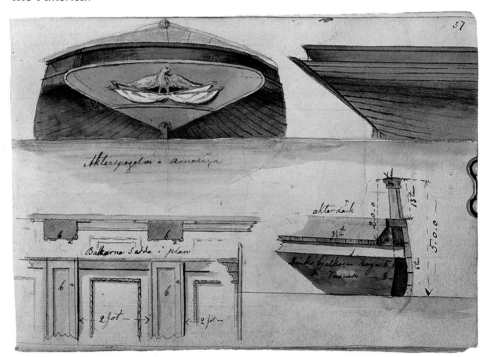

3.4 Among the 80 Swedish craftsmen who travelled to London for the Great Exhibition of 1851 were boat-builder Fredrick Andersen and designer Pehr Wilhelm Cedergren. Their interest in naval architecture took them to Britain's foremost shipbuilding centers, including Portsmouth and Cowes, where they did a thorough inspection of the *America*. They were very impressed: " . . . the American shipbuilder, Steers, will probably change the art of ship designing through the excellent construction of the schooner *America*." Cedergren did a series of detailed studies of the yacht's construction and rig, from which Andersen was to base his own schooner *Sverige*.

When she next raced, it was in another international contest, but this time as an English boat against an invading Swede. In 1851, Johan Frederick Andersen, a Swedish shipbuilder, and Pehr Wilhelm Cedergren, a marine artist, came over for the Great Exhibition and, during their tour of British shipyards, studied *America*. They may have been part of the throng at the Portsmouth dockyard when she was hauled for repairs. Back home, they announced that George Steers was revolutionizing shipbuilding through a refinement of the wave-line theory, and proposed that to be competitive, Sweden build a vessel along the same idea. A syndicate commissioned Andersen to build a slightly larger schooner using this theory, and the result was *Sverige*, who shared with her inspiration a patriotic name and much the same looks, though she had a deeper forefoot and a longer bow. She sailed to Cowes, and after long negotiations raced against *America* in a good breeze on 12 October 1852.

3.5 *Sverige,* the Swedish challenger not only shared *America*'s looks, but her taste in patriotic names.

Leading by nine minutes at the end of the 20-mile run, *Sverige* carried away her main gaff, was passed, and lost by twenty-six minutes. Soon after, de Blaquiere made a public challenge for a match to be sailed before 16 November, carefully excluding American yachts and ones that exceeded *America*'s tonnage. He found no takers.

During the next eight years, *America* all but vanished from the record of English yachting. De Blaquiere put her up for sale, apparently because he had remarried and was facing military duties involving the Crimean War, but she was not purchased until 1856 and apparently sat unused during the interval. The new owner, Henry Montagu Upton, the second Viscount Templeton (whose title and wealth, like de Blaquiere's, originated in Ireland), renamed her *Camilla*. Lord Templeton used her rarely, and she spent most of the next two years on the mud at Portsmouth and Cowes, closed up and rotting.

America was neglected because she had succeeded to the ambiguous status that is reserved for all trend-setters past their prime. As time went on, her performance in August 1851 came to be regarded by the English as freakish, for other U.S. yachts appearing in England did not do quite so well. One of these visitors was the George Steers-designed centerboard sloop *Sylvie* (also called *Silvie*), which had been built next to *America* at William Brown's shipyard. Much feared before she arrived in 1853, *Sylvie* was generally regarded as a total failure and could not find an English buyer after finishing only second in the Squadron Cup race. The crisis was over; English shipbuilding had recovered.

In 1858, Lord Templeton sold *Camilla* a to shipbuilder named Henry Sotheby Pitcher, who rebuilt her at his shipyard near Gravesend, on the Thames. Although there were no major changes to her shape, the hull was thoroughly reconstructed. The bottom was now elm and oak, the frames English oak, the topsides teak. The bases of the masts were found to be rotten, so the spars were cut down by 5 or 6 feet and taller topmasts were rigged. New flax sails replaced the tattered cotton originals. Sometime during this interim period the great golden eagle was removed from her transom. The eagle ended up in the bar of the Eagle Hotel, in Ryde, on the Isle of Wight. In 1912, the Royal Yacht Squadron purchased it and presented it to the New York Yacht Club.

After rebuilding *Camilla*, Pitcher sold her to Henry Edward Decie in July 1860. Not much is known about the background of this mysterious character except that he was a twenty-eight-year-old former Royal Navy officer. The Service had released him, he claimed, because he had accidentally attacked a Brazilian warship while commanding a patrol boat searching for pirates along the coast of South America. Taking into account the mix of ambition, romanticism, and negligence that surrounded Decie's ownership of the former *America*, that story is credible.

In August *Camilla* won a race off Plymouth, and two months later she left Southampton with Decie; a woman who was Decie's mistress or wife, her six children, and a crew of thirteen. The yacht worked her way to Lisbon and the Cape Verde Islands during the fall and winter, and on 25 April 1861 anchored at Savannah, Georgia. Decie's purpose could not have been other than to provide some service to the rebels, for although Fort Sumter had been fired on during his Atlantic crossing, the coming of the Civil War had been anticipated for months. Claiming to be an English nobleman, he attracted considerable attention, but the main appeal to the Confederacy was the famous speed of his yacht. In May, the government purchased her under terms that are unclear. In his extremely thorough account of the schooner's career under Decie, published in *The American Neptune* in 1967, Thomas R. Neblett concludes that the purchase price was $60,000 with $26,000 down, the remainder to come after her return from a special mission to Europe, plus $6000 for fitting-out expenses. One condition seems to have been that Decie would continue in command, for he remained *Camilla*'s captain until February 1862.

On 25 May, *Camilla* went to sea bound for Ireland. Her passengers

included Edward Clifford Anderson, a civilian who had been directed by
President Jefferson Davis to guarantee that military supplies were being
purchased by an unreliable Confederate agent in England, and Lieutenant James H. North of the Confederate Navy, who carried $600,000 in
bills of exchange and a letter of credit for purchasing or building warships.
North's wife and children were on board as well, for it was expected that
he would remain in Europe to supervise construction of warships. After a
crossing complicated by Decie's careless navigation and casual leadership,
the schooner reached Queenstown, Ireland, on 23 June. Despite her
worn sails and peeling paint her Union Jack and Royal Victoria Yacht
Club burgee convinced customs officials that she had, as Decie said,
strolled over from Cowes for a little competition. As a log had not been
kept, there was no way to disprove this claim. North and Anderson immediately went ashore on their separate missions, and Decie went racing,
finishing second on corrected time in a fleet of four on the twenty-eighth.

Camilla arrived at Cowes on 6 July. There she awaited dispatches and
equipment to carry back to America, meanwhile taking long, easy
daysails on the waters where she had earned her reputation. In her only
race, she was badly beaten in a match for stakes of £200 by *Alarm*, the
rumored challenger of a decade earlier that had been thoroughly
*America*ized with a schooner rig and a long, sharp bow. Reportedly,
Camilla was fast enough, but her crew was sloppy. Decie was equally
careless in his role as a Scarlet Pimpernel, showing much more interest in
the yachting side of the voyage, which the Confederates must have con-

sidered a cover, than in the secret mission. He was slow preparing for the voyage back to America, he refused to take aboard some cartridges that Anderson wanted to ship back to the Confederacy, and he skipped an appointment with agents at which he would pick up dispatches.

On 15 August, *Camilla* set out cross-channel for Cherbourg, and the next that is known of her is a customs inspection in Jacksonville, Florida, on 25 October. At about this time, the sale to the Confederacy was completed, and the schooner—by one account now renamed *Memphis*—went into service as a blockade runner based in Jacksonville. She sailed in at least two missions (one of which took her as far as Hampton Roads, Virginia).

In March 1862, when Jacksonville was taken by Union troops, her fleeing crew removed her spars, drilled five holes in her bottom, and scuttled her in Dunn's Creek, about 70 miles up the St. John's River from the city. A Union Navy lieutenant named Thomas H. Stevens found her with only her port rail showing and, after a week of hard work, raised her using improvised pumps. It is more than likely that the exhausting recovery would not have been undertaken had she been just any vessel, for in his letter of commendation to Lieutenant Stevens — the remarkable coincidence in names between him and two of the original owners must be noted — Flag Officer (later Admiral) Samuel F. DuPont mentioned "the historical interest which attaches to this vessel and the incidents attending her career." She was renamed *America*, her spars were stepped, and she was towed to Port Royal, South Carolina. None the worse for wear once she was dried out, she served in the Union blockade near Rattlesnake Shoal, off Charleston, from late June 1862 until May 1863, with November and December off for an overhaul in New York. Judging from official dispatches, her service was busy, and she frequently used her three guns to get the attention of Confederate blockade runners, three of which she captured or forced to run ashore.

3.7 This cannon is a model of the 24-pounder Dahlgren deck gun carried on board *America* during her blockade service in the Civil War.

48

On 1 May 1863, *America* was ordered to sail to Newport, Rhode Island, to serve as a training ship for midshipmen at the United States Naval Academy, which had been relocated from Annapolis, Maryland. At this time there occurred one of those curious encounters between old and new that mean little historically but much dramatically. In late June 1863, while returning to Newport from a training cruise that included a fruitless hunt for a Confederate privateer, *America* anchored with several other war vessels in a strong southeast wind off New Haven, Connecticut. Sailing by that day was fifteen-year-old Nathanael Greene Herreshoff, who was cruising in a 28-foot sloop, *Kelpie*, with his blind brother John. In 1937, after he had retired as the world's foremost yacht designer and builder, Nat Herreshoff remembered with total recall the details of his first sight of the vessel whose cup he helped defend eight times. "We passed the war vessels at anchor a little farther out than the breakwater is now," he wrote to a friend in a letter, a copy of which is now in the G.W. Blunt White Library at Mystic Seaport, "and all were pitching and diving and straining at their cables."

For the next three years, *America* carried midshipmen on training cruises, impressing on the young sailors not only something of the ways of sailing men but also the aroma of U.S. maritime history. One alumnus of *America*'s fo'c's'le wrote, "I know in my early service days we gloried in no other thing which floated, save the *Constitution*, *Cumberland*, and *Monitor*, and looking back I can recall many a night when the peace and quiet of Gardiner's Bay would be broken by the chorus of a hundred boyish voices singing:

> Where did she come from? New York town!
> Who was her skipper? Old Dick Brown!"

3.8 During the summer of 1863, *America* sailed on the Naval Academy cruise, accompanying the sloops-of-war *Marion* and *Macedonian* to New York, Newport, Portsmouth, New Hampshire, and here.to the Boston Navy Yard.

49

Cambria.   Madgic.   Phantom.   Light-Ship.   Silvie.   America.   Dauntless.   Idler.   Magic.   Tidal Wave.

THE RACE FOR THE QUEEN'S CUP—ROUNDING THE LIGHT-SHIP.—DRAWN BY CHARLES PARSONS, FROM A SKETCH MADE ON BOARD A. S. HATCH'S YACHT "CALYPSO."—[SEE PAGE 554.]

Her value as a relic must have been greater than her worth as a training ship, for in 1866 the Navy laid her up at Annapolis near the *Constitution* and other schoolships. Four years later, her status as a national symbol led Admiral David Porter, the Naval Academy's former superintendant and now the commander of the Brooklyn Navy Yard, to recommission her at a cost to the government of $19,000 so that she could sail in the first race for the "*America* Cup," on 8 August 1870.

As in the race in which *America* won the trophy back in 1851, a solitary foreign yacht owned by an heir to a railroad fortune — James Ashbury's *Cambria* — was pitted against a large homegrown fleet. Again as before, most of the race was sailed in cramped, crowded, tide-swept waters — now in New York Harbor. The similarities ended there. This time (and for twenty-three other times until 1983), the visitor was unsuccessful. The race was won by a slippery centerboard schooner named *Magic*, which had been much altered since her launching in 1857. *Cambria* finished eighth on elapsed time and tenth on corrected time. *America*, commanded by Old Dick Brown's son Charles, was fourth out of fifteen finishers on both elapsed and corrected time. This was an excellent, perhaps even amazing, showing, given that she was a nineteen-year-old boat that had not raced in a decade; in fact, like *Cambria*, she was sailing her first race in the United States. Nevertheless, the legend for

3.9 In 1870, the first challenge for the America's Cup was made by Englishman James Ashbury in his yacht *Cambria*. In a sentimental gesture, the Navy put *America* in racing condition, and sent her to New York to join the N.Y.Y.C. fleet for the contest. She finished fourth.

invincibility that surrounded her led many to castigate her crew of midshipmen and the Navy itself because she had not won.

America remained in Navy service for the next three years, apparently doing little more than some daysailing on Chesapeake Bay. In 1873, claiming that she was too costly to maintain for the limited service she offered, the Secretary of the Navy had her put up for auction. Navy officers fumed "We may next expect to see the old *Constitution* advertised," one wrote — but the government calmly responded that more than $30,000 had been spent solely on repairs in the four years since 1869, and major work was still needed.

Events soon suggested not only that this figure was inflated, but that it was part of a smokescreen to cover up a transaction reeking of favoritism. When several potential bidders made inquiries, they were told that *America*'s title could not be guaranteed since, after her capture in 1862, there had never been a prize court hearing to test a claim of ownership by a Georgian named Gazaway B. Lamar. Hearing this, all but one of the prospective owners cautiously backed out. The sole bid was for only $5000 from John Cassels, who was soon revealed as a front for his friend and former Civil War commander Benjamin F. Butler and Butler's business partner, Jonas H. French. The names of Cassels and French did not again appear in connection with *America*.

The key figure was Butler. He was a friend of Lamar, who had offered to withdraw his claims if Butler could arrange to purchase the yacht; he was a friend of Navy Secretary George M. Robeson, who ordered the

3.10 Although the N.Y.Y.C. Cruise of 1872 did take the squadron to Newport for a week of racing in August, there is no evidence that *America* was able to join them. Perhaps the event just didn't seem right without her.

51

3.11 The Honorable, and formidable, Benjamin Franklin Butler (1818-1893), was a lawyer, Civil War general, Governor of Massachusetts, unsuccessful presidential candidate, yachtsman, and showman.

sale; and, like Robeson, he was an old enemy of Admiral Porter, who had succeeded in making the yacht a Navy tradition. An 1876 Congressional investigation of this transaction and others that lined Secretary Robeson's pockets made it clear that a private interest had succeeded in swiping one of the Navy's most prized monuments. Ironically, the buyer did not get what he thought he was getting, for the Navy removed from *America*'s bilge some lead ballast that, presumably, was installed during the 1870 refit. Butler was loaned 20 tons of empty bomb shells, which was still far from sufficient. The delivery crew nursed the badly under-ballasted schooner north in a gale and squalls, and once she was knocked over until her cockpit took water; but she survived and was reballasted with lead and shell casings in Boston.

By the time she was taken over by Butler, *America* had served as a racing and cruising yacht, as a secret courier, as a warship under two flags, and as a training vessel. In her twenty-three years, she had been owned by a total of seven owners, including two governments. For the remainder of her seventy-three years, she would have only three owners and serve only one role: the reminder of a day of glory.

Ben Butler took full advantage of his yacht's fame. Born in 1818, he had become a lawyer and politician in Massachusetts. His ambition, and the flexibility he showed in following it, were as notorious as his rough and tumble tactics. A Democrat in the 'fifties, he quickly acclimated himself to the political demands of the Civil War and became a general in the Massachusetts volunteers. He commanded occupying forces in Maryland and in New Orleans, where he was known as "Beast" Butler because of measures that were considered harsh, among them prohibiting southern women from insulting Union troops in public (for this Jefferson Davis officially declared him an outlaw). Butler was less successful on the battlefield, and Lincoln released him before the end of the war. He was elected to the House of Representatives in 1866 and, except for one term, stayed there until 1879, a year after he resigned from the Republican Party because he thought it too conservative. Three years later he was elected governor of Massachusetts. In 1884, he was the unsuccessful presidential candidate of the radical Greenback Party.

Whether as an occupying general, a radical Republican thundering for the impeachment of Andrew Johnson, or a candidate for office, Butler inspired as much hate as he did admiration through the extremity of his views and the vituperativeness with which he pursued them. One of Butler's victims was Richard Henry Dana, Jr., author of *Two Years Before the Mast*, who ran against him in the Republican Congressional primary in 1868. Butler pilloried Dana across eastern Massachusetts as an aristocratic stuffed shirt, and, for his pains, Dana was beaten by a margin of seven to one. Eight years later, Butler broke Dana's heart by conspiring to defeat his appointment as ambassador to the Court of St. James, which Dana thought was due him because of his cultured breeding and anglified ways.

Butler enjoyed the sea. As a boy, he had cruised to Newfoundland in his uncle's fishing schooner, and later he found time between his political, legal, and business obligations to do a little sailing on Massachusetts Bay. He kept a fleet of boats moored off the mansion he built near his granite quarries on Cape Ann. *America* was his jewel, and not only because, as the yachting writer William U. Swan put it, "She brought him a certain celebrity at a time when he found publicity desirable." While he and his yacht made a strange couple, this was not the first time that the vessel had been a projection of someone's dreams. The same could be said of John Cox Stevens, Henry Decie, and perhaps even the U.S. Navy. Yet Butler's ownership was different in three ways: he owned her for a much longer time; he shamelessly showed her off; and he assiduously repaid her with loving care.

3.12 In July of 1875, the Isles of Shoals Regatta was sponsored by the owner of the Oceanic Hotel on Star Island, but the results were so confused and protested, that a rematch had to be called. *America*'s only competition was Rufus Hatch's centerboard schooner *Resolute*, and Ben Butler won the punchbowl handily.

3.13 This is one of very few early photographs of *America* that show her as altered by Donald McKay in 1875, but before she was rerigged by Edward Burgess in 1885.

For most of the twenty summers until his death in 1893, *America* and Butler were almost inseparable. Though he cared little about yacht racing (and knew even less), he entered her in a total of twenty-eight races, in which she won five and placed second or third in five more.

In 1875, she took part in a controversial race off New Hampshire's Isles of Shoals. She was third to finish and fourth on corrected time, but was disqualified along with every other entry but one for not rounding a mark, which had drifted four miles. Rather than present the trophy — a silver-plated punch bowl donated by the owner of an island hotel — to the one boat that somehow found and rounded the mark, the judges called off the entire fiasco. A week later, Butler and a character named Uncle Rufus Hatch, owner of a bigger yacht named *Resolute*, held a more successful match for the cup. *Resolute* was first to finish, but *America* won on her handicap, and tourism on the islands benefitted.

3.14 In 1885, Edward Burgess, designer of the America's cup defender *Puritan*, was hired by Butler to overhaul *America*. Among other alterations, he reset her masts slightly forward of plumb, and fitted her with a pole bowsprit.

3.15–17 This series of photographs shows the yacht *America* in the far more relaxed service of General Butler. Guests enjoy relaxing interludes at anchor, under the huge boom canopy, and pleasant sails out from her Cape Ann anchorage.

3.18 The last major alteration to *America* took place in 1887, when Ben Butler had her painted white.

Besides those official races, he sometimes sailed alongside the fleets in races that he could not enter, for example, during the New York Yacht Club Cruise (which, despite its name, is a series of port to port races). He was never a member of the club, which had its share of rough characters but tended to spurn public figures, and *America*'s heritage was Butler's only calling card in its high circles. In 1876, the N.Y.Y.C. — whose Vice-Commodore, H. Nicholson Kane, had commanded *America* as a midshipman in 1866 — allowed *America* to start five minutes after the two official contestants in the second race of the America's Cup match. The race committee took her time and, to almost universal delight, she finished only seven minutes behind the defender and nineteen ahead of the Canadian challenger.

3.19 *America* on port tack. 18 August 1891.

Claiming that this informal race proved that yacht design had not advanced in twenty-five years, Butler offered to race any boat in the world on a 50-mile course, half upwind and half downwind. Nobody took up the challenge, perhaps out of respect for *America*'s history. Misinterpreting this reaction to indicate fear, Butler naively told the N.Y.Y.C. in 1885 that he would be pleased to defend what he called the Queen's Cup against a well-regarded English challenger, *Genesta*, but *America* was soundly defeated by the eventual defender, *Puritan*.

Besides having dreams of America's Cup glory, Butler enjoyed odd contests. In 1882, he raced 225 miles out into the Atlantic against the 1700-ton full-rigged ship *North American*. *America*'s captain made no effort to sail ahead, but rather showed which was fastest by circling the ship five times. *America* then sailed off on a cruise to the Gulf of St. Lawrence. In other years, *America* cruised to Nova Scotia and the Caribbean, getting as far as Vera Cruz.

3.20 *America* with all sail set. 6 September 1897.

Unlike the Stevens syndicate, Butler obviously regarded *America* as much more than a gamble. One year, she turned up at a joint regatta of the N.Y.Y.C. and the Eastern Yacht Club, of Massachusetts, proudly flying a 22-foot banner on which her name was printed in 24-inch letters. A yachting writer sniffed that it was "the East River excursion barge variety," but Butler was delighted. Where he showed his greatest devotion was in her upkeep. In 1875 he had Donald McKay, the great builder of clipper ships, modify her rig, add two cabins, and replace the tiller with a steering wheel. As a point of maritime history, this project was Donald McKay's last. Five years later, another Boston shipyard added three more cabins, replaced some rotting planks, and lengthened the schooner's bow and stern to stretch her deck to 107 feet 6 inches and provide her with

3.21 Oil painting of
America, attributed to
Clement Drew, ca. 1880.

looks that were more up to date. In 1885, the bottom was re-coppered and the old-fashioned single-headsail rig was replaced with two jibs.

In the summer of 1885, after *America* was badly beaten by the Cup-defending sloop *Puritan*, in a race off Marblehead, Massachusetts, Butler asked *Puritan*'s designer, Edward Burgess, to bring her completely up to date. Burgess gave her a more powerful clipper bow and a new keel that carried 25 tons of lead in a bulb at the bottom. With all that outside ballast, she could carry more sail, so Burgess gave her a longer bowsprit and longer topmasts and gaffs. The Burgess rig had an entirely different look: instead of raking aft, it raked slightly forward of plumb. The last significant change made by Ben Butler was her color. In 1887 he had her painted white.

There was little chance to test the new rig, for as Butler aged, *America* sailed less and less. Leaving her one day in September 1892, he was heard to say, "Good bye, old girl. God only knows when I shall ever tread your decks again." He died in January 1893, and for four years *America* lay under a canvas cover near Boston's Chelsea Bridge. His son Paul, who was interested in canoes (he invented the sliding seat for sailing canoes), had little time for her. He eventually turned the schooner over to his nephew Butler Ames, who recommissioned her in 1897 and did some racing, winning the Corinthian Yacht Club's Nash Cup. Coming forty-six years after the Squadron Cup race, this was her last win. In 1898, she was sent south to join her owner, who was a volunteer officer in the Spanish-American War, but got only as far as Montauk, where she took soldiers daysailing. It could be said, then, that she once again was a military vessel.

Also once again, she was able to carry the flag of the N.Y.Y.C. after Butler Ames joined the club in 1898. When she joined the club's fleet at New London, she was greeted by crowds singing songs in her honor and patting her sides. After the races, she sailed to New York and took Sir Thomas Lipton for a sail. On 26 July 1901 — about one month shy of the fiftieth anniversary of the Squadron Cup race — she sailed her fifty-first and last race. Fittingly, it was against the yacht club's flagship, which beat her by twenty minutes.

3.22 After a half century of active sailing, *America* was laid up for fifteen years at Boston by Butler Ames, who then sought to sell her. She was rescued from packet service in the Cape Verde Islands by Charles H.W. Foster, who purchased her for the Eastern Yacht Club.

For the next fifteen years she lay under wraps in Boston until, in 1916, Butler Ames commissioned Edward Burgess's brother Walter to sell her. Some Cape Verdians soon made a downpayment; they would use her as a packet between the Cape Verdes and New Bedford, Massachusetts. When the word got out, Charles H.W. Foster, a member of the Eastern and New York Yacht Clubs who was dead set against her leaving the country or going into trade, bought her and arranged that another vessel take her place in the original deal. Foster turned her over

3.23 In 1921, the Eastern Yacht Club donated *America* back to her old home, the U.S. Naval Academy in Annapolis, where she was opened to visitors as an exhibit vessel.

to a holding company centered on the Eastern Yacht Club, and in 1921 this group decided to donate her to her old home, the U.S. Naval Academy. More than enough funds were raised to make the repairs needed for her to reach her destination. Towed by a Navy submarine chaser, the old schooner made a triumphant nineteen-day trip down the East Coast to enthusiastic receptions at yacht clubs, seafront towns, and bridges. Reaching Annapolis on 29 September 1921, she went on permanent exhibit in the Academy's inner basin, accepting visitors.

She was not well maintained. In 1940, she showed signs of serious decay, and to keep her from sinking was hauled and stored in a shed at the Annapolis Yacht Yard. Pressured by President Franklin D. Roosevelt, who wanted to see her in a National Naval Museum, Congress appropriated $100,000 for a thorough overhaul, but war needs took a higher priority.

3.24 Badly in need of maintenance, *America* was hauled out at Trumpy's Annapolis Yacht Yard in 1940. Unfortunately, war broke out before the Navy could commit funds to her restoration.

3.25 Here are the remains of *America*, being scrapped in 1945, after she was crushed when snow collapsed her storage shed in the winter of 1942. The Trumpy Yard received credit from the Navy for the sound wood and lead that were recovered—a total of $990.90.

On 29 March 1942, the shed's roof collapsed under a wet, heavy snowfall, and *America*'s rotted timbers gave way under the load. Busy with a war on two fronts, the Navy waited more than three years to make up its mind about the fate of the remaining splinters. A surveyor reported that, to float again, she would have to be almost completely rebuilt at a cost of $200,000 to $300,000. He recommended scrapping her and building a scale model out of what little sound wood remained. The Chief of Naval Operations agreed, but action was postponed when members of the yachting community went into an uproar at the news. On 18 October 1945, Herbert L. Stone, Editor of *Yachting*, complained to Commodore P.H. Magruder about how "shamefully neglected" she had been by the Navy. The decision was postponed, but on 20 November 1945, the Chief of the Bureau of Ships ordered the scrapping. When the job was finished in 1946, the yard received $990.90 credit for the sound wood and lead that were recovered. The model was constructed, and sits now in the Naval Academy's museum. In 1967, a near-replica of *America* was built to remind people of the marvelous history of the original.

America's value far outlasts any models or reproductions, and far outweighs the paltry sums of money surrounding her demise. In one form or another and under one name or another she lived for ninety-five years, and her story continues to survive — even thrive. She is an enthralling symbol combining bold ambition, the romance of the far horizon, high national purpose, and breakthrough technology. The men who built, bought, and sailed *America* did not merely make and use a tool with which to accomplish their own small aims: win a race, run a blockade, publicize a political campaign. In spite of themselves, each succeeded in becoming part of an extraordinary adventure, the *America* adventure, which will be retold again and again as long as men and women sail for pleasure.

3.26 Schooner Yacht *America* signed "T. Willis."

ACKNOWLEDGMENTS
AND SOURCES

I am pleased to thank Ben Fuller, Curator at the Mystic Seaport Museum, and Tom Aageson, of the Mystic Seaport Museum Stores, for allowing me to contribute my part to this publication. I also wish to thank the following librarians for their assistance: at the G.W. Blunt White Library, Mystic Seaport Museum, Douglas L. Stein, Curator of Manuscripts, Dorothy Thomas, Manuscripts Assistant, and Paul O'Pecko, Reference Librarian; at the New York Yacht Club, Sohei Hohri, Librarian and Curator; and at the Stevens Institute of Technology, Jane F. Hartye, Special Collections Librarian. Dana Rousmaniere was a tireless reseach assistant.

John Rousmaniere

Books and Periodicals

Adams, Charles Francis. *Richard Henry Dana: A Biography*. 2 vols. Boston: Houghton, Mifflin, 1890.

Albion, Robert Greenhalgh. "New York and its Rivals." *Journal of Economic and Business History* III no. 4 (August 1931).

_____. *The Rise of New York Port, 1815–1860*. New York: Scribner's, 1939.

Bennett, Daphne. *King without a Crown: Albert, Prince Consort of England, 1819–1861*. Philadelphia: J.B. Lippincott, 1977.

Boswell, Charles. *The America: The Story of the World's Most Famous Yacht*. New York: David McKay, 1967.

Bruzek, Joseph C. "The U.S. Schooner Yacht *America*." *U.S. Naval Institute Proceedings* vol. 93 no. 9 (September 1967).

Butler, Benjamin F. *Butler's Book*. Boston: Thayer, 1892.

Chapelle, Howard I. *American Sailing Craft*. New York: Kennedy, 1936.

_____. *The History of American Sailing Ships*. New York: W.W. Norton, 1935.

_____. *The Search for Speed under Sail, 1700–1855*. New York: W.W. Norton, 1967.

Cutler, Carl C. *Greyhounds of the Sea: The Story of the American Clipper Ship*. Annapolis, Md.: Naval Institute, 1930.

Day, Thomas Fleming. "Men Who Have Made Yachting: George Steers." *The Rudder* vol. 17 no. 2 (February 1906).

Dear, Ian. *The America's Cup: An Informal History*. New York: Dodd, Mead, 1980.

_____. *The Royal Yacht Squadron, 1815–1985*. London: Stanley Paul, 1985.

DeSaix, Pierre. "Tank Testing *America*: Some Interesting Comparisons with Modern Yachts." *Yachting* vol. 122 no. 1 (September 1967).

Dictionary of American Biography.

Griffiths, John W. *Treatise on Marine and Naval Architecture, or Theory and Practice Blended on Ship Building*. New York: n.p., 1850; 3rd edition, New York: Appleton, 1852.

Laing, Alexander. *Clipper Ships and Their Makers*. New York: Putnam's, 1966.

Longford, Elizabeth. *Queen Victoria: Born to Succeed*. New York: Harper and Row, 1964.

National Cyclopedia of American Biography.

Mainero, Frank A. "But There is a Second *America*." *The Log of Mystic Seaport* 19 (Spring-Summer 1967), 41–45.

Morrison, John H. *History of American Steam Navigation*. New York: Sametz, 1903.

_____. *History of New York Ship Yards*. New York: Sametz, 1919.

Nash, Howard P., Jr. *Stormy Petrel: The Life and Times of General Benjamin F. Butler, 1818–1893*. Rutherford, N.J.: Fairleigh Dickinson University Press, 1969.

Neblett, Thomas R. "The *America*: A New Account Pertaining to Her Confederate Operations." *The American Neptune* vol. 27 no. 4 (October 1967).

Nevins, Allan, ed. *The Diary of Philip Hone*. 4 vols. New York: Dodd, Mead, 1936.

Nevins, Allan, and Milton Halsey Thomas, ed. *The Diary of George Templeton Strong*. 4 vols. New York: Macmillan, 1952.

Parkinson, John, Jr. *The History of the New York Yacht Club*. 2 vols. New York: New York Yacht Club, 1975.

Rousmaniere, John. *America's Cup Book, 1851–1983*. New York: W.W. Norton, 1983.

_____. *The Golden Pastime: A New History of Yachting*. New York: W.W. Norton, 1986.

Russell, John Scott. *The Modern System of Naval Architecture*. 3 vols. London: Day, 1865.

Stephens, William P. *Traditions and Memories of American Yachting*. Camden, Me.: International Marine, 1981.

Stone, Herbert L., William H. Taylor, and William W. Robinson. *The America's Cup Races*. New York: W.W. Norton, 1970.

Streeter, John. "The Secret of *Sverige*'s Past: A Swedish Challenger Races the *America*." *The Log of Mystic Seaport* vol. 29 no. 3 (October 1977).

Thompson, Winfield M., and Thomas W. Lawson. *The Lawson History of the America's Cup*. Boston: privately published, 1902.

Thompson, Winfield M., William P. Stephens, and William U. Swan. *The Yacht America*. Boston: Lauriat, 1925.

Turnbull, Archibald Douglas. *John Stevens: An American Record*. New York: Century, 1928.

Whipple, A.B.C., and the Editors of Time-Life Books. *The Racing Yachts*. Alexandria, Va., Time-Life Books, 1980.

Newspapers

Bell's Life in London, 1850–1852. Yachting clippings collected in scrapbooks in the library of the New York Yacht Club; microfilm in G.W. Blunt White Library, Mystic Seaport Museum.

New York Herald. Miscellaneous clippings from New York periodicals. In scrapbooks in library of the New York Yacht Club; microfilm in G.W. Blunt White Library, Mystic Seaport Museum.

Unpublished Sources

Herreshoff, Nathanael G. Letter to Henry C. White, 28 September 1935. Copy in Manuscripts Collection, VFM 1098, G.W. Blunt White Library, Mystic Seaport Museum.

Leavitt, John F. "Notes on American Yachting." Unpublished essay. Copy in Manuscripts Collection, RF 19, G.W. Blunt White Library, Mystic Seaport Museum.

Sherar, J.W. "The *America*." An essay submitted to the Head of the Department of English, History, and Government, United States Naval Academy, March 1952. Copy in Manuscripts Collection, RF 465, G.W. Blunt White Library, Mystic Seaport Museum.

Steers, James R. Journal of transatlantic crossing in yacht *America*, 21 June – 11 July 1851. Manuscripts Collection, Log 368, G.W. Blunt White Library, Mystic Seaport Museum.

Stevens, Edwin A. Letter to Mary Stevens, 29 August 1851. Copy in Stevens Collection, Stevens Institute of Technology.

U.S. Navy. Correspondence concerning disposition of yacht *America*, 18 July 1945 to February 1946. Copy in Manuscripts Collection, VFM 529, G.W. Blunt White Library, Mystic Seaport Museum.

Wilson, Robert N. Letter to F. DeR. Furman, Dean, Stevens Institute of Technology, 10 October 1932. In Stevens Collection, Stevens Institute of Technology.

LIST OF ILLUSTRATIONS

All dimensions are in inches, height before width. Abbreviations: M.S.M. = Mystic Seaport Museum; N.Y.Y.C. = New York Yacht Club; l.o.a. = Length over all. The slash mark / indicates line endings on the original.

Pencil, chalk, and gouache drawings
Signed "J.E. Butterworth, 1851"
Courtesy Private Collection

2.13 *America* sailing for the cup
Watercolor
Signed "J.C. Schetky — 1851"
Courtesy Private Collection
(11 1/2 x 23 1/2)

2.14 "PRIDE/THE SCHOONER YACHT
'WYVERN' R.Y.S. 205 TONS"
Published 19 May 1849 by Fores,
41 Piccadilly, London
Colored lithograph by T. Picken/
Day & Son
After painting by N.M. Condy
Courtesy N.Y.Y.C. (15 1/2 x 19 1/2)

2.15 THE CUTTER YACHT 'VOLANTE'
48 TONS R.T.Y.C."
Published 8 June 1852 by Fores,
41 Piccadilly, London
Colored lithograph
After a painting by T.S. Robins
Courtesy N.Y.Y.C. (15 1/2 x 20)

2.16 "SCHOONER YACHT 'AMERICA'
OFF DUNNOSE I.W."
Colored lithograph
After painting by I.M. Gilbert
Courtesy N.Y.Y.C.
(11 x 12 3/8 trimmed)

2.17 (Also cover) *The Illustrated London News*,
Engraving
9 August 1851 and 30 August 1851
M.S.M. 75.187.35 a/b

2.18 *America* sailing for the cup, 1851
Ink and watercolor
Signed "Frank H. Schell"
Courtesy N.Y.Y.C. (12 x 18 1/2)

2.19 Ensign from *America*, 1851
Courtesy N.Y.Y.C. (22 x 34)

3.1 Sheet music cover: "THE /AMERICA
SCHOTTISCH./DEDICATED TO/
COMMODORE JOHN C. STEVENS./
Composed and arranged/FOR THE/
Piano Forte,/BY/WILLIAM
DRESSLER./NEW YORK./
PUBLISHED BY WM. HALL & SON,
239 BROADWAY."
Colored lithograph by Sarony & Major,
New York
M.S.M. 75.187.24 (12 1/2 x 10)

3.2 "THE SCHOONER YACHT 'AMERICA',
170 TONS/ FORMERLY THE
PROPERTY OF COMMODORE J.C.
STEVENS NEW YORK YACHT
CLUB/To Captain the Honorable John
de Blaquiere"
Colored lithograph by Day & Son
Published 5 September 1851 by
Ackermann & Co., 96 Strand, London
After painting by T.G. Dutton
Courtesy N.Y.Y.C. (15 1/2 x 21 7/8)

3.3 Cutter *Arrow*
Pencil, chalk, and gouache
J.E. Buttersworth, 1851
Courtesy Private Collection

3.4 Details of the yacht *America*
Pencil, ink, and watercolor
Pehr Wilhelm Cedergren, ca. 1851
Courtesy Statens Sjöhistoriska Museum,
Stockholm, Sweden

3.5 "The 'SVERIGE' 280 TONS, WINNING
THE ROYAL THAMES YACHT
CLUB MATCH ON JUNE 1st 1853"
Colored lithograph by T.G. Dutton
Published 12 May 1854 by Rudolf
Ackermann, 191 Regent St., London
After painting by T.S. Robins
Courtesy N.Y.Y.C. (22 x 30)

3.6 "The Schooner Yacht Alarm, R.Y.S.
248 Tons."
Colored lithograph
Published 5 November 1852 by Fores,
41 Piccadilly, London
After painting by J.M. Gilbert
Courtesy N.Y.Y.C. (15 3/4 x 19 1/2)

3.7 Cannon model
M.S.M. 75.187.38 (l.o.a. 16")

3.8 *America* at the Charlestown Navy Yard,
1863
Photograph, silver print
M.S.M. 36.28

3.9 "The Race for the Queens Cup —
Rounding the Lightship — Drawn by
Charles Parsons, from a sketch made on
board A.S. Hatch's yacht 'Calypso'."
Engraving
Harper's Weekly Magazine,
27 August 1870, p. 553
M.S.M. 76.189 (10 1/2 x 14 1/2)

3.10 "THE YACHT SQUADRON
AT NEWPORT"
Colored lithograph
Published in 1872 by Currier & Ives,
125 Nassau St., New York
M.S.M. 83.89.3 (23 1/2 x 33 1/4)

3.11 Portrait of Benjamin F. Butler
Engraving
Butler's Book, by B.F. Butler
Published in 1892 by A.M. Theyer & Co.,
Boston

3.12 "Oceanic Prize/Won By/Yacht America,
89 Tons./against the/Resolute. 119
Tons./in a Sweepstakes Race/over 36
mile course at the/Isle of Shoals/
Aug 2nd 1875"
Silver-plated punch bowl trophy by
N. Harding & Co.
M.S.M. 80.36 (16 x 25 1/2)

3.13 "Sch Yacht America as she was re-
conditioned/after the war by Gen
Ben Butler/The most famous yacht
in the world."
Photograph, albumen print
Edwin Hale Lincoln, ca. 1884
M.S.M. 80.79.1498

3.14 Schooner yacht *America* at anchor, ca. 1886
Photograph, silver print
M.S.M. 77.139

3.15 Cockpit of schooner yacht *America* at
anchor, ca. 1886
Photograph, silver print

M.S.M. 77.140

3.16 Deck of schooner yacht *America*, looking
forward, ca. 1886
Photograph, silver print
M.S.M. 77.142

3.17 Cockpit of schooner yacht *America*,
under way, ca. 1886
Photograph, silver print
M.S.M. 74.272

3.18 *America* on starboard tack
Photograph, silver print
Frank H. Child, Newport, R.I., ca. 1890
M.S.M. 54.2

3.19 *America* on port tack
Photograph by Henry G. Peabody,
18 August 1891
Photolithograph from *Representative
American Yachts, A Collection of One
Hundred Views*, published by Henry G.
Peabody, 122 Boylston Street,
Boston, 1891
M.S.M. 59.453.19 (6 5/8 x 9 1/8)

3.20 *America* with all sail set
Photograph, albumen print
N.L. Stebbins, 6 September 1897
M.S.M. 59.580

3.21 *America*
Oil painting on canvas
Attributed to Clement Drew, ca. 1880
M.S.M. 56.1054 (22 x 30 1/8)

3.22 *America* under wraps in Boston
Photograph, silver print
Henry Donald Fisher, 1913
M.S.M. 76.208.377

3.23 *America* at U.S. Naval Academy, June 1928
Photograph, silver print
M.S.M. 46.190.3

3.24 *America*, hauled out in Annapolis,
3 April 1941
Photograph, silver print
Courtesy U.S. Naval Academy Museum

3.25 *America*, at Trumpy's Boatyard, after
29 March 1942.
Photograph, silver print
Courtesy U.S. Naval Academy Museum

3.26 Schooner Yacht *America*
Oil painting with embroidery and satin
applique
Signed "T. Willis"
M.S.M. 75.187.34 (15 3/4 x 23 1/2)

3.27 "THE CLIPPER YACHT 'AMERICA'/
Built by Mr Geo. Steers of New York for
Jn C. Stevens Esq. and associates of the
New-York Yacht Club"
Colored lithograph
F.F. Palmer and N. Currier
Published by N. Currier, 152 Nassau St.,
New York
M.S.M. 72.516 (15 3/8 x 19 7/8)

Back Cover: *America* sailing with her successors
Oil on canvas
Artist unknown
Courtesy N.Y.Y.C.

66

America: Sources for Plans

America was designed by cutting a model, which is now lost. What we know of her shape today is based on drawings made from that builder's model, from the lines drawn full size from which her molds were made, or from measurements made when she was hauled out for painting or repairs.

The first published plan was by J.W. Griffiths in his *Treatise on Marine and Naval Architecture,* 1852 edition. Drawn for publication, it shows minimal information, but was undoubtedly based on data furnished by Steers, a friend and colleague of Griffiths, if not from the designer's model itself.

Far more detailed is the New York Yacht Club's plan drawn by Nelson Spratt, and reproduced here. Spratt was an associate of Steers, possibly the supervisor of his mold loft, a model maker and expert draftsman. He worked with Steers on at least one other project, the sloop *Julia* of 1854, which one source credits Spratt with designing. The plan produced by Spratt shows both lines to the inside of planking (which he could have gotten from the model), and lines to the outside, which could be estimated or, more easily, have been taken from the mold loft floor where she was drawn full size. These lines have been traced by David W. Dillion and are available from *WoodenBoat* magazine. At 1/2" to the foot, they show subtleties of shape hard to see in smaller-scale drawings.

When *America* went to Europe she was measured twice or perhaps three times. Discrepancies among these different drawings, and between these and the two from New York, are due to several causes. Alterations may have been made to *America* in the mold loft or once she stood in frame, not an uncommon practice. Takeoffs from the vessel could vary greatly in quality, depending on time available and the workmanship of the measurers. And, finally, errors could creep in when a drawing was being made.

The first time *America* may have been measured was when dry docked at the naval dockyard in Le Havre for painting, before she went to England. These lines last were in the possession of maritime historian Capt. Arthur H. Clark in 1917.

America was again dry docked in the Portsmouth Naval Yard in England for some minor repairs between her victory of 22 August 1851 and a match race with *Titania* on 28 August. At the request of its commanding officer, Admiral William Loring, she was measured by British Admiralty draftsmen. It was the "Loring" lines that the Swedish artist, P.W. Cedergren, copied, and on which the Swedish schooner *Sverige* was based. And it is his work that pins down the date that the Admiralty drawing was made, for his sketchbook has a painting of her under sail on 12 September 1851. Cedergren and his companion, shipbuilder J.F. Andersen, may have been among the crowd that saw her in dry dock. They certainly managed to board her, and obtain as well the Admiralty drawings long enough to trace them. Cedergren did two sail plans as well, one with and one without the flying jib detested by Captain Dick Brown and his crew. The Admiralty lines were discovered and traced by Howard I. Chapelle in 1933, and are available from the Smithsonian's Museum of American History's maritime division.

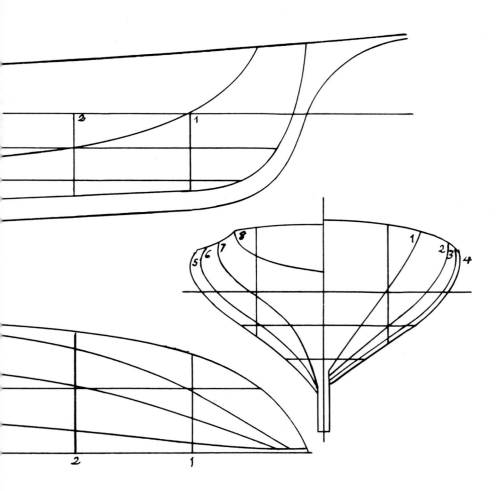

Cygnet

Schooner designed by George Steers, 1844, for William Edgar. 53' 2" long, 45 tons. One of the eight original vessels of the New York Yacht Club fleet. This small schooner shows the form typical of revenue cutters and pilot boats, the speediest small schooners of the early nineteenth century. The widest midship section is ahead of the middle of the vessel, and the bow is relatively blunt compared to the *America*'s. She shares the same deep V midsection, a shape proven to be efficient to windward in the light displacement Baltimore Clippers.

scale 1/4"=1'

Lines plan of *America*
Pencil and ink drawing,
  scale 1/2"=1'
Nelson Spratt
Courtesy N.Y.Y.C.
(15 5/8 x 52 5/8)

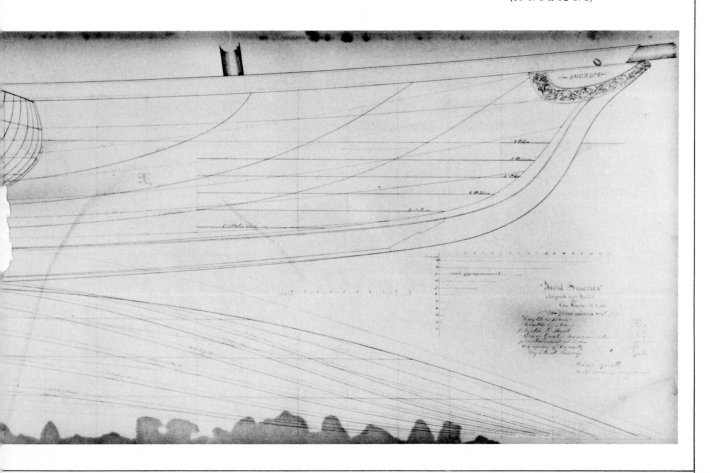

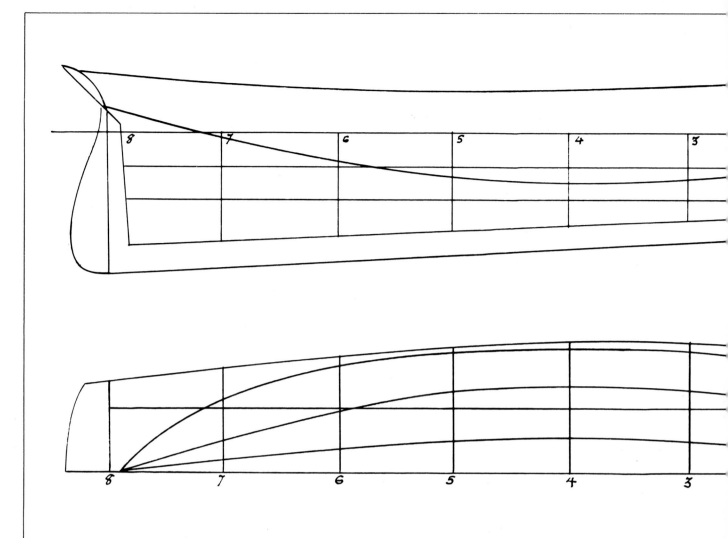

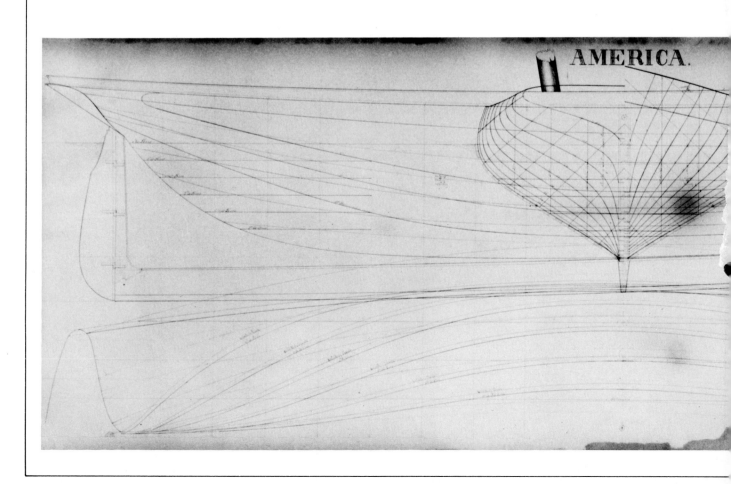

AMERICA.

She was measured again by Henry S. Pitcher at his yard in Northfleet on the Thames in 1859, when she was being rebuilt. The "Northfleet" lines are in the W.P. Stephens Collection at Mystic Seaport Museum, and were used by Stephens in his biography of the vessel written in 1924.

Finally, after *America* returned to the United States, as a prize of the United States Navy, Admiral Daniel Braine had her measured before she was sold in 1873. A copy of this drawing, dated 22 July 1876, is also in the W.P. Stephens Collection at Mystic.

Sail and Rigging Plans:

America's original sails were made by Rubin H. Wilson of Port Jefferson, Long Island. The New York Yacht Club's drawing, reproduced on page 16 purports to be the original sail plan, and a sailmaker's plan it certainly is, obvious from its simplicity and notations for another sail on the reverse. It differs in several important details from the plan published in *The Yacht "America"* in 1924, said to be from a photo of the original plan taken in 1901, before it was lost in a fire. This main topsail is a lug type, highly unusual for American vessels of the period. The sails are also two to four feet larger in their various dimensions than are dimensions given in later sail and rigging plans. However, the measurement on Wilson's plan may have been maximum or "not to exceed" dimensions. The sails may also have shrunk some after a season's use. Whether or not this is the plan referred to in the sailmaker's son Robert N. Wilson's letter to Stevens Institute, is also a mystery.

Mystic Seaport's Stearman drawing of October 1851 is the best record of rigging details and construction specifications we have. Done, like the Spratt drawing, after the vessel had achieved fame, it is a painstakingly careful record of the details of the vessel while they were fresh in the minds of her builders and riggers. It shows the nonexistent but intended main topsail, and a fore and mainsail slightly smaller than the Wilson drawing, but larger than the later Ratsey sail plan. However, the jib shown is two to three feet smaller than both the Wilson and Ratsey plans. Interestingly enough, it also shows no jib club, something *America* certainly carried in her New York debut, and later, in Europe.

The reasons Spratt and Stearman had for making their drawings did not survive with their work. Both may have been produced purely because of the interest *America* generated after her victory. Or they may have been commissioned by one of the syndicate members, or Steers himself, as a record of the schooner.

The Ratsey sail plan, drawn by George Ratsey in 1852 from dimensions obtained from the Admiralty take off (and probably obtained when he made her a main topsail and flying jib), came to the U.S. branch of the firm, and was donated to Mystic Seaport by Colin E. Ratsey. It is the one traced by both W.P. Stephens and Howard I. Chapelle.

B.A.G. Fuller

Sources:

Herreshoff, Lewis "Yachting in America," in Sullivan, Sir Edward, and others. 2 vols. *Yachting: The Badminton Library of Sports and Pastimes.* London: Longmans Green and Co., 1894.

Unpublished:

Webe, Dr. Gösta, "*America-Sverige*, Industrial Espionage, 1850's Fashion." Unpublished paper. Curatorial Department, Mystic Seaport Museum.

Stephens, William P. Letter to L. Francis Herreshoff, 18 December 1945. William P. Stephens Papers, G.W. Blunt White Library, Mystic Seaport Museum.

Hedengren, Torsten R. Letter to William P. Stephens, 29 April 1941. William P. Stephens Papers, G.W. Blunt White Library, Mystic Seaport Museum.

Specifications on Rigging Drawing of AMERICA
By John F. Stearman, October 31st 1851.

RIGGING PLAN OF AMERICA

Dimensions of Materials used in the construction of the yacht AMERICA
Keel, Stem & Stern-post sided Seven inches and a half.
After end – twenty-two inches. Bottom of Keel four inches thick – tapered
from the Garboard Streak downwards.
Deck beams of yellow pine – 9 x 5 1/2 inches – Round 4 1/2 inches –
Deck knees sided 5 inches – Hacometac – Boossom – Lodger – Knee
between each beam – Deck plank – white pine – 2 3/4 inches thick
3 3/4 inches wide –   Waterways on the Main Deck of white
Pine – 7 3/4 inches deep up and down –
Break of Quarter Deck – 7 3/4 inches – Plank on the top side 3 inches
thick – bottom 2 1/4 – 2 1/2 & 2 3/4 inches – Ceiling plank – 2 ins yellow pine –
Clamps 3 inches thick 3 Streaks – Hacmetac dead wood at each end –
Distance of Frames from centre to centre 21 inches – Floor timbers
sided 6 and 7 inches – the rest of the frame sided 5 inches –
Hacmetac at the Fore end –
Foremast 79 1/2 ft long – Mainmast 81 feet long – mast heads 7 feet each –
Mainboom 58 feet long – Main Gaff 28 feet long – Fore Gaff 25 feet long
Bowsprit 37 feet long – 17 ft outboard – Main topmast – 32 feet long
Rail 13 inches high forward – 13 ins in the centre & 6 1/2 ins Aft.
Cockpit Combings 8 inches high – Companion way Combings 19 inches high on
the after end – Fore end 7 inches high – Skylight Combings 9 inches high –
Hatch Combings 16 inches above deck – 5 1/2 inches thick –
Plankshear 3 inches thick – Rail 3 ins – Bulwarks White pine 7/8 thick

Rake of Mast 2 3/4 inches to a Foot
Built by George Steers of New York
In the Year 1851

Scale 1/4 of an inch equal to One Foot

Other dimensions and notes on drawing:

Bowsprit of yellow pine 16 x 16 (at stem head to) 10 1/2'' (at end)
Jib stay 10'' rope, (bob stay) 10'' rope
Stem 1 1/2'' on the front side
(Fore mast details:) 20 1/2'' (at partners), Neck of Mast 13 3/4 Hounds 1 3/4
7/8 iron rod (from jib stay) set up by a Turnbuckle to head of / mast

Fore and Main Throat Haulyard Blocks are 12 ins – Treble
Also the Peak Haulyard Blocks attached to the Mast
Two single ones to each side of the Gaffs
Jib also has 2 single 12'' blocks.
Masts of Norwegian Pine
Boom, Gaffs & Topmast of Spruce.
Bowsprit has a 3 inch hole through it – in order to dry it in the center –
The Sails are made of Colt's Cotton Duck, No. 2

Duck for Sails 22 inches wide –
Rake of Masts, 2 3/4 inches to a foot. –

Fore and Main Rigging 6 1/2 inch rope –
Main top and lift – 4'' rope –

Topmast Stay 2 3/4'' rope
Spring stay 5'' rope
Haulyards 3 1/2'' Manilla rope

(Topmast details) 4 3/4 (at base), 6 3/4 (at partners)
(Main mast details) 20 1/4''(at partners), 13 1/2''(at neck), 9 1/4'' (at head)
(Main boom details) 8''(inboard), 13'' (max), 7''(outboard)
(Main gaff details) 6 1/2''(inboard), 6 1/2''(max), 4'' outboard

Top and lift – 4'' rope
(reefs) 8 ft each

Bonnet of Jib, Bonnet of Foresail 12 ft
(Foot of Jib) 43 ft, (Foot of Foresail) 40 ft

61 Tons of Ballast in all. (40 tons stowed in mound at
foot of mainmast, 21 tons between timbers)

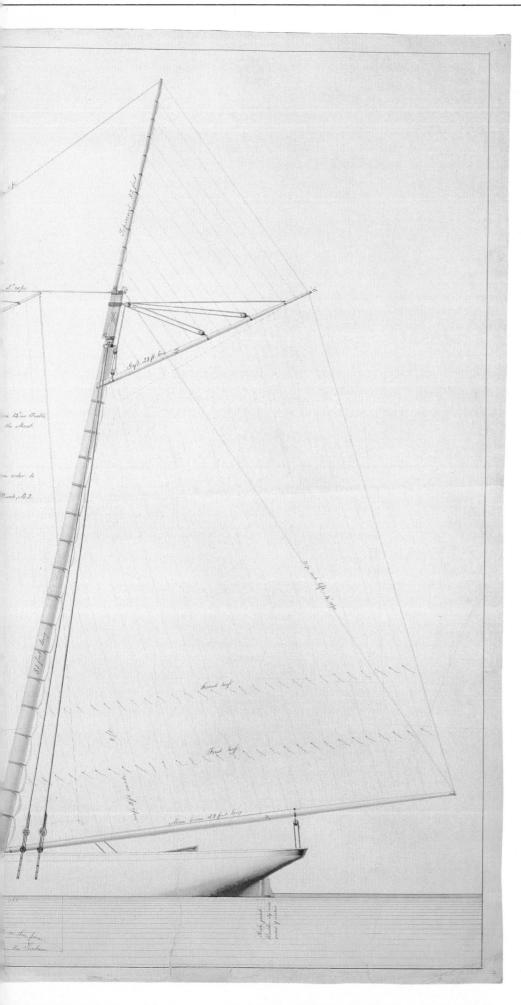

Rigging plan of *America*
Ink and watercolor drawing,
  scale 1/4"=1'
"Drawn by John F. Stearman/
 Mechanical Engineer,
 31 Lexington Avenue,
 New York City,
 October 31st 1851."
M.S.M. 79.22 (29 x37 1/4)

Dimensions of Materials used in the construction of the yacht America

Keel, Stem & Stern-post sided Seven inches and a half.

Depth of Keel in centre, below the Garboard Streak - Twenty-seven inches

After end - twenty-two inches. Bottom of Keel four inches thick & tapered

from the Garboard Streak downwards.

Deck beams of yellow pine - 9 x 5½ inches - Round 4½ inches -

Deck knees sided 5 inches - Hacmotac - Bosom & Lodger - Knee

between each beam - Deck planks white Pine - 2¾ inches thick.

3¾ inches wide -   Waterways on the Main Deck of white

Pine - 7¾ inches deep up and down -

Break of Quarter Deck. 7¾ inches - Plank on the top side 3 inches

thick - bottom 2¼ - 2½ & 2¾ inches - Ceiling plank 2 ins yellow pine.

Clamps 3 inches thick 3 Streaks - Hacmotac dead wood at each end -

Distance of Frames from centre to centre 21 inches - Floor timbers

sided 6 and 7 inches - the rest of the frame sided 5 inches -

Hacmotac at the Fore end -

Foremast 79½ ft long - Main mast 81 feet long - mast heads 7 feet each -

Main boom 58 feet long - Main Gaft 28 feet long - Fore Gaft 25 feet long -

Bowsprit 37 feet long - 17 ft outboard - Main topmast 52 feet long -

Rail 13 inches high forward - 13 ins in the centre & 6½ ins Aft.

Cockpit Combings 8 inches high - Companion way Combings 19 inches high on

the after end - Fore end 7 inches high - Skylight Combings 9 inches high -

Hatch Combings 16 inches above deck - 5½ inches thick -

Plankshear 5 inches thick - Rail 3 ins - Bulwarks White pine 7/8 thick -

Rake of Mast 2¾ inches to a Foot -

Built by George Steers of New York

In the year 1851.

Scale ¼ of an inch equal to One Foot -

Drawn by Jno. F. Reimers,
Mechanical Engineer. 31 Lexington Avenue, New York City, October 31st 1851.

Octagonal Head. 9½ inches

Neck of Mast 13¾. Hounds 13¾

Topmast Head

Halyards & Shrouds

24 ft long

Fore and Main Throat Haulyard Blocks
Also the Peak Haulyard Blocks attached
Two single ones to each of the Gafts.
Gaft also has 2 single 12" blocks.
Hounds of Norwegian pine.
Boom. Gafts & Topmast of Spruce.
Bowsprit has a 5 inch hole through each
dry it in the centre -
The Sheets are made of belt's botton

Duck for sails. 2½ inches wide -
Rake of Mast. 2¾ inches to a foot.
Fore and Main rigging 6½ inch rope.
Main top & lift 4" rope.

Mouth of Apron

Bonnet of Foresail

Jib stay 10 inch rope

Bonnet of Jib

12 ft

43 ft

Bowsprit of yellow pine. 17 ft outboard

Rail 5" thick

Butts 7/7

Plankshear 5" thick

Bulwarks of white pine 7/8 thick

46 ft

20 ft

Load-water-line

LINES AND
SAIL PLAN
OF *AMERICA*

The survival of documents like this sailplan is remarkable when we consider that these were working drawings, never thought of as "works of art" in their day. British sailmaker George Ratsey drew this plan over 130 years ago, used it to do some sail work for the schooner, then set it aside for future reference. Though worn, torn and badly waterstained, the drawing was saved and eventually it descended to the American branch of the Ratsey firm. It was recently donated to Mystic Seaport Museum by Colin E. Ratsey. The drawing has now been cleaned and restored to the limits of modern science, but it will always show the signs of its age and use.

Standard Grade

It is important to know what is expected of you. This page shows you how the English course is structured, how to do extra study for folio pieces and how to begin revision for examinations.

English

In English you will be given a grade in **reading**, **writing** and **talking**. These three elements are of equal value, contributing one-third each towards your overall grade.

Coursework accounts for two-thirds of your final grade: half of your **reading** and **writing** grades come from your folio; all of your **talking** grade is assessed in class.

Reading – folio

You are required to submit **three critical evaluations on texts** you have studied during your two-year course. Two must be from **prose**, **drama** and **poetry**, and the third can be from any genre, including **media**, or it could be an **imaginative response** to a text.

Writing – folio

Your writing folio consists of two pieces of writing. One should be broadly **transactional** / **discursive** in nature (giving information or expressing a point of view); the other should be primarily **expressive** / **imaginative** (a reflection on personal experience while conveying your thoughts and feelings or a specific genre, such as a short story).

Talking

Talk is graded through a series of targeted assessments in which your teacher will focus on your participation in **group discussions** or the delivery of **individual talks**.

Exams

Exams account for **one-third of your final grade** – 50% of your exam assessment is reading and 50% is writing.

Reading exam

Your reading exam consists of **two close reading papers** where you read a passage and then answer questions designed to test your understanding of the material.

Everyone sits the General Paper, which covers Grades 3 and 4. Depending on your potential achievement you either sit the Credit Paper, Grades 1 and 2, or the Foundation Paper, Grades 5 and 6. You will be awarded the highest grade achieved from the two papers you sit.

Writing exam

You are required to select a **single task** from a range of options and produce an essay within one hour and fifteen minutes. Your work is graded from 1 to 7.

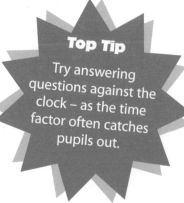

Top Tip

Try answering questions against the clock – as the time factor often catches pupils out.

Success guides

Leckie × Leckie

Standard Grade
English

Frank Fitzsimons × John Mannion

with contributions from Larry Flanagan

Contents

Writing skills

Writing

Reading: Responding To Literature

Reading: Prose

How to begin your revision

Know your course requirements

- If you **know the requirements of the course** then you will stand a much better chance of meeting them.
- Make sure that you **understand how your course is set out**.
- Ask your **teacher for advice** on what you can expect to face in your exams.
- **Look at past exam papers** fairly early in your course, since these will help you to understand what you have to aim for to get a good mark.

Complete your coursework

You cannot get a final grade unless all your folio is completed. You can always submit re-drafted assignments, with your teacher's agreement, to get better grades, providing that you are not overdoing it by racing to catch up with your coursework in several subjects. If you fall behind with your assignments, you risk producing poor ones by rushing them.

Produce an exam revision timetable

- **Time management is crucial** at every stage in your revision, not just in the exams.
- **Leave yourself time to relax** and do not overdo it! If you try too hard, you could end up doing your best work outside the exam room because you are too tired in the exam.
- Go to bed in good time and do not stay up late doing last-minute revision.
- Allow a few days in your revision timetable in which you do nothing at all. You will **recharge your batteries** and be the better for it.
- If you do not understand something, have a short break. Your brain unconsciously puzzles things out while you are doing something else. When you start your revision again the problem may seem simple to solve.
- Doing **a little study often** is better for the mind than doing a lot rarely. That is how people learn foreign languages.

Top Tip

Revise all aspects of punctuation early in your course. This will help you to produce better coursework and it will also give you more confidence for your final exams.

Team work

Pair up with a friend if this helps to motivate you. Why not proof-read each other's work? You will get better at spotting your own mistakes.

Catching up on missing assignments or producing better ones

You may have missed an assignment for a variety of reasons. Maybe you are dissatisfied with a folio assignment that you rushed. Perhaps you thought that you could have done a better assignment. Check with your teacher if you can work on a missed assignment at home or continue to re-draft work until you are satisfied with it. However, your teacher will have to be assured that the final piece is your own work because he or she has to sign a form to this effect for the SQA.

Punctuation again!

You cannot get good grades in English unless you can punctuate your writing skilfully and correctly. You may be still surviving on skills learned in Primary!

Why use punctuation?

- When you speak, you punctuate naturally through your pauses and body language.
- However, **when you write you have to help your reader understand what you mean through a variety of punctuation marks**.
- The more you know about punctuation, the better you will be able to express yourself.
- Pupils who use semi-colons and colons stand out from others, especially if they use these punctuation marks effectively.

> Markers can miss good points and ideas in your writing when their attention is continually drawn to punctuation errors.

Clarify ideas

Writing is a second-hand way of getting our meaning across to others; we need to punctuate our work to help our audience understand us.

Remember that when we let our writing pass into the hands of others, our punctuation marks and the words we use are all that there is to communicate our message. We are no longer in a position to correct any errors, as we would be if we were speaking directly to our audience.

To sum up: **we use punctuation marks to clarify** the points and ideas that we want to communicate to others.

Internet

Visit www.leckieandleckie.co.uk for links to helpful sites on punctuation. You'll find the links for the Standard Grade English Success Guides in the Learning Lab section of the site.

Begin all sentences and are used at the beginning of lines of verse.

Are used for **initials of people's names and places**. Remember that 'I' needs a capital letter too.

Are used when you begin **direct speech**; for example: Julia asked, 'Have you begun your revision for English yet?'

Have to be used for adjectives from **proper** (specific) **nouns**; for example: English, French, Elizabethan and McDonalds.

Capital letters

Need to be used in the **first and main words of titles** of books, newspapers, films, groups and programmes, etc.

Are used when writing letters with 'Dear' and 'Yours . . .'.

Are used for **days of the week, months, holidays** and **special days**.

Are used as **acronyms** for organisations; for example: BBC, NATO and GMTV. Note that you do not need a dot after each letter if it is a well-known organisation.

Top Tip

Get into the habit of proof-reading your work. Target the errors that you usually make.

Quick Test

1. Why is punctuation necessary?
2. List four occasions when you would use capital letters.
3. Correct the following sentences:
   a) 'what's the capital of portugal, lauren?'
   b) my favourite song at the moment is 'i knew i loved you' by savage garden.
4. Which words need a capital: hamburger restaurant, monday, summer, the atlantic, westlife, rspca, sea, christmas, louise?

Punctuating sentences

Full stops

A **full stop** is the main punctuation mark that **signals the end of one idea and the beginning of another**.

Sentences help to complete ideas in your writing. You can use full stops to make strong points in your writing, because they slow readers down.

Change your sentences by making some long and some short; **variety** helps to keep your audience interested in what you have to say. Try to be **expressive** through your choice of punctuation.

Read your work aloud and listen to where one idea ends and another begins. Each idea is a sentence. Trust your ears.

Top Tip

Select the punctuation mark that best fits the meaning and purpose. The more expressive you are, the better your writing will be.

Semi-colons

Semi-colons join two or more closely related ideas:

- Steve worked hard for his results; he stuck to his revision plan.
- Spring has come early; the trees have begun to blossom and the grassy banks are full of daffodils.

Semi-colons separate sets of items in a list when there are commas within the sets or lists:

- When you unpack your new computer you will find everything you need: multi-coloured leads; the plugs for your monitor and base unit; the speakers with their leads; a microphone, if this is included, with a stand; manuals for your computer and, if you are lucky, lots of interesting software.

NB: You do not need a capital letter after a semi-colon.

Colons

Colons are two dots, one above the other. They are used to:

- **introduce a list**
  You should bring to your exam: a watch, two pens, a ruler, tissues and hope!

- **introduce quotations**
  Hamlet ponders: 'To be or not to be? That is the question.'
  (It is also acceptable to use a comma here.)

- **expand on the meaning of a previous idea**
  Tracy scored the highest grade in the exam: it was an A*.

A dash can also do the job of a colon by emphasising the sentence that follows:

- Tom had achieved fantastic results in his exams – he got As in five of them.

- **punctuate dialogue in plays**
  Macbeth: If we should fail?
  Lady Macbeth: We fail!
                  But screw your courage to the sticking place, And we'll not fail.

Other punctuation

Exclamation marks

Exclamation marks help to express surprise, anger, fear, joy and most other emotions. For example: Louise! It is good to see you!

Question marks

Question marks can be used for **rhetorical questions** where no direct reply is expected, only mental agreement; for example: 'Who could defend a statement like that?'

They can also be used for **requests for information**: 'What time is it?'

You do not need a question mark for an indirect question: 'Siobhan asked me for a pen.'

Look at how professional writers use punctuation as you read their work. Pause over some passages and think about the effectiveness of the punctuation.

Top Tip

To get high grades in Standard Grade you will need to vary the length of your sentences and the style of your punctuation.

Quick Test

1. Explain one of the things that semi-colons can do.
2. What does a full stop do?
3. Can a colon introduce a list of items?
4. Can colons be used to introduce a quotation?
5. Give one other purpose for a colon.

Answers 1. They link two closely related phrases or separate sets of items in a list where there are commas within the sets. **2.** It marks the end of a sentence. **3.** Yes. **4.** Yes. **5.** It links another phrase which expands upon the meaning of the first, or punctuates dialogue in plays.

Speech marks and commas

The skilful use of punctuation marks can improve your expression

Commas

Commas separate items in lists:
- I would like three hamburgers, a cheeseburger, a large serving of fries and a coffee.

Commas clarify sentences that could be misleading:
- After a period of calm, students returned after the fire alarm.

Commas need to be used in direct speech:
- Elaine was curious about the previous evening and asked, 'Where did you get to?'
  'The shopping centre,' John replied.

Commas can be used to mark off words, phrases, and connectives in sentences:
- Billy, who did not like to be made fun of, was angry.
- On the other hand, there was no harm in what Carly said.

Top Tip

Be careful not to use commas instead of full stops in sentences.

Speech marks

There are four main rules for setting out speech:

1. Use **inverted commas** for the words spoken: Catherine said, 'I haven't seen you in ages!'
2. **Direct speech must be separated from the rest of the writing by a punctuation mark**; see the comma in the example above.
3. Remember to **use a capital letter** when you begin the direct speech: Catherine said, 'It's ages since I last saw you.'
4. Each time you introduce a **new speaker**, begin a new line and indent. That is, begin the speech of your new speaker three letter spaces to the right of the margin.

Quotation marks

- Quotation marks are **inverted commas for words or phrases cited from texts**. Use single inverted commas for speech and double inverted commas for speech within speech. For example: Jane shouted to her husband in the next room, 'Your mother phoned and she said, "When are you going to visit me?" Colin, I thought that you called in on her last week.'

- **Remember to close quotation marks**. It is confusing for readers and markers if you fail to do so! To show that you are ending a quotation, place the final full stop on the outside of the inverted comma; for example: In *My Fair Lady* Eliza Doolittle shows her independence from Professor Higgins when she says, 'I can do without you'.

Eliza Doolittle.

Title marks

- In secondary schools, **inverted commas** are used to signify book titles, stories, newspapers, magazines, television programmes, movies or shows. For example: 'My Fair Lady' is the title of the musical or 1964 film version of the play, 'Pygmalion'.

- In your writing always use title marks to show the difference between **eponymous characters** and the names of the work in which they appear. For example: Macbeth is a character whereas 'Macbeth' is a play. (Eponymous characters share their names with the titles of their texts.)

- The convention (or accepted rule) for titles in universities is to underline them, e.g. <u>Hamlet</u> and <u>Macbeth</u>. The main thing is to **remain consistent** in your method of identifying titles.

- Note that if you use italics for titles then this is acceptable for printed work.

Quick Test

1. Identify three uses for commas.

2. Make up a sentence in which you use all four rules for setting out speech.

3. What do you need to use when you write out the title of a film, book or story?

Answers 1. They can mark off a list and phrases within a sentence; they are used within direct speech. **2.** Phil said, 'Buy the latest team shirt.' / 'It is too expensive,' said Paul. **3.** Title marks, underlining or italics.

Apostrophes

Apostrophes help to show that something belongs to someone (possession) or to shorten words (contraction).

Its and *it's* can be confusing words.
- If you wrote, 'I emptied a box of its contents', you would not need an apostrophe because *its* in this instance is a possessive pronoun.
- If you say, 'It's going to rain all day', you need an apostrophe because you mean *it is*.

Apostrophes of possession

Top Tip
Abbreviated words are only to be used in informal writing. We use them when we speak or write to friends or family. Avoid using shortened words in your assignments and exams unless you are asked to do so.

Possessive pronouns

Pronouns like these do not need apostrophes to show ownership:
- **my**, e.g. The watch is mine.
- **his or hers**, e.g. The computer is hers.
- **yours**, e.g. The bag is yours.
- **its**, e.g. The box was emptied of its contents.
- **ours**, e.g. The car is ours.
- **theirs**, e.g. The house is theirs.

Apostrophes of ownership for one person or thing

If there is a **single owner, place the apostrophe before the 's'**:
- Tim's video player
- Christine's house

Apostrophes of ownership for more than one owner

If there is **more than one owner**, you need to **put the apostrophe after the 's'** to show that you mean a plural owner:
- The Jacksons' video
- The Smiths' house

If a person's name already ends in 's', you can do one of two things:
- James's haircut or James' haircut

Whichever style you go for, remain consistent.

If a plural noun does not need an 's' to make it plural, you should place your apostrophe before the 's':
- The men's business venture
- The children's playground
- The women's society
- The people's champion

Expression

You can **vary your expression by using an apostrophe**. For example, 'The claws of the cat' becomes 'The cat's claws' with an apostrophe.

If you are unsure of whether to use a possessive apostrophe then write your sentence the long way round. For example, 'Dan's new house' becomes 'The new house of Dan'.

Always ask yourself why you are inserting an apostrophe. Do not put it in just for good measure.

Apostrophes of contraction

Apostrophes are used to show that one or more letters have been missed out.

Contractions combine two words into one with an apostrophe.

- I'm = I am
- They're = They are
- Won't = Will not
- Doesn't = Does not
- Can't = Cannot
- Would've = Would have

Apostrophes when writing the time or dates

- 'I will see Dave at 7 o'clock.' This is the short way of writing 'seven of the clock'.

Missing numbers in dates can be suggested by an apostrophe:

- 21st of September '99
- 3rd of November '01

Apostrophes in plays

Playwrights such as Shakespeare shortened their words to allow their verse to remain in **iambic pentameter**. Shakespeare tried to divide his blank-verse lines into ten syllables, that is, five feet of two syllables each.

Take this example from *Romeo and Juliet*, in which Romeo wants Juliet to exchange vows:

- Romeo: 'Th' exchange of thy love's faithful vow for mine.'

Apostrophes in dialect

Apostrophes are used a great deal by writers when they try to represent local dialect:

- ' 'ow's it goin' me ole mate?'

William Shakespeare

Quick Test

True or false?

1. Possessive pronouns can take apostrophes.

2. Apostrophes lengthen words.

3. Apostrophes can help to show ownership.

4. If a person's name ends with an 's', you can put the apostrophe after it.

5. I ca'nt is correct.

6. Apostrophes of possession can help to vary your sentences and make them shorter.

Answers 1. False. **2.** False. **3.** True. **4.** True. **5.** False. **6.** True.

Sentences

Sentence types

Sentences can be put into four groups according to what they do. They can be **statements** (which give information), **exclamations** (e.g. My Goodness!), **instructions or commands** (e.g. Insert your card this way up.) or **questions**. Sentences are also grouped into structures: simple, compound, complex and minor.

1. **Simple sentences** must contain:
   - **a subject** (what / who does the action)
   - **a verb** (the action)

They can have other parts as well, such as:
   - **an object** (the person or thing acted upon)
   - **a complement** (additional information about the subject)
   - **adverbials** (additional information about the verb)

When they form part of other sentences, simple sentences are usually referred to as **clauses**.

2. **Compound sentences** **join two or more sentences together**. The two parts are joined by **coordinating conjunctions**, such as 'and', 'but' or 'or'. For example: Do you want to catch the bus or will you walk home?

3. **Complex sentences** have **two or more clauses joined by subordinating conjunctions**, such as 'although', 'because' or 'if'. The **main clause** makes sense on its own. The **subordinate clause** does not make sense on its own; for example:

   I didn't see you at the party **although** I looked everywhere.

   If you read in this light, you'll hurt your eyes.

4. **Minor sentences** usually consist of a single verb or verb phrase. They are often used in instructions or commands, for example: Listen.

> **Top Tip**
> Examiners are looking for a variety of sentence styles in your writing. Avoid too many sentences joined by coordinating conjunctions. Remember that short, sharp sentences can be very effective.

> Note that the subordinate clause can occur at the beginning of the sentence as well as at the end.

The anatomy of a sentence

The **different parts of speech**, such as **noun**, **pronoun**, **adjective**, **verb** and **adverb**, **conjunctions** and **prepositions**, can be single words or short phrases:

- adjective   noun   verb   adverb
  Old   Alex   walked   slowly.

- Last Wednesday   the   early   train   was derailed   unexpectedly.
  adverbial phrase   *adjective* *noun*   *verb*   *adverb*

It is important to remember that you can only tell what part of speech a word or phrase is when it is in a sentence. For example:

London looks like a noun because it is the name of a place, but in the sentence *I caught the London bus* it is an adjective.

Walk looks like a verb because it is an action, but in the sentence *They went for a walk* it is a noun.

Variety within sentences

As well as using all the different sentence types, you will impress examiners if you **vary the internal structure of your sentences**. Two ways of doing this involve:

- placing the most important information at the beginning of the sentence
- withholding important information until the end to create suspense.

For example: *Passing my driving test was probably one of the proudest moments of my life* places emphasis on the passing of the test; whereas *One of the proudest moments of my life was probably passing my driving test* uses exactly the same words but places the emphasis on how the speaker felt.

The passive voice

The **passive voice places emphasis on the thing done rather than the person or thing performing an action**. It uses part of the verb *to be*, such as *is* or *was*, plus a past participle, such as *heard* or *taken*. For example:

- Two pills are to be taken twice per day.
- The glass was broken.

However, **overuse of the passive should be avoided**. Writing is rather flat if you don't know who is doing what.

The use of pronouns

Pronouns stand in for nouns, e.g. I, you, he, she, it, we, they, him, her, its, himself. In a compound sentence it often makes sense not to repeat the noun. However, if there is more than one character involved, **pronouns can become confusing**. Can you understand the following sentence?

> Patrick gave the CD to Joe but he was annoyed when he didn't tell him that he had recorded it.

Its and it's

Its is a possessive pronoun which causes problems because of its similarity to *it's* – the short form of *it is*, e.g. *It's annoying when the dog loses its bone.*

If you can't decide which version you should use, try expanding the short form to its longer form, e.g. **It is** *annoying when the dog loses* **it is** *bone*. The first it's makes sense but the second one doesn't.

Quick Test

True or false?

1. Independent clauses can make sense on their own.

2. 'When you look into them' is a sentence.

3. The sentence, 'Write your name in block capitals' is a statement.

4. Varying your sentences can improve your expression.

Answers 1. True. 2. False. 3. False: it is a command or an instruction. 4. True.

15

Spellings

Methods of learning tricky spellings

1. Look up words in **dictionaries** and check their spellings. Dictionaries work on the alphabet principle for each word and finding words becomes easier with practice. Carry a small dictionary with you. Relying on teachers and others to spell words for you means that you will never really learn them. Aim to be an independent learner.

2. The **Look–Say–Cover–Write–Check** method is successful as long as you have spelled the word correctly in the first place. Learning words by repeating this process does work.

3. Try writing a crazy but **memorable sentence** using each letter of the word (a **mnemonic**). For example, a mnemonic for the word believe could be: *Big Elephants Look Inside Elephantine Vases Everywhere*. However, only use this method for the few words that are the biggest problems for you, otherwise you will have too many strange phrases to remember.

4. Use the **sound of words** to help you spell them. Work your way through each syllable as you aim to spell the word. This works for many words and is always worth trying before using other methods.

5. For **tricky plural endings**:
   - If a noun ends with a 'y' and it has a letter such as 't', 'r' or 'n' before the 'y', you need to add 'ies' to the plural. For example: *diary – diaries; curry – curries; company – companies; city – cities*.
   - If the last letter before the 'y' is a vowel (a, e, i, o, u) you have to add an 's' to make the plural. For example: *boy – boys; journey – journeys; key – keys; guy – guys; monkey – monkeys*.
   - Words which end in 'fe', such as *knife*, take 'ves' in plurals; similarly, words ending in 'f', like *shelf* or *half*, change to *shelves* and *halves* in plurals.

6. Use **'i' before 'e' except after 'c'**; for example; *thief* and *sieve*, but *receive*.

7. **Proof-read** your work for words that you are likely to spell incorrectly. Make a list of these words from a number of subjects and focus on learning them.

Word families

A good way of improving your spelling is to realise that words belong to **word families**. This means that, if you know the basic word, you will have a good idea about other similar words. For instance, the spelling of *criticism* is easier if you remember that it is related to *critic*. Here are some other useful word families.

- **act**, actor, action, activity, react, reaction
- **assist**, assistant, assistance
- **balance**, imbalance, unbalanced
- **bore**, boring, boredom
- **call**, recall, calling
- **child**, children, childhood, childlike, childish, childless
- **claim**, reclaim, reclamation, disclaim
- **cover**, discover, discovery, uncover
- **critic**, criticism, criticise, critique
- **electric**, electrical, electricity, electrician, electronic, electrocute
- **examine**, examination, examiner, examinee
- **fill**, fulfil, fulfilling, fulfilment
- **give**, given, forgive, forgiveness
- **govern**, governor, government

- **hand**, handler, handy, handicraft
- **hero**, heroic, heroism
- **joy**, joyful, enjoy, enjoyment
- **light**, lightening, lightning, delighted, enlighten
- **machine**, machinery, machinist
- **medic**, medical, medication
- **native**, nation, national, nativity
- **nature**, natural, unnatural, denatured
- **obey**, disobey, disobedient
- **operate**, operator, cooperate, cooperation
- **pack**, packet, package
- **pain**, painkiller, painful, painless, painstaking
- **pass**, passage, passenger
- **press**, impress, depression, repress, express
- **prison**, imprison, imprisonment

- **prove**, approval, disapprove
- **public**, publication, publicity, publicise
- **relate**, relative, relation
- **shake**, shakily, shaken
- **sign**, signatory, signature, signal, resign, resignation
- **sum**, summary, summation, assume, assumption
- **syllable**, monosyllable, monosyllabic, polysyllabic
- **take**, mistake, mistaken, overtaken, overtaking, partaking.

Quick Test

1. What is the difference between an *examiner* and an *examinee*?
2. Can you think of any other words that make this distinction?
3. What connection can you see between the meanings of the words *operate* and *cooperation*?
4. Can you explain why *fulfil* and *fulfilment* are spelled differently from *fulfilling*?

Answers 1. An *examiner* is the person doing the examining; an *examinee* is the person being examined. **2.** Nominator, nominee; payer, payee; trainer, trainee. The other half of the pair for words like *refugee* and *evacuee* is not used. **3.** They both have to do with work. **4.** The 'l' is doubled in *fulfilling* to keep the 'i' sound short.

Words often misspelled

Commonly misspelled words

A–F

accommodation
actually
alcohol
although
analyse
analysis
argument
assessment
atmosphere
audible
audience
autumn

beautiful
beginning
believe
beneath
buried
business

caught
chocolate
climb
column
concentration
conclusion
conscience
consequence
continuous
creation

daughter
decide
decision
definite
design
development
diamond
diary
disappear
disappoint

embarrass
energy
engagement
enquire
environment
evaluation
evidence
explanation

February
fierce
forty
fulfil
furthermore

G–O

guard

happened
health
height

imaginary
improvise
industrial
interesting
interrupt
issue

jealous

knowledge

listening
lonely
lovely

marriage
material
meanwhile
miscellaneous
mischief
modern
moreover
murmur

necessary
nervous

original
outrageous

P–R

parallel
participation
pattern
peaceful
people
performance
permanent
persuade
persuasion
physical
possession
potential
preparation
prioritise
proportion
proposition

questionnaire
queue

reaction
receive
reference
relief
research
resources

S–W

safety
Saturday
secondary
separate
sequence
shoulder
sincerely
skilful
soldier
stomach
straight
strategy
strength
success
surely
surprise

technique
technology
tomorrow

unfortunately

Wednesday
weight
weird
women

Top Tip

English is a notoriously difficult language to spell; however, with effort you can overcome most obvious misspellings. Why not go through the lists here and try some of the exercises suggested on page 16? The main learning method is: Look–Say–Cover–Write–Check.

Common homophones and confusions

Homophones sound the same, but have different meanings.

a lot, allot (*never alot as a single word*)
advise, advice (*verb, noun*)
affect, effect (*to influence, a result*)
allowed, aloud (*permitted, out loud*)
bean, been (*as in baked bean, part of the verb to be*)
beech, beach (*tree, seashore*)
blue, blew (*colour, air moved*)
board, bored (*wood or group of managers, uninterested*)
bought, brought (*purchased, carried*)
break, brake (*damage, slow down*)
by, buy, bye (*next to or responsible for, purchase, farewell*)
cell, sell (*enclosed space, dispose of for money*)
cent, scent, sent (*coin, smell, dispatched*)
cereal, serial (*grain, a story in parts*)
choose, chose (*present tense, past tense*)
cloth, clothe (*material, to dress*)
conscience, conscious (*sense of right or wrong, aware*)
course, coarse (*route or direction, rough*)
dear, deer (*beloved or expensive, animal*)
fate, fete (*destiny, celebration*)
flour, flower (*bread ingredient, part of plant*)
grate, great (*metal grid, very large*)
hair, hare (*on head, animal*)
herd, heard (*group, listened to*)
here, hear (*this place, listen*)
him, hymn (*that man, religious song*)
hole, whole (*pit, complete*)
hour, our (*time, belonging to us*)
it's, its (*it is, belonging to it*)
key, quay (*lock opener, boat dock*)
knight, night (*wears armour, darkness*)
knot, not (*rope tie or nautical speed, negative*)
know, no (*be aware, negative*)
made, maid (*built or done, servant*)

main, mane (*important, lion's hair*)
meet, meat (*come together, animal flesh*)
might, mite (*may or strength, small insect or small amount*)
morning, mourning (*early part of day, grieving*)
new, knew (*recent, was aware*)
pane, pain (*part of window, hurt*)
peace, piece (*quiet, segment or part*)
place, plaice (*location, fish*)
plane, plain (*flat surface or short for aeroplane, not beautiful or large expanse of flat land*)
practise, practice (*to practise, a practice*)
quiet, quite (*not loud, fairly*)
read, reed (*e.g. read a book, kind of grass*)
rein, rain, reign (*horse equipment, water, royal rule*)
right, write (*correct, use pen*)
rode, road, rowed (*used vehicle, carriageway, used oars*)
scene, seen (*part of play, looked at*)
see, sea (*look, body of water*)
sew, so, sow (*use needle and thread, therefore, plant seed*)
site, sight (*place, vision*)
source, sauce (*origin, food supplement*)
stair, stare (*steps, look hard*)
steel, steal (*metal, take*)
sum, some (*total, a few*)
sun, son (*thing in sky, male descendant*)
tail, tale (*part of animal, story*)
their, they're, there (*belonging to them, they are, that place*)
too, two, to (*in addition, 2, in the direction of*)
vain, vein (*self admiring, blood vessel*)
waist, waste (*below stomach, not used*)
week, weak (*seven days, without strength*)
where, wear (*which place, clothes*)
you, yew, ewe (*person, tree, female sheep*)
you're, your (*you are, belonging to you*)

Synonyms

Synonyms are words that have similar meanings, for example:

- beautiful – pretty, nice, fine, good-looking, elegant, lovely, fair

- display – show, exhibit, exhibition, spread, open, expose, demonstration, layout.

Structures

Connective words link phrases, sentences and paragraphs together.

Ordering your ideas

Words that help to put your ideas in order

- *firstly, then, so far, secondly, in the end, next, eventually, subsequently, at last, at length, afterwards*

Words for exceptions

- *only, if, unless, except (for), save for*

Making points and giving examples

Words used to argue and make points

- *consequently, thus, so, as a result, because, as, hence, therefore, since, until, whenever, accordingly, as long as*

Words to help you give examples

- *for example, for instance, such as, take the case of, thus, as (evidence), to show that, as revealed by*

Words for extra points or ideas

- *and, too, what is more, also, furthermore, and then, again, moreover, as well as, in addition*

Words to emphasise points

- *above all, in particular, notably, specifically, indeed, more important, especially, significant(ly), in fact*

in addition
take the case of
as a result
above all
therefore

Paragraphing

Paragraphs are necessary to break the text flow and help the reader to follow the writer's meaning.

- Paragraphs are **groups of sentences connected by the same topic**. Each paragraph carries a main idea.
- The main sentence of a paragraph is often found at the beginning and it is called a **topic sentence**. For example: *Successful students plan their revision in each subject. They plan how much time they have available and then try to cover a number of areas in each subject.*
- Any paragraphs following the first paragraph will need to **begin on a new line, indented 2 cm from the page margin**.
- You can link your paragraphs together skilfully by using the **connecting words** found in the boxes on these pages.

Being persuasive and analytical

Words to persuade

- of course, naturally, obviously, clearly, certainly, surely, evidently

Words to help you show an opinion or analyse

- it would seem, to suggest, one might conclude / propose / deduce / infer / imply / say / consider

Comparing and contrasting

Words to make a contrast or show what is different

- but, nevertheless, alternatively, despite this, on the contrary, however, yet, the opposite, instead, whereas, to turn to, although, still, on the other hand

Words to compare things in your writing or show what is similar

- equally, in the same way, as with, likewise, similarly, compared with, an equivalent

Essay endings

Words to sum up or end with

- in brief, in summary, throughout, in all, on the whole, to sum up, overall, finally, to conclude, to recap, in the end

```
in summary
on the whole
to conclude
```

Top Tip

Use appropriate and varied connective words in your essays to signpost your arguments.

Quick Test

1. Why use paragraphs?

2. Identify two words that can help you to compare pieces of writing.

3. What is the difference between comparing and contrasting?

4. Give two words that help to emphasise points in writing.

5. What do the words furthermore and moreover help you to do?

Answers 1. Paragraphs help readers to follow your ideas. They also break up the text according to topics. **2.** Any of the following: in the same way, similarly, equally, as with, likewise, compared with, an equivalent. **3.** To compare is to look for similarities and to contrast is to look for differences. **4.** Any of the following: indeed, in particular, above all, notably, specifically, more importantly, especially, significantly, in fact. **5.** They help you to make extra points or ideas.

Improve your style

Control

Teachers and examiners are looking for control in your writing. This means an awareness of the effect that **different writing techniques** can have and **deliberate use of them**.

Vocabulary and choice of words

The words you choose need to be **appropriate** for the task and as **accurate** as possible. For example, does your character get into a car, a battered old Ford, a people carrier or an oversized all-terrain vehicle? Do characters 'say' things all the time or do they 'mutter', 'mumble' or 'shout'?

Varying sentences and paragraphs

You already know about using different types of sentences, but you should also think about the **rhythm of your writing**. Large stretches of **long sentences can create a sense of continuity and flow**, but they can also become monotonous.

Try short sentences for emphasis. Even more emphatic than the short sentence is the short paragraph.

A single sentence paragraph really stands out.

You can build up tension by using short, snappy sentences that make the reader pause over each detail:

> 'I ran. Ran for all I was worth! Sometimes I stumbled over tree roots. Branches slashed my face. Something was rapidly hunting me down. Twigs and branches snapped in the desperate rushing behind me. A savage, wolf-like howl tore the air. Something clasped my leg! "God help me!" I screamed, as I gasped for breath.'

Varying sentence structures

The first part of a sentence tends to contain the subject. In the middle of the sentence there is often known information – the new information comes at the end. From time to time you can vary this order. Compare the impact of: *As I put the car into gear the engine went 'thunk'* with *'Thunk' went the engine as I put the car into gear*.

You also have a great deal of choice when it comes to the placing of **adverbial phrases**. These tell you about things like time, mood and manner. For example:

- *With deliberate slowness,* Dr Shrike marked out the area he was going to cut.
- Dr Shrike, *with deliberate slowness,* marked out the area he was going to cut.
- Dr Shrike marked out the area he was going to cut *with deliberate slowness.*

Descriptive writing

The power of descriptive writing comes in the **accurate choice of nouns and verbs**. Adjectives and adverbs can help to pin down what you say even more accurately. Always make sure that your adjectives or adverbs are doing some work. For example, *he walked slowly* could be conveyed with the single verb *he strolled*; *a gnarled oak* will create a much clearer picture in your readers' minds than *a big twisted tree*. Finally, remember to **appeal to all five senses in descriptive writing**.

Some pitfalls to avoid

- Do not confuse big words with a sophisticated style. Remember that you want to give your readers as clear a picture as possible.
- Do not overdo any one effect. If all your sentences have an unusual structure, people will find it distracting.
- Use figurative language sparingly. One well-chosen simile or metaphor will stand out like a rose in a desert.

Top Tip

A clear, fluent, written style is something that you are going to have to work at. Examine the style of the writers you are studying and think about phrases, words and punctuation that could work for you.

How to improve your expression

Clarity and brevity

- Keep what you write **brief**, **simple** and **clear**.
- **Avoid long-winded, pompous sentences**; for example: *I remained in my abode and passed the time watching uninteresting programmes while looking at the little box in the corner.* This is tedious; try this instead: *I stayed at home watching boring programmes on TV.*

Clichés

Clichés are **tired expressions and imagery** that have **lost impact because of overuse**. Avoid the following:

like the plague
food for thought

like two ships that pass in the night
leaves much to be desired

Writing effective sentences

In a stylish, effective sentence:

- the beginning is the second-most important part;
- the middle is the least important part;
- the end is the most important part.

Take, for example, this line from Shakespeare's *Twelfth Night*:

'Some are born great, some achieve greatness and some have greatness thrust upon 'em.'

Avoid overworked words because they can be boring and repetitive, e.g. got, get, nice, good, totally, a lot of, kind of.

Avoid using tautologies – that is, repeating yourself unnecessarily, e.g. final end, sad misfortune, puzzling mystery.

Also try to **avoid reinforcing words** with words that would be better left out; your writing will have more impact without them. Word-reinforcement to avoid includes: totally wrong, absolutely fantastic, seriously consider.

Circumlocutions

Circumlocutions are **roundabout ways of saying things**. Again, stick to simple words or expressions, as these are usually more effective:

- in a majority of cases = usually
- in the event that = if
- owing to the fact that = because

- in less than no time = quickly
- on the grounds that = because
- with the exception of = except.

Top Tip

Try to improve your expression as you develop the habit of proof-reading your work. The Russian writer Chekhov said, 'Rewrite everything five times!'

Quick Test

1. Reduce these phrases to one word:
   - **a)** due to the fact that
   - **b)** pink in colour
   - **c)** in this day and age.

2. What is the danger of overdoing description?

3. Identify a cliché and explain why you should try to avoid clichés in your writing.

Answers 1. a) because **b)** pink; **c)** now. **2.** The readers could lose sight of your meaning. **3.** There are numerous examples of clichés; for example, 'shot in the foot'. The image has no impact and will simply pass readers by, or worse, bore them.

Test your progress

Use the questions to test your progress.
Check your answers at the back of the book on page 94–5.

Punctuation and sentences

1. Try to sum up in a sentence why you need to punctuate your writing.

   ....

2. Identify five instances where you would need a capital letter.

   ....

3. Correct the following sentences by putting in capital letters where they are necessary:

   • jemma read Great Expectations for her english coursework. she had never read charles dickens before; she may read another one of his novels before easter.

   ....

4. Identify four of the five punctuation marks that can complete a sentence.

   ....

5. Explain one of the uses that semi-colons can serve.

   ....

6. What is a rhetorical question?

   ....

7. Identify one use for colons.

   ....

8. Give three of the four rules of direct speech.

   ....

9. What are the two main purposes of apostrophes?

   ....

10. Where does the apostrophe need to go with plural nouns that do not need an 's' to make them plurals?

    ....

11. Identify three of the four types of sentences grouped according to what they do.

    ....

12. Point out the main and dependent clauses of this sentence:

    • I will go to see the new movie at the cinema as soon as I have done the washing up.

    ....

Spelling and expression

13. Point out two methods of learning tricky spellings.

    ....

14. What is before 'e' except after 'c'?

....

15. Why do the following plurals end in 'ies': twenties, lorries, cities, injuries and berries?

....

16. Why do the following plurals end in 's': journeys, trolleys, donkeys, chimneys, toys?

....

17. What do 'here', 'there' and 'where' have in common?

....

18. Correct the following spellings: begginning, apperance, intrested, grammer, tonge, definately, neccesity, rythm, sentance.

....

19. What are synonyms?

....

20. Why are homophones confusing?

....

21. What are connectives?

....

22. What is the purpose of connectives in writing?

....

23. Why is it necessary to use paragraphs?

....

24. What is a topic sentence?

....

25. Briefly explain what 'control' means in writing.

....

26. Reduce this circumlocution to one word: 'on the grounds that'.

....

27. The following piece of writing has ten errors involving punctuation. Write it out correctly.

The opening line of Tennysons poem the eagle is very striking.
'He clasps the crag with crooked hands'
The most noticeable thing about it is the use of the word hands where the reader might have expected something like talons or claws. The second thing that makes the line striking is the alliteration on the letter c. The repeated cs give the line a harsh sound which is in keeping with the eagles harsh environment.

How did you do?

1–9	correct	start again
10–15	correct	getting there
16–22	correct	good work
23–27	correct	excellent

25

Transactional writing

What you are expected to do

The task for your W1 folio piece is to **produce a piece of writing that either conveys information or deploys ideas, expounds, argues and evaluates**. (You may choose to tackle another piece of writing like this in your exam.)

What you can write about

A transactional piece, W1, could be:

- an informative piece on a topic that interests you
- a piece of writing in which you give your view on a subject, for example, animal experimentation
- a discursive essay exploring two sides of a topic.

How you will be graded

To achieve Grades 1–3 you will need to:

- **research** your chosen topic carefully and then **use ideas and evidence** effectively
- **organise** your writing so that it is a detailed response to the task, with significant points being highlighted
- **interest** your readers and sustain points
- use an **appropriate** range of **punctuation** to make your meaning clear
- use **your own words**
- show both **elaboration** and **conciseness** in your writing
- use **wide-ranging vocabulary** in which syntax, spelling and punctuation is **accurate** and **varied**
- consciously use language to achieve sophisticated effects
- produce a **well-structured** piece of work
- write between 600–800 words.

Top Tip

Always consider the purpose and intended audience of your writing.

Top Tip

Develop your paragraphs in a variety of ways: provide evidence, give examples, use statistics, compare and contrast, illustrate with anecdote, question and answer. Remember that good paragraphs have effective topic sentences.

Organising transactional writing

Consider the **task and topic**, and think about the **appropriate form of writing**: an article, essay, letter, etc. Topics that would meet the requirement for a W1 piece might include:

- an informative piece on an activity you are involved in
- a biography of someone in your family
- your viewpoint on a controversial area, such as the use of CCTV and issues of privacy.

Researching your topic

Once you have chosen a topic, do the **research**: see experts who know the topic, go to libraries, use the Internet, look in encyclopedias, write to associated organisations.

Make notes on one side of a piece of paper; number any pages that you use. Alternatively, make a mind-map if you prefer. Instructions on how to produce a mind-map are given on pages 38–41.

Planning your writing

Once you have completed your notes, look over them and **plan your piece of writing** on a single sheet of paper. Number your points; this could be organised as a brainstorm.

Drafting your essay

Remember to **write your title** when you write or type your first draft. If you hand-write your work, leave every second line blank for proof-reading and alterations; this will make it easier to check your work at each draft. **Always proof-read your work for spelling, punctuation and expression**. Remember to proof-read your final draft again for the errors that you are likely to make.

A plan for a discursive essay

Introduction – Introduce the topic and state your attitude clearly.
Paragraph 2 – Introduce your first point in support of your viewpoint.
Paragraph 3 – Make a second point in support and develop your stance.
Paragraph 4 – Produce a final argument in support of your view.
Paragraph 5 – State an opposite view and then refute it.
Paragraph 6 – Conclude with a strong re-statement of your view and a summation of your key points.

Top Tip
Always produce at least two drafts of your work. Your second draft should be your best one.

Quick Test

1. What is it that you are doing when you look over your work again?
2. How many drafts should you make of your work?
3. Identify three places where you could find information for your chosen topic.

Expressive writing

Describing personal experience

What you are expected to do

A personal experience essay is one of the options for your second, W2, folio piece. Your task is to write an essay in which you not only **describe a personal experience** but, more importantly, **express your thoughts and feelings**, and **reflect upon the event** detailed in your writing.

It is crucial that your essay does not simply re-tell a story. The marker will be looking for evidence of **how the experience has affected you** and will expect to see aspects of your personality shine through the words you use. You should therefore attempt to **write sensitively about yourself** and **be genuine in your thoughts, feelings and reactions**.

Good essays will **reveal insights gained by the writer** as a result of the experience being described and **show a high degree of self-awareness**. Your sense of involvement will be clear from your writing.

How you will be graded

As well as the key issues of accurate punctuation and effective paragraphing, a good personal experience essay will:

provide a concise account of the event with a clear sense of involvement

be well sustained

demonstrate a degree of insight

have some style to it

show self-awareness

express your personal feelings and reactions with a degree of sensitivity

What you can write about

There is no set task for your folio work, so **the choice is yours**. In the exam you may be offered an assignment which lets you write a personal experience style essay, and in such a situation it would be important to stick to the task.

Pupils often choose to write about **an event that they remember vividly**, either because it was a particularly exhilarating time, such as a public performance, or because it was an extremely emotional time, such as a family bereavement. However, **be careful not to overdo any sense of emotion** – good or bad – as this can lead to quite clichéd writing.

Top Tip

Be genuine in a personal essay. Markers can almost always spot when a student has invented an experience.

Planning

As with all writing, your essay will benefit from some **pre-writing planning**. An important feature that markers look for is **structure**. This can be difficult to achieve if you do not prepare properly.

Time spent on preparation is time well spent!

Begin by creating a title that sets out your task. It does not have to be clever or intriguing: the title is not part of your essay but part of your planning! Once you have your 'working title', brainstorm some ideas around it; you could use a spidergram. From here you can begin to structure your essay into clear paragraphs.

Plan your paragraphs.

Use effective word choices to convey your thoughts and feelings.

Choose a vivid experience.

How To Write a Successful Personal Essay

Be genuine in your response.

Let your personality shine through.

Reflect on how the experience has affected you.

Quick Test

1. A personal experience essay is a work of fiction. True or False?

2. Clichéd writing means
   a) writing that is fresh and original
   b) writing that uses worn out phrases and predictable events
   c) writing that has a twist in the tale

3. 'Insight' means a) self awareness or b) good vision.

4. What is the best way to ensure a sense of structure to your essay?

5. What is the best way to convey thoughts and feelings?

Answers 1. False. **2.** (b.) **3.** (a) **4.** Planning. **5.** Effective word choice.

Creative writing

What you are expected to do

A second option for your W2 piece is to produce a creative piece of writing in a **specific literary genre**, the most popular of which is the short story.

- In this task you will be **assessed on the quality of your writing**.

- There is **a wide range of possibilities regarding what you may write about** because there are no restrictions on form, content or genre. The key requirement is that the piece should be broadly expressive in nature. For example, a letter of complaint to your local council would not meet this requirement (although it could be a W1 piece); however, an imaginary letter home from a soldier suffering in the trenches would be acceptable.

- **Dramascripts** and **poetry** are acceptable forms for this assignment, but you would be well advised to check with your teacher before considering either of these options.

- **The SQA do not specify any particular length** for your work in terms of words or pages. The general rule is that work should be of an appropriate length for the task. As a general rule, however, around 800 words should be sufficient for a story; obviously you would use fewer words for poetry.

- What is most important is that the written piece has **clear aims**, a **specific purpose**, and that it is **effectively written**. If your work is **convincing and concise** then the examiner will give it a high grade.

- **Imaginative responses to literature** are also permissible, but again be advised by your teacher in this area. Writing the next chapter to a novel – for example, what happens to George from John Steinbeck's *Of Mice and Men* – is the type of work that could be considered for inclusion in your writing folio. However, it would be assessed as a piece of original writing not as a critical response to the text.

Remember that you can word-process your work, which makes re-drafting much easier.

Internet

Go to the Learning Lab at www.leckieandleckie.co.uk for links to examples of excellent short stories.

What you can write about

Here are a few suggestions that you could choose from for a fictional piece of writing:

| write the opening of a novel, introducing the key character | keep an imaginary diary | write a one-act play | write a short horror story with a 'twist in the tale' |

Here are a few short story titles to get you going if you are stuck for ideas:

- 'My Last Day on Earth'
- 'Strange Meeting'
- 'Emergency on Alpha Minor'
- 'Danger in Venice'
- 'The Visitors'
- 'A Day in My Life as a Dog'

How you will be graded

To achieve Grades 1–3, you will need to:

- write in the appropriate manner for the genre and purpose selected
- use a varied range of sentences and vocabulary to keep your audience's interest
- keep punctuation accurate and produce logical paragraphs to make your meaning clear
- develop characters and settings within your narrative
- use literary devices such as similes and metaphors effectively
- write with flair and originality
- show assured control in your writing, with a wide range of expression to achieve effects
- show an awareness of tone in words and sentences
- use the conventions of your selected genre effectively
- be accurate in punctuation and spelling

Internet

If you would like to read an excellent story with an ingenious ending, read Liam O'Flaherty's The Sniper. You can find the link in the Learning Lab.
This story has a very short timeframe: its action takes place over a few hours. You could do the same in your story by writing about a single incident or an episode that lasts for only a few hours.

Quick Test

1. Which of the following would not be accepted as a 'specific literary genre'?
   a) Short story
   b) Discursive essay
   c) Poem
   d) Diary entry

2. What is the term for checking over your work and making corrections?

3. Using a variety of sentence structures will help do what?

4. Short stories may only be written in the folio. True or False?

5. Re-drafting work is made easier by using what tool?

Answers 1. (b) **2.** Proof-reading. **3.** Keep your reader interested. **4.** False. **5.** Word processing.

31

Writing short stories

Planning

Brainstorm or create a **spidergram** (or **mind-map**) of your ideas on a blank sheet of paper. Sometimes stories can come from a character; sometimes they can come from a specific situation such as a shipwreck or a sudden discovery. Once you have a few ideas, try to think of a title because this may help you to focus on the plot and characterisation of your story.

The **plot** is the plan or outline of your story.
- What will be the climax of your plot when your story reaches a crisis?
- What will be the result of the climax?
- From whose point of view is the story going to be told?

Style of narration

Decide if the style of narration is to be in the first or third person. A **first-person narrator** tells the story from within the story; a **third-person narrator** stands outside the story. How much will your narrator know and see? Will the third-person narrator be able to know everything that the characters are thinking? These are matters of **perspective**. Will the narrator be biased or objective in their viewpoint?

Top Tip

Try to use a few **literary devices**, such as similes, metaphors and alliteration, to create effects in your writing.

Characters

You will need a main character and two or three other important characters. You could include some minor ones, too. Create a brief **profile for each character** because this will enable you to be realistic in your portrayal of them. Have a checklist for each character, covering, for example, age, appearance, habits, job, traits, ambitions, hobbies, likes and dislikes, motivation, etc.

Setting

Where is the story going to be set?
- Will it be set at **home or abroad**?
- Is the story going to be set in the **present, future or past**?
- Will your story be **drawn from everyday life**?
- Perhaps you would prefer a fairy-tale setting **drawn from your imagination**?

How are you going to **describe the setting**? Will you suggest the setting through minor details in your writing, or will you be more elaborate in the details you give to describe the setting? If necessary, do a little research to make your setting convincing.

Genre

Choose a genre for your story. Is your story going to be:

an adventure?   a comedy?   a detective mystery?

science-fiction?   a romance?

You can be even more specific within your genre by going for a sub-division within it, for example, a romantic comedy.

Structure

Ensure that you have a clear beginning, middle and end in your story.

You need to bait your story with a good 'hook' at the beginning, to make your readers want to read on.

> You could begin in the middle of **an exciting incident.**

> If your story involves suspense, try to include 'a twist in the tale'. Alternatively, you could give a moral to your story.

> You could use an **unusual** description or start from an unusual perspective, to **intrigue** the reader.

Look at examples in the stories you read.

Use of time

How are you going to tell your story? Will you tell your story in a **linear** (straightforward) way or through **flashbacks**? The plots of most stories, novels and plays are written in a linear manner, i.e. the plots and characters move forward naturally in time. In contrast, a novel such as *Wuthering Heights* (1847) by Emily Brontë moves forwards and backwards in time as various first-person narrators relate significant events in the novel.

Top Tip
The last part of your sentence usually carries the most impact, so recast your sentences to maximise your impact.

Quick Test

1. How is a first-person narrative told?

2. What does the term 'genre' mean?

3. What do you need at the beginning of a story to keep your readers interested in reading further?

4. What does it mean to 'elaborate'?

5. How can you make your characters believable?

Answers 1. By a character in the story, using 'I'. 2. A kind of writing, for example, detective stories, romance, science-fiction, etc. 3. An interesting 'hook' that will seize the reader's attention. 4. It means going into detail or extensive description. 5. Build up a profile for them; try to give them realistic speech.

Test your progress

Use the questions to test your progress.
Check your answers at the back of the book on page 95.

Writing

1. How many writing pieces contribute to your folio grade?

....

2. What is the word length that you should be aiming for?

....

3. What does 'transactional' mean?

....

4. What does 'expressive' mean?

....

5. What does 'imaginative' mean?

....

6. Give two examples of what you could write about as a W1 piece.

....

7. Give two examples of what you could write about as W2 piece.

....

8. Why is it important to express your thoughts and feelings in a personal experience type essay?

....

9. What does 'insight' mean?

....

10. What danger lies in being over emotional in your writing?

....

11. Why should you use a genuine experience in a personal experience essay?

....

12. Indicate two ways that paragraphs can be developed.

....

....

13. Similes are comparisons. How do they differ from metaphors?

....

14. Why should you use figurative language in your work?

....

15. What does 'hook' mean in terms of stories?

....

16. What is meant by 'setting'?

....

17. What are the main styles of narration?

....

18. If a narrator is outside the story, what is he or she?

....

19. What does 'plot' mean?

....

20. Give a method by which you can plan your story.

....

21. Explain what is meant by 'control' in writing.

....

22. If writing is 'linear', what is it?

....

23. If your task is 'discursive', how is it written?

....

24. Give three sources where you could find information on a topic.

....

25. Will an imaginative story be suitable for a W1 piece?

....

26. Other than short story, name two genres that would be acceptable as a specific literary form.

....

27. Are you allowed to word process your folio pieces?

....

28. What does 'proof-read' mean?

....

29. Other than the folio, where else are your writing skills assessed?

....

How did you do?

1–9	correct	start again
10–15	correct	getting there
16–22	correct	good work
23–29	correct	excellent

Critical essays

What is a critical essay?

Your ability to respond thoughtfully to literature is tested through the writing of **critical essays**. A critical essay is your written response to a text that you have studied, based on a set task. The 'text' may be a novel, a short story, poetry, a play or even a film. In the essay you **evaluate** the text and attempt to **demonstrate your understanding** of its main ideas and your **analysis** of the writer's technique and craft. You are also expected to reveal your **genuine personal reaction** to the text.

1: Planning

- Examine **key words** and **phrases** in the task to help you focus on your answer.
- **Brainstorm** an essay plan with your essay question in the middle of a blank piece of paper.
- Aim for **three or four main arguments** and group your points around them. Remember to include a note of any **sources used** and to acknowledge any **quotations**.

2: Writing an introduction

Sometimes it is hard to start essays. A good way to begin is to **answer the question briefly in the opening paragraph**. Look at your notes and mind-maps to help you.

The following example is of an opening paragraph for an essay question on *Educating Rita*. The question asks: *Re-read the early and last scenes of* Educating Rita. *Explain what Rita gains and loses in her determination to become educated.*

> '*Educating Rita by Willy Russell tells the story of Rita White, a 26-year-old hairdresser, who is trying to "find herself". Rita's gains can be summed up as follows: ...*'

3: The main body

Work through **each main argument** from your introduction as **fully** as you can. Once you think that you have proved an argument sufficiently, move on to your next argument. Do not hammer away at the same point for too long.

Remember that your technique must be **point**, **evidence** and **comment**:

- make a key point in your argument;
- support it with evidence from the text;
- and then comment on the matter.

Use a wide range of **connective words** to link your points and arguments together (see pages 20–21). These words will bring your essay together. The skilful use of connectives can help the **fluency of arguments** in essays and make them easier to read.

Top Tip

Get an idea of what good essays look like. Ask your teacher for good examples of work by former pupils.

4: Conclusions

Your essay needs to embody a sense of **finality**. This should be reflected in the tone of your conclusion:

- Conclude by **summing up your arguments and findings**.
- **Give your views** on the text(s) that you are writing about.
- It is important to **explain what you gained** from reading the text(s).

Types of response

Imaginative responses to literature

This is an option for your reading folio. It is important to remember that while you will need to display some skill in the form chosen – dramascript, extra chapter, letter, report, etc. – the piece of work is still essentially a response to the text read. Your work will need to **demonstrate a thorough familiarity with the original text** through appropriate references and allusions, and you will need to be **sensitive to the mood and tone** of the original piece.

Media and imaginative responses

Writing a critical evaluation of a media text requires the same approach as for a literary text, with a focus on the task set. It is especially important that you do not simply re-tell the story (narrative) of a film you have studied. Use of appropriate **critical terminology** is essential: for example, *mise en scène*, representation, editing, camera angles, lighting, sound, etc. You need to **prepare thoroughly** in order to tackle a **critical evaluation** of a media text.

The term 'text' can refer to any form of writing and you should refer to your books, stories or poems as texts in your writing. Films, for the purpose of the folio requirements, are referred to as media texts.

Quick Test

1. What should you focus on in essay questions?

2. What does 'text' mean?

3. How many main arguments should you aim for?

Mind-maps for essays

Re-read your text

Whether you are reading a play, poem, novel or short story, you must **re-read your text** for **a deeper understanding of your essay question or task**.

- When creating a task for a folio piece, many teachers concentrate on a **writer's technique** and how this **aids our understanding of the text**.
- For plays, teachers may focus on **conflict as a central issue** and ask you to examine how the writer develops this through **characterisation and plot**.
- For novels, you might be expected to show how a **theme, character, imagery** or **mood**, has been represented.
- For poetry, you will certainly be looking at **the poet's choice of words** and **use of imagery and figurative language**.

One of the best ways of making notes for your essay is to produce a memorable mind-map or spidergram.

When to use a spidergram/mind-map

If your essay title asks you to write about a character, theme or any aspect of a text that you are studying, you could do a mind-map like the one on the opposite page. **Study your essay question** and try to build up relevant comments by **looking carefully at key words and phrases in your question**. Check your ideas again by **re-reading key parts of the text**.

Study the characters

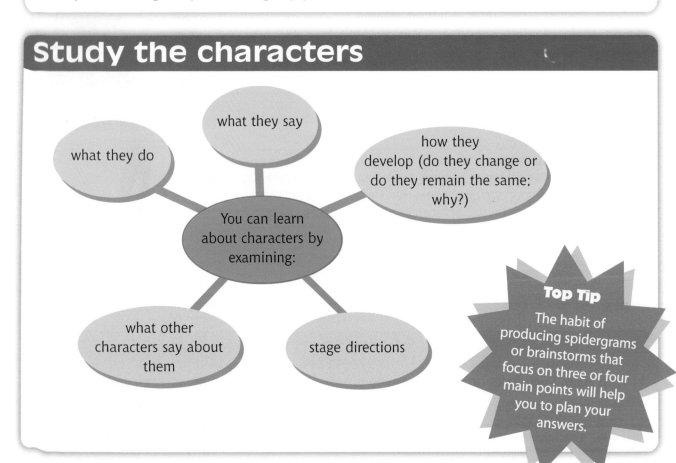

what they say

what they do

how they develop (do they change or do they remain the same; why?)

You can learn about characters by examining:

what other characters say about them

stage directions

Top Tip

The habit of producing spidergrams or brainstorms that focus on three or four main points will help you to plan your answers.

Build your mind-map as you read

A mind-map for a character study

Go through the text and look at the places where your character speaks or others speak about him or her. Build your mind-map up gradually, as follows:

1. Use white paper without lines – it helps you think more clearly.

2. Use a pencil and a rubber – it is quicker and you can also add colours.

3. **Begin in the middle of the page** with a title (use the words of the task to create a suitable title) and put the most important information around the title.

4. Work your way out to the **margins**, where you should put **the least important information**.

5. Your **first five minutes** are likely to be the **most productive** so do not stop for anything. You can make your map pretty and memorable afterwards. Remember that the **colours** you choose for various topics of your mind-map can be meaningful because everything can be given an appropriate colour.

6. **Make connections between ideas by running branches off your main ideas**. Draw connecting branches to other main ideas if it seems sensible. It will then take on the character of a colourful tube map; you can then add appropriate pictures and images.

7. Keep mind-maps to one piece of paper. If you run out of space, tape another sheet of paper on to the side of the paper where you are running out of space. It does not matter how big your piece of paper is as long as your mind-map is on one side of paper. You can always carefully fold it up afterwards.

Top Tip

Try to get an overview of the themes of your particular play. Then see how a character relates to these themes.

Quick Test

1. What is gained by a re-reading of a text, before attempting a task?

2. How can you keep comments relevant to the task?

3. List three ways that we learn about characters.

4. Where should the title or topic of the mind-map be placed?

5. Why should you not stop during the first five minutes of brainstorming a mind-map?

Test your progress

Use the questions to test your progress.

Check your answers at the back of the book on page 94.

Question A

Choose just one answer: a, b, c, or d.

1. Which of the following is not suitable as a subject for a mind-map?
   a) discussing a theme
   b) exploring a character
   c) telling the story of a play or novel
   d) investigating imagery

2. Before you begin a mind-map, you should:
   a) make sure you have suitable pens and paper available
   b) check the key words of the question for suitable headings
   c) brainstorm ideas
   d) sharpen your pencils

3. What is the point in colouring in a completed mind-map?
   a) it looks good.
   b) the colour makes it easier to remember.
   c) the different colours are a way of grouping ideas together.
   d) to make it look like a map of the London tube

4. A mind-map is a good method of planning because:
   a) it helps you see the connections between ideas
   b) it makes a memorable revision aid
   c) unexpected connections sometimes come up
   d) it's a more creative approach than just jotting down points

Question B

Study the notes below on *Macbeth* and then complete the task that follows.

Question: 'Are the witches responsible for the tragedy of *Macbeth*?'

- Sailor speech shows that they can't directly change fate.
- Temptation – Use the truth against him, Thane of Cawdor greeting is true when they utter it.
- Temptation 2 – All three warnings are true. Just not what Macbeth expected.
- Effect on Macbeth – Witches not present at murder – his decision.
- Effect on Lady Macbeth – Letter describes meeting – she persuades Macbeth.
- Conclusion.
1. Rearrange these notes as a mind-map.

2. Which version is easier to follow?

Question C: Folio practice task

Planning an essay

Use a mind-map to plan an essay that discusses Shakespeare's presentation of the main character of the play you have studied. (If you haven't studied a play by Shakespeare, simply adjust the task to suit a play that you have read.)

Consider:

- How we are introduced to the character.
- How the character changes.
- Key relationships.
- Important plot developments.

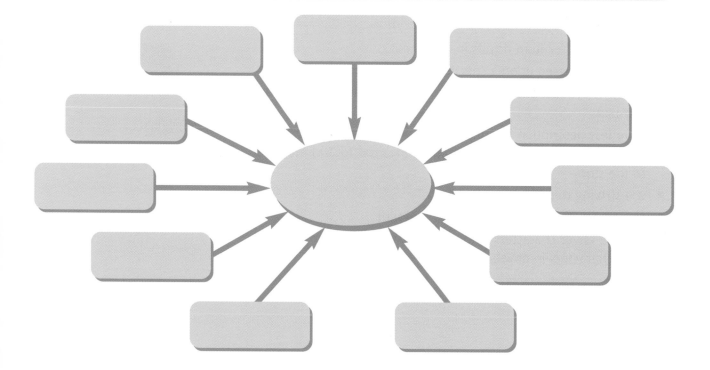

Studying prose

Novels and short stories (prose) are studied as part of the Standard Grade course.

How you will be graded

You will be assessed on your ability to show through your writing your understanding and appreciation of texts that you have read.

- convey a strong sense of genuine personal response
- demonstrate thorough familiarity with the text(s)
- show insight into the implications and relevance of a text

To achieve Grades 1–3, you should aim to:

- respond in a thorough fashion to the specific task
- comment on its style, structure and characters
- make accurate and effective use of critical terminology
- discuss the writer's use of language

Comparing novels and stories

Novels and stories have **plots** and **stories**, may include **dialogue**, have **characters** and set out **themes** and **ideas**.

Short stories differ from novels in that they:

- are usually based upon a specific incident or point in time
- usually have just one main plot and no space for sub-plots or sub-texts
- have less description because there is less space: any description needs to be economical and essential in order to add meaning to the story
- use striking details
- sometimes have more fragmented dialogue
- include fewer characters who do and say more in less space than characters in novels.

What to look for in characters

When you are studying the characters in your novel, you should look out for the following things.

- The **names of characters** sometimes tell you more about them. For example, Pip from *Great Expectations* is named after a seed. One of the novel's main themes is his development and growth as he changes from a lower-class boy to a gentleman. The novel charts the education of his heart as well as his mind.

- **Flat and round characters**. E.M. Forster created these terms to describe types of characters found in novels in his book *Aspects of the Novel* (1927). Flat characters do not develop in novels and are generally not as important as round characters, who develop because they change in the course of a novel. The same terms can be applied to characters in short stories.

- **How a character interacts with other characters** and **what other characters say about him or her**. This can help readers to understand other aspects of a character's personality.

- Any **direct comments** on the character by a **third-person narrator**.

- If the character that you are studying is the narrator of your story, **how far can you trust** what he or she says? Do they have **self-knowledge** or do they have a lot to learn? Could they be termed **an unreliable narrator**?

- What characters look like: the **physical appearance** of characters given in their description often tells us more about them.

- What a character **says and does**; much can be inferred from talk and action.

First- or third-person narrator

Do writers tell the story from the point of view of a character within the story as 'I' or 'me' – that is, as a first-person narrator? Or is the story told by a third-person narrator, who looks at what is going on from outside? The **writer's choice of who tells the story** can determine how we see, understand and interpret characters, as well as themes and ideas within a story.

First-person narrators usually have **a limited point of view**. They are so close to what is happening that they cannot see everything that is going on or know what other characters are thinking. Yet first-person narrators can **reveal much more of themselves**.

Third-person narrators can see and know much more. They can know everything if the writer wants them to. This last kind of narrator is called an **omniscient narrator**.

It is important to understand that whatever the first- or third-person narrator thinks is **not necessarily what the writer thinks**. Show in your writing that you understand that **writers adopt masks by using narrators** in their stories.

Top Tip

Always check to see if a story is written in the first or third person.

Quick Test

1. What does 'genre' mean?

2. What does 'prose' mean

3. What is a first-person narrative?

4. What is a third-person narrative?

Themes and mood

Themes

Themes are **ideas or messages that writers explore in their stories**. The novel is a form of writing that allows writers to examine more than one theme.

For example, in *Roll of Thunder Hear My Cry* (1976), Mildred D. Taylor explores the theme of **growing up** and the coming of age of its main character, Cassie Logan. She experiences **racism** in 1930s' Mississippi, despite her family's best efforts to shield her from its worst aspects. Among other themes, the novel also examines the characters' **attachment to the land**, **family roots**, **independence** and the **self-respect** that comes from owning parcels of land.

Top Tip

Choose a passage that moves you from a text that you are reading and try to work out how the writer created the mood and atmosphere of the passage.

Mood and atmosphere

Writers try to create a mood and atmosphere in stories and novels to **illuminate the feelings and actions of their characters**. Mood and atmosphere, through the skilful use of description, helps to **set the tone** for a piece of writing. This creates a **frame of mind** for the reader and a **sense of expectation of what is to follow**.

Mood and atmosphere can be achieved by using the following literary effects:

- the **careful choice of words** (diction) helps to suggest an atmosphere and tone
- the **length and variety** of sentences; for example, short ones can suggest tension
- **repetition** in sentences of words and phrases
- **similes** (comparisons using 'as' or 'like') **metaphors** (stronger comparisons in which you say something *is* something else)
- **monologues** (speaking to oneself) and dreams and day-dreams are good ways of revealing the motives and desires of characters
- **personification** (giving human feelings to animals or inanimate objects)
- **oxymorons** (combining contradictory words and phrases to cause an effect)
- **assonance** (combining words with rhyming vowel sounds, e.g. fowl owl)
- **alliteration** (using words together that repeat the first sound of the word, e.g. lovely lush leaves)
- **motifs** (words, ideas and imagery which recur in texts)
- the use of the **senses**: sound, touch, sight, smell and taste
- the **tone** of the narrator and his or her closeness to, or distance from, the action

(Some of the above effects are explained in more detail on pages 54–55.)

Dialogue

In novels, dialogue is more than mere communication: it makes characters seem more vivid and lifelike.

Characters' **aims, motives, personalities** and **outlooks** are revealed through what they say and the words and phrases that they use. Dialogue shows **what characters think about other characters**. This also helps us to make up our minds about them, and to understand how they relate to the main themes, messages and ideas in a story.

Third-person narration

The following is an example of third-person narration and characterisation from Doris Lessing's *Flight*:

He moved warily along the hedge, stalking his granddaughter, who was now looped over the gate, her head loose on her arms, singing. The light happy sound mingled with the crooning of the birds, and his anger mounted.

'Hey!' he shouted; saw her jump, look back, and abandon the gate.

Her eyes veiled themselves, and she said in a pert neutral voice: 'Hullo, Grandad.' Politely she moved towards him, after a lingering backward glance at the road.

'Waiting for Steven, hey?' he said, his fingers curling like claws into his palm.

'Any objection?' she asked lightly, refusing to look at him.

He confronted her, his eyes narrowed, shoulders hunched, tight in a hard knot of pain which included the preening birds, the sunlight, the flowers. He said: 'Think you're old enough to go courting, hey?'

First-person narration

The following is an example of first-person narration and dialogue from Sylvia Plath's *Superman and Paula Brown's New Snowsuit*. (The narrator has been wrongfully accused of spoiling Paula Brown's snowsuit.)

A mouthful of chocolate pudding blocked my throat, thick and bitter. I had to wash it down with milk. Finally I said, 'I didn't do it.'

But the words came out like hard, dry little seeds, hollow and insincere. I tried again. 'I didn't do it. Jimmy Lane did it.'

'Of course we'll believe you,' Mother said slowly, 'but the whole neighbourhood is talking about it. Mrs Sterling heard the story from Mrs Fein and sent David over to say we should buy Paula a new snowsuit. I can't understand it.'

'I didn't do it,' I repeated, and the blood beat in my ears like a slack drum. I pushed my chair away from the table, not looking at Uncle Frank or Mother sitting there, solemn and sorrowful in the candlelight.

The staircase to the second floor was dark, but I went down the long hall to my room without turning on the light switch and shut the door. A small unripe moon was shafting squares of greenish light along the floor and the window-panes were fringed with frost.

Quick Test

1. Theme refers to:
   a) the storyline of a novel or short story
   b) the overall topic that the writer is exploring
   c) the end of a story

2. Short sentences might create what kind of mood in prose writing?

3. Why is dialogue important for establishing characters?

4. What is first-person narration?

5. As well as identifying literary terms and techniques, what else must you do?

Short stories

Using short stories in the folio

When writing a critical evaluation of a short story for a folio piece, it is important that you **do more than simply re-tell the narrative** of the text (storyline).

Attention must be paid to features such as **dialogue**, **characterisation**, **setting**, and **theme**. The endings of many short stories contain 'twists' that also would invite comment in a critical essay.

Pay particular attention to the *Details of task*, as set out by your teacher and attempt to **deal with the specific requirements of the assignment**.

A folio task might look like this:

Details of task

Write about a short story that you thought was unusual in some way but which had an important message. Consider the writer's use of language, setting, structure, character, incident, humour and imagery. Remember to state your overall opinion of the story.

How to plan your essay

Look at the essay plan below, which uses the short story 'Hunter of Dryburn'
by Brian McCabe, to respond to this task.

Creating an essay plan becomes straightforward if you use the task as a guide.

Once your paragraph plan is created, use PEC to write the full essay.

Hunter of Dryburn

In this short story, which is written in Scots, a lonely man holds a one-sided conversation with a young couple who have inadvertently ended up in the village of Dryburn and have gone into a local pub for a drink. It becomes clear that the man, the 'hunter' of the title, is searching for some greater purpose to his life but appears to be trapped by the circumstances of living in a 'dump' like Dryburn.

Hunter of
Dryburn

Brian McCabe

The essay plan

Paragraph 1: Introduction

Use the task to help you write your opening paragraph. Give the title and author and say what you intend to do in your essay, e.g.

> *'Hunter of Dryburn' by Brain McCabe is a short story that I thought was unusual in a number of ways but which contained an important message. In this essay I will look at the writer's use of language, setting, structure, character, incident, humour and imagery and consider how effective he has been in conveying his viewpoint.*

Paragraph 2: 'language'

Explain what you thought was unusual about the story, e.g. that it was written in Scots. Say how this added to your enjoyment and how it made the characters realistic. Remember to use some quotations.

Paragraph 3: 'setting'

Write about the setting. Explain how we know that 'Dryburn's a dump' and why Dryburn is a good name for the village.

Paragraph 4: 'structure'

Now explain the unusual structure of the story, i.e. that it is a dramatic monologue. Quote examples of how the writer lets you know that other people are there.

Paragraph 5: 'character'

Write about the character of the Auld Man. Explain how we know why he was like this.

Paragraph 6: 'incident'

There is one central incident in the story – the auld man's death. Say what happened and give your opinion about who was to blame.

Paragraph 7: 'humour'

Give examples of the funny parts in the story and say how they added to you enjoyment.

Paragraph 8: 'imagery'

Now deal with the end of the story and the fact that the storyteller can't imagine a lion. Explain the point that the writer is trying to make. Give your overall opinion of the story.

Top Tip
It is much easier to write a good essay when you have enjoyed a story. If you are given a choice, pick a favourite text.

Top Tip
Remember to give examples and use quotations from the text to back up your point.

Quick Test

1. What are the most popular areas for comparison between two short stories?
2. Why should you pick a text you have enjoyed when writing a critical essay?

Answers 1. Character and theme. 2. It will be easier to write about.

Test your progress

Use the questions to test your progress.
Check your answers at the back of the book on page 95.

1. What does 'plot' mean?

   ....

2. What does it mean to 'contrast'?

   ....

3. Explain the term 'genre'.

   ....

4. What is meant by a 'writer's craft'?

   ....

5. Explain what 'irony' means.

   ....

6. What are 'transitions'?

   ....

7. What are the main styles of narration?

   ....

8. From which viewpoint does a first-person narrator tell a story?

   ....

9. Does the author believe what a narrator believes?

   ....

10. What type of narrator can see most in a story?

    ....

11. Give three ways of understanding a character.

    ....

12. What is an 'omniscient narrator'?

    ....

13. What is meant by the terms 'flat' and 'round' characters?

    ....

14. Define what 'dialogue' means.

    ....

15. Why do writers use dialogue?

    ....

16. Briefly explain the rules for how dialogue should be set out on the page.

....

17. What is a monologue?

....

18. How can dialogue help you to learn more about characters?

....

19. Identify three similarities in novels and short stories.

....

20. Point out three differences between short stories and novels.

....

21. Why do short stories concentrate on mainly one plot?

....

22. Point out three ways in which writers create mood and atmosphere in their stories.

....

23. What is 'diction'?

....

24. Mood and atmosphere sets up a frame of mind and an expectation of what is to follow in a text. True or false?

....

25. Mood and atmosphere can be achieved through the skilful use of description or imagery. True or false?

....

26. Imagery is used only for poetry and not in novels or short stories. True or false?

....

27. Explain the difference between 'alliteration' and 'assonance'.

....

28. What is a theme?

....

How did you do?

1–9	correct	start again
10–15	correct	getting there
16–22	correct	good work
23–28	correct	excellent

Critical evaluations

What you may study

The play that you study will be determined by what your English teachers have in their library; Shakespeare's *Macbeth*, the 'Scottish play', is a popular choice.

As you read the play, try to get the gist of what characters are saying before you read passages again for a more detailed understanding. Also make use of any general notes in your books to guide your understanding.

How you will be graded

Support your points with textual evidence on the play's language, themes, characters or structure.

Demonstrate a thorough familiarity with the text.

Show through your critical and personal response how meaning is made in the play.

To achieve Grades 1–3, you will need to show that you are able to do some of the following:

Provide a well-structured response to the task.

Show that you understand the play and the implications from its themes and relevance for our times.

Show an awareness of the writer's use of linguistic devices and make effective use of critical terminology.

Top Tip

You can find out about a character from any imagery associated with the character.

Writing a critical evaluation on a play by Shakespeare

The plays most often studied are:
- *Julius Caesar*
- *The Merchant of Venice*
- *Macbeth*
- *The Tempest*
- *Romeo and Juliet*
- *A Midsummer Night's Dream*
- *Twelfth Night*

Shakespeare's choice of language

Shakespeare used **three styles of writing** in his plays. Here are a few examples from *Twelfth Night*:

1: Poetic verse (rhymed)

Verse which is often used to signal the end of a scene, such as a curtain call, or for heightened dramatic effect. Take, for example, this rhyming couplet from *Twelfth Night*:

> *Duke Orsino:* Away before me to sweet beds of flowers:
> Love-thoughts lie rich when canopied with bowers.

2: Blank verse (unrhymed)

Verse intended to represent the rhythms of speech. It is usually used by noble characters, who are given elevated speech to show their feelings and mood:

> *Duke Orsino:* If music be the food of love, play on.

Note how the speech is in **iambic pentameter**. That is, it has ten syllables to the line in which five are stressed. The rhythm pattern is ti-tum, ti-tum, ti-tum, ti-tum, ti-tum. Sometimes you'll find more or fewer stresses to the lines, yet the overall pattern will be even.

3: Prose

Ordinary language used by characters of all ranks, but uneducated characters tend to use it. It can also be used for comic exchanges between characters, for plot development, and for speech which lacks dramatic intensity:

> *Viola as Cesario:* Save thee, friend, and thy music. Dost thou live by thy tabor?
> *Feste:* No, sir, I live by the church.
> *Viola:* Art thou a churchman?
> *Feste:* No such matter sir: I do live by the church; for I do live at my house, and my house doth stand by the church.

Quick Test

1. What are the three styles of writing used by Shakespeare?
2. How do you support points made in a critical essay?
3. What is poetic verse often used to signal?
4. What is blank verse intended to represent?

Answers 1. Poetic verse, blank verse and prose. **2.** By producing textual evidence. **3.** The end of an act or a scene. **4.** The natural rhythms of speech.

Shakespeare – structure and theme

Plot structure

Shakespeare liked to stress the comedy or seriousness of many scenes within his plays by making **dramatic contrasts**. He did this by **placing a serious scene after a comic scene** and vice versa.

Main characters are introduced to the audience. **Order reigns** and the world and nature are in natural harmony.

Problems are revealed. Things begin to go wrong. Confusions, murders, deceit, pranks and other complications begin.

As events progress there is **chaos** and **a loss of order and harmony**. The natural world appears out of sorts.

Things come to a head in the play's **climax**. ('Climax' comes from the Greek word for 'ladder'.) If you are reading a tragedy, then several more deaths occur now, including a main character like Macbeth. The climax is the moment of the **highest dramatic intensity in the play**, particularly for the main character.

Order is re-established with the right people in control again. Nature is again at one with the main characters. Comedies usually end in several, usually three, marriages.

Conflict

As with any play **conflict** is a **central concern** in Shakespeare's texts. This can take a number of forms:

Perhaps the most obvious source of conflict is when **the central figure is in a direct clash with another major character**. Whatever the source of conflict, the play will work towards **the resolution of the conflict** in its narrative / storyline.

Conflict can be within a single character who is **torn between two desires**.

A writer may use a number of characters to explore a **basic clash between two ideas**, e.g. good and evil.

Themes

Shakespeare's plays are rich with thematic content and **often several issues will be explored** within a single text. A number of themes also appear in more than one play.

Recurring thematic concerns of Shakespeare include:

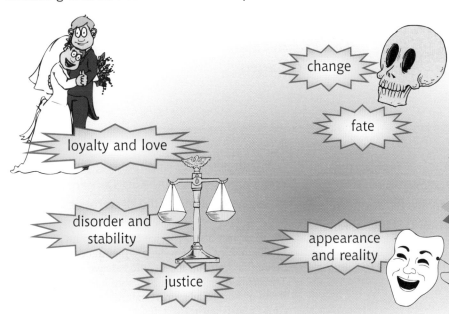

loyalty and love

change

fate

disorder and stability

appearance and reality

justice

self-knowledge

Your own study of Shakespeare is likely to focus on a single text and within that study you will concentrate on the appropriate themes.

Top Tip

To attune yourself to the language of Shakespeare, a good exercise is to translate six-line passages into modern English.

Top Tip

To understand Shakespeare, aim to get a rough idea of what is going on in the play. Once you have this idea, you can then deepen your understanding by reading for more meaning in imagery and word choices.

Internet

Websites for help with Shakespeare plays can be accessed through the Learning Lab at www.leckieandleckie.co.uk

Quick Test

1. What is the most frequent source of conflict in a play?

2. What function has the end of a play in terms of conflict?

3. What is a theme?

4. Where would you find the 'climax' of a play?

5. What does 'plot' mean?

6. What does 'context' mean?

7. What is 'textual evidence'?

Answers 1. Between two characters. **2.** To resolve the main conflict. **3.** It is the play's main message or idea. There can be several themes in a play. **4.** Near the end. **5.** The plan or outline of the play. **6.** The events and ideas around the time when the text was written. **7.** Brief quotations from the play that are used as evidence for points in essays.

Shakespeare – imagery

Figures of speech

Shakespeare uses figures of speech – that is, imagery or word pictures – to do the following:

| say more about points made in dialogue and action | reinforce and enhance the audience's ideas of the characters | magnify or draw attention to themes or issues in the text |

To do this, Shakespeare uses:

Motifs

Motifs are characters, themes or images that **recur** throughout a text. For example, disguise is a running idea in *Twelfth Night*. In *Macbeth* there are several motifs. One is 'fair and foul' and another is sleep:

- To the Weird Sisters, who characterise evil, what is ugly is beautiful, and what is beautiful is ugly: 'Fair is foul and foul is fair.'

- Macbeth and Lady Macbeth reign in restless ecstasy after murdering King Duncan. Macbeth soon says to illustrate the sleep motif:

> Me thought I heard a voice cry, "Sleep no more!"
> Macbeth does murder sleep – the innocent sleep,
> Sleep that knits up the ravelled sleave of care,
> The death of each day's life, sore labour's bath,
> Balm of hurt minds, great nature's second course
> Chief nourisher in life's feast.
> (*Macbeth, Act 2, Scene 2, lines 34–39*)

Similes

Similes are comparisons using 'as' or 'like'; for example: 'The moon is like a balloon.'

Metaphors

Stronger comparisons saying something *is* something else: 'The moon is a balloon', 'The world is a stage.'

Personification

Giving human feelings to animals or inanimate objects: 'The sun smiled.'

Oxymorons

These are words and phrases that you would not expect to see yoked together to cause an effect. For example, as soon as Juliet hears that Tybalt, her cousin, has been killed by Romeo, her grief and outrage is tempered by her disbelief that Romeo could carry out such a deed: 'Fiend angelical, dove-feathered raven, wolvish-ravening lamb, ... A damned saint, an honourable villain!' (*Romeo and Juliet, Act 3, Scene 2, lines 75–79*)

Top Tip

Get a recording of a play from your local library and listen to parts of the play as it is read. It will help your understanding.

Extended Metaphors

A metaphor that is used extensively throughout a passage.

An example of Shakespeare's imagery

In the following speech from *King Lear*, Kent is enquiring of a Gentleman whether Cordelia, the daughter of King Lear, has been upset by a letter describing her father's condition.

Kent:	O, then it mov'd her?
Gentleman:	Not to a rage. Patience and sorrow strove
	Who should express her goodliest. You have seen
	Sunshine and rain at once: her smiles and tears
	Were like a better way. Those happy smilets
	That play'd on her ripe lip seem'd not to know
	What guests were in her eyes, which parted thence
	As pearls from diamonds dropp'd. In brief,
	Sorrow would be a rarity most belov'd,
	If all could so become it.

King Lear, Act 4, Scene 3

Top Tip

If the audience knows more about the development of the plot than the characters do, then this is known as **dramatic irony**.

The Gentleman attempts to describe Cordelia's **conflicting** emotions in a number of ways. First he uses **personification** to make the struggle in her mind between patience and sorrow seem more vivid.

He then moves on to **metaphors** of 'sunshine' and 'rain' to express these emotions. In order to give an impression of the strength of her emotions, he again uses **personification** to characterise the smilets (small smiles) that 'played' on her lips, and the tears that were 'guests' in her eyes. Finally, he uses a simile to describe the richness and beauty of Cordelia's tears, which part from her eyes as 'pearls from diamonds dropp'd'.

This moment is very moving. It is an example of Shakespeare's dramatic technique that he has Cordelia's reaction described rather than calling upon an actor to play it.

Quick Test

Circle the correct answer:

1. Shakespeare uses imagery:
   a) to make his writing pretty
   b) to fill up space
   c) to enhance our understanding of a character, theme or point

2. A simile is a figure of speech which:
   a) draws a comparison using 'as' or 'like'
   b) allows characters to smile
   c) has to do with singularity
   d) makes a comparison using 'is' or 'are'

3. The term 'imagery' means:
   a) looking in mirrors
   b) word pictures
   c) writing prose

Answers 1. (c) 2. (a) 3. (b)

Using PEC

PEC for critical evaluation

In all your critical evaluations, it is important that you consider the words of the task carefully. This will give your essay a clear sense of purpose, which is one of the key features that a marker will be looking for.

Consider the example below, which is based on the play *An Inspector Calls* by J.B. Priestley and illustrates how you should approach critical evaluation.

Details of task

Choose a play that you feel has an important social message for our time. Consider in some detail how the dramatist uses the issue of conflict between the characters to explore the theme. How successful has the dramatist been?

Firstly, use a spidergram (mind-map) to plan your work.

Top Tip

As with any genre, when you write essays on plays you should use the PEC method:
- make a point
- give evidence for your point
- comment on your evidence.

What the message is – social responsibility

Title: 'How J.B. Priestley uses conflict between his characters to explore an important social message.'

Conflict between:
Goole and Mr Birling
Goole and Gerard
Goole and Sheila
Goole and Eric
Goole and Mrs Birling

Other conflicts:
Sheila and Eric and their parents
Sheila and Gerard

Introduction

Use the words of the task to assist with your opening paragraph. In the following example, the underlined words have been lifted from the task.

A <u>play that has an important social message for our time</u> is 'An Inspector Calls' by J.B. Priestley. In this essay <u>I will consider in some detail how the dramatist uses the issue of conflict between the characters to explore the theme</u> of social responsibility and comment on <u>how successful he has been.</u>

Now, using PEC, you can begin to write the body of your essay:

Point

A key conflict in the drama is between Inspector Goole and Mr Birling. The writer uses this clash to illustrate the uncaring nature of Mr Birling and men like him.

Explanation

The Inspector accuses Birling of having unfairly sacked a young female worker for simply standing up for her rights. Birling is unrepentant, however, and justifies his sacking of the girl by saying: 'She'd had a lot to say – far too much – she had to go.' When told that this act was the first in a chain of events that apparently led to the girl's tragic suicide, Birling remains defiant: 'I can't accept any responsibility.'

Comment

However, it is clear that the Inspector feels that Birling, and the others at the dinner party he interrupted, need to learn to take responsibility for those around them. He says, later, 'We are members of one body. We are responsible for each other.' This is the important social message that the writer wishes us to learn.

Repeat this pattern for the other key points from your plan.

Conclusion

It is important in your conclusion to draw together the key points of the task and to highlight your personal evaluation of the writer's success:

J.B. Priestley has been extremely successful in using conflict between his characters to explore the central theme of social responsibility. Although the play was written over fifty years ago and is set during an even earlier period, the message that we need to consider ourselves as members of one community, one world, has never been more relevant.

Top Tip

Keep quotations relevant and brief. Aim to use single words and phrases, and certainly no more than a sentence or two, to prove your points. Remember to comment on the quotations that you use.

Quick Test

1. What does PEC stand for?
2. What should you back up your points with?
3. What is the purpose of the conclusion?

Answers 1. Point, evidence, comment. 2. Evidence from the text. 3. To draw together the key points of your argument and sum up your personal evaluation of the text.

57

Test your progress

Use the questions to test your progress.
Check your answers at the back of the book on page 95.

1. Name two possible sources of conflict in a play.

....

2. What must you remember to do with any quotations you use?

....

3. What are the main genres of Shakespeare plays?

....

4. List the three styles of writing Shakespeare used in his plays.

....

5. Where did Shakespeare use poetic verse?

....

6. What is the purpose of blank verse?

....

7. What does Shakespeare like to establish at the beginning of his plays?

....

8. What happens next?

....

9. What is the 'climax' of a play?

....

10. What could happen during the climax of a play?

....

11. Briefly explain what usually happens at the end of a Shakespeare play.

....

12. What is a 'theme'?

....

13. Identify three themes that can be found in Shakespeare's plays.

....

14. What type of themes might you expect to find in a comedy?

....

15. Briefly explain what is meant by 'dramatic contrast'.

....

16. Why did Shakespeare build dramatic contrasts into his plays?

....

17. Explain what is meant by 'self-knowledge'.

....

18. Briefly sum up the typical structure of a Shakespeare play.

....

19. What is meant by the term 'figure of speech'?

....

20. What is a simile?

....

21. Why is a metaphor a stronger comparison?

....

22. What is an extended metaphor?

....

23. What is meant by 'personification'?

....

24. Define an oxymoron.

....

25. What is a motif?

....

26. Give two reasons why Shakespeare uses imagery in his plays.

....

27. Shakespeare uses a great deal of irony in his plays. What is irony?

....

28. What is dramatic irony?

....

29. Why and where would you expect to find passages rich in imagery?

....

30. Briefly sum up what is meant by imagery.

....

How did you do?

1–9	correct	start again
10–15	correct	getting there
16–25	correct	good work
26–30	correct	excellent

Studying poetry

Chaucer SHELLEY
WORDSWORTH t.s eliot
coleridge Keats

What you have to study

Poetry is a significant part of Standard Grade English courses. Typically, at least one of your Reading folio pieces will be in response to a poem (the maximum number will be two).

The **type of poems** that you will study will range extensively, from **ballads** (narrative or story poems) to **sonnets** (serious poems that explore deep themes, such as love and death) to **free verse**.

You will be expected to make considered responses to them on the basis of content, theme and technique.

Responding to a poem

Study the poem very carefully.

- Consider briefly **what you think the poem is about**. You are looking for an **overview** at this stage. This early view of the poem may change once you have studied it in greater detail.

- Examine **how the poet gets their meaning across** through their choice of **form, language, imagery** and **themes**.

- Consider the poem's **tone**. For example, what is the **attitude** of the speaker towards the topic or theme? What is their attitude to you? Does the poem's tone change in the poem? Go through each area as fully as you can.

- Once you have studied the text, **consider your views again** on the poem, stating what the poem is about. Consider, in particular, **what you may have learned** from the poem.

Top Tip

Do not merely identify figures of speech and other poetic techniques, but show how they affect meaning in the poem.

Top Tip

Try to write a poem of your own using a specific form – there is a lot to be learned about poetry by trying to write your own poem. You may even find that you enjoy writing poetry.

How you will be graded

Show that you have **engaged with the poems** by giving a sustained and developed response to key words and phrases in your task. More sophisticated answers will display an **enthusiastic personal response** with close textual analysis.

Display **analytical and interpretive skills** when examining the **social, moral and philosophical significance** of the poem.

Explore the poems and **show insight.** Again, more sophisticated responses will show greater insight or exploration of the poems.

To achieve Grades 1–3, you will need to:

Give a **sophisticated personal response** that is **convincing and imaginative,** showing a high degree of **empathy.**

Explain how the poet has **used language and imagery** in the poem. In other words, you will need to be able to **identify word choices (diction)** and what they may suggest. You should also show how the poet uses **figures of speech,** such as similes, to add meaning to his or her **ideas and messages** in the poem(s).

Identify with the **poet's intentions** or the **view of the narrator** in the poem.

Say something about **the poet's purposes and intentions.** What is the poet setting out to achieve?

Quick Test

1. How many folio pieces may be in response to poetry?
2. What kind of poem is a ballad?
3. What is empathy?

Writing about poetry

Tips on writing about poetry

One of the biggest problems in writing about poetry is finding phrases that enable you to express your ideas and make your writing flow. You should aim to **integrate useful phrases** into your writing so that you can explain yourself with ease in critical essays. Beware, however, of always using the same phrases, which would lead to a mechanical style.

The following framework is not really meant as a substitute for your structure, but to provide a helping hand if you get stuck.

- **Introduce points** that you want to make by using some of the phrases given below; change them around or simply add them together. The more fluent you are the more impressive your points will be.

- Good grades in critical evaluations are achieved through **knowing your texts** and being able to **express your points in a fluent manner**. You will also be judged on your **punctuation**, **use of language** and the **quality of your expression**.

- Look out for **useful ways of expressing your ideas** and make a note of them. Successful pupils are able to make their points in essays in a fluent and knowledgeable manner.

1: Introductory phrases

- The poem ... is about ...

- The poem is narrated in the first / second person. This enhances the poem's meaning because ...

- The form of the poem is (a ballad / sonnet / two-, three-, four-, five-line stanzas / free verse) ... This is an appropriate form for the poem because it helps readers to appreciate ...

Top Tip

Remember PEC:
- make a **point** to address your question
- give a word, phrase or line of **evidence** for it
- **comment** on your evidence and link it to the task.

Top Tip

It is important to be precise when writing about poetry. Remember that 'verse' means the whole poem or a collection of poems. You should use 'stanza' when you want to describe a part of a poem, such as a four-line 'quatrain'.

2: Phrases for the middle of a piece of writing

- The theme / idea of ... is present / repeated in both poems. For example, the poet contrasts ... with ...

- The poet uses appropriate language to convey a feeling of ... For example ...

- The caesura after ... helps an audience to understand that ...

- The use of alliteration / assonance / onomatopoeia with ... shows that ...

- The poet's use of imagery (similes / metaphors / personification) can be seen with ... This shows / intensifies the idea of ...

- Another interesting example of this is ... This emphasises / shows / reinforces / gives a sense of / refers to ...

- The poem's meaning is enhanced / deepened with ... An example of which is ...

- This refers to the main idea of ... For example, this can be seen with ... .

- The poem reflects the narrator's / poet's feelings on ... of ...

- The poet reminds the reader of ... with ...

- The poet draws attention to the fact that ...

- The poet compares ... with ...

3: Phrases to sum up your arguments and views

- The poem's / narrator's tone is one of ... This helps the reader / audience to appreciate the/ how ...

- From reading these poems I learned that ...

- The tone(s) in each poem is / are ... This / these show(s) that ...

- To sum up, I would say that the poet feels ... about his / her subject. The poet wants us to understand / feel the ...

- My final view of the poem(s) is that it is / they are ...

- Both / each of the poems show ... This shows the poet's feelings of ...

Quick Test

1. What does PEC stand for?
2. Find out what the term 'caesura' means.
3. Find out the number of lines in a sonnet.
4. What is alliteration?
5. What is a writing frame?

Poetic techniques

Discussing poetic technique

For a poetic form (sonnet, dramatic monologue) essay, you need to:

- have a good grasp of the rules of the form, e.g. rhyme scheme or use of persona
- be able to discuss how each poem uses the form
- be able to discuss how the poets adapt the form for their own purposes
- be able to assess the effectiveness of the use of the form.

Top Tip

Make sure you show **how** poetic techniques add meaning to a poem.

Some essential poetic terms

Use of letter and word sounds

Alliteration: the same consonant at the beginning of words repeated for an effect, e.g. *fireside flickers*.

Assonance: repetition of vowel sounds for an effect, e.g. *icy winds knife us*. The repetition of the vowel 'i' helps stress the coldness of the 'winds'.

Onomatopoeia: words which sound like their meaning, e.g. *buzz* and *click*.

Rhythm and rhyme: the poem's pace when read aloud, and word endings that sound alike for an effect.

Imagery

Metaphor: a strong comparison where 'is' or 'are' is used or implied. *Juliet is the sun.*

Personification ('person-making'): giving an animal, idea or object human feelings to enhance an emotion, feeling or effect, e.g. *Arise fair sun and kill the envious moon.*

Oxymoron: figures of speech in which contradictory, opposite words are yoked together for an effect. For example, The Beatles, the great 1960s' pop band, famously had a hit song and a film entitled *A Hard Day's Night*. Oxymorons can also be **paradoxes** to enliven prose, but some have turned into clichés, e.g. *act naturally*, *living dead*, etc.

Simile: a comparison using 'as' or 'like', e.g. *My love is as deep as the sea.*

Punctuation and form

Ballad: a story poem that usually features dramatic stories about ordinary people.

Couplet: a two-line stanza that rhymes.

Verse: an entire poem or collection of poems or poetry.

Caesura (or cesura): means 'a cutting'. It can be any type of punctuation in poetry that causes the reader to pause. Poets use them to end-stop their lines and to emphasise points and ideas in their poetry. A caesura can add a great deal of meaning if placed in the middle of a line.

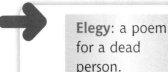

Elegy: a poem for a dead person.

Enjambment (or run-on line or stanza): one line runs into another to achieve a poetic effect. It is often used to aid rhythm and help enact something.

Free verse: irregular stanzas filled with lines of varying length. The lines are like waves coming in along a sea-shore: each has natural rhythm and is just long enough. The form suits conversational and argumentative poems. Free verse, or *vers libre*, was the most popular form of poetry in the twentieth century and remains so today.

Lyric: a poem that sets out the thoughts and feelings of a single speaker.

Quatrain: four lines of a poem that rhyme. It is the main unit in English poetry.

Stanza: a clear section of a poem, usually two or four lines.

Sonnet: usually a 14-line poem about a serious theme such as love or death.

Triplet (or tercet): a three-line stanza. It is a form suited for comic poetry. Poets sometimes reverse the expected content, e.g. Seamus Heaney's 'Mid-Term Break'. The effect can be very poignant.

Narrative stance and attitudes within poems

Dramatic monologue is a poem spoken by the first-person narrator, who is not the poet. The poet adopts a persona and addresses an unspeaking implied listener. A dramatic monologue is often written in the present tense, as in a speech made on stage.

Robert Browning's 'My Last Duchess' is a well-known poem in Scottish schools that uses dramatic monologue. The poem is spoken by a Renaissance duke who had his last wife killed for being too easily pleased and not appreciating his aristocratic heritage. The implied listener is an ambassador who has come to arrange the duke's next marriage. The poem makes good use of a dramatic situation – the two men are looking at a portrait of the duchess and the persona's attitude is cruel. There is an interesting use of run-on lines and rhyme.

Tone: a poet's or a narrator's attitude towards their subject and audience. Tone can change within a poem to emphasise changes of meaning.

The poet's use of diction (words deliberately chosen for their associations and sounds) can affect the **tone** of a poem. Contrasts between multi-syllable and one-syllable words can very quickly change the mood of a poem. In Carol Ann Duffy's poem 'Education for Leisure', the contrast between the multi-syllabic 'pavements suddenly glitter' and the mono-syllabic 'I touch your arm' is very chilling.

Internet

Links to useful exercises, ideas and help with poetry and texts can be found at Leckie and Leckie's Learning Lab.

Quick Test

1. What is a simile?

2. Explain what empathy means.

3. Give an example of onomatopoeia.

4. What is the difference between 'verse' and a 'stanza'?

5. What is a suitable subject for a sonnet and why?

Answers 1. A comparison using 'as' or 'like'. **2.** An appreciation of a writer's or narrator's concerns and ideas. **3.** Any word that sounds like its meaning, e.g. buzz. **4.** 'Verse' is an entire poem or collection of poems; a 'stanza' is a section of a poem. **5.** 'Love' or 'death' because sonnets usually have serious subject matter.

Two poems to study

Six O'Clock News

this is thi
six a clock
news thi
man said n
thi reason
a talk wia
BBC accent
iz coz yi
widny wahnt
mi ti talk
aboot thi
trooth wia
voice lik
wanna yoo
scruff. if
a toktaboot
thi trooth
lik wanna yoo
scruff yi
widny thingk
it wuz troo.
jist wanna yoo
scruff tokn.
thirza right
way ti spell
ana right way
ti tok it. this
is me tokn yir
right way a
spellin. this
is ma trooth.
yooz doant no
thi trooth
yirsellz cawz
yi canny talk
right. this is
the six a clock
nyooz. belt up.

Tom Leonard

Half-Caste

Excuse me
standing on one leg
I'm half-caste

Explain yuself
what yu mean
when yu say half-caste
yu mean when picasso
mix red an green
is a half-caste canvas
explain yuself
wha yu mean
when yu say half-caste
yu mean when light an shadow
mix in de sky
is a half-caste weather
well in dat case
england weather
nearly always half-caste
in fact some o dem cloud
half-caste till dem overcast
so spiteful dem dont want de sun pass
ah rass
explain yuself
wha yu mean
when yu say half-caste
yu mean tchaikovsky
sit down at dah piano
an mix a black key
wid a white key
is a half-caste symphony

Explain yuself
wha yu mean
Ah listening to yu wid de keen
half of mih ear
Ah lookin at yu wid de keen
half of mih eye
and when I'm introduced to yu

I'm sure you'll understand
why I offer yu half-a-hand
an when I sleep at night
I close half-a-eye
consequently when I dream
I dream half-a-dream
an when moon begin to glow
I half-caste human being
cast half-a-shadow
but yu must come back tomorrow
wid de whole of yu eye
an de whole of yu ear
an de whole of yu mind

an I will tell yu
de other half
of my story

John Agard

What the poems are about

1. Both poems deal with issues of **language**, **power** and **prejudice**.

2. Leonard ironically **reverses the usual dialects** associated with authority and reading the news (received pronunciation and standard English). He wants us to think about issues of truth and authority when we only hear the news read by people with received pronunciation or standard English.

3. Leonard argues that it is wrong and prejudiced to believe that these dialects are the only ones capable of expressing the truth and so be taken seriously.

4. The **tone** of Leonard's poem is one of **anger against the prejudices** of society where working-class dialects are not taken seriously and given no respect.

5. Agard's narrator eloquently shows, through a number of unusual and convincing comparisons, that it is **wrong to label anyone by using the term 'half-caste'**. The unquestioned use of such terms can lead to **prejudice**.

6. Agard and Leonard show us that **power, authority and prejudice are linked with language and how we use it**. They warn us against blindly accepting some dialects, such as standard English, as voices of authority and correctness while excluding others and their speakers as only worthy of ridicule. **The 'truth' can be expressed in other dialects too.**

How meaning is expressed

1. The impact of each poem's argument is enhanced through being spoken by a **first-person narrator**.

2. Both poems are appropriately set out in **free verse**, in which the **dialect is defiantly proclaimed and phonetically spelled** in lines of varying length. The narrowness of the poems' lines contrast with other poems written in standard English.

3. The rules of standard English have no place in these poems as there is **no punctuation, nor capital letters**. The narrators make their points with **questions**, **arguments** and **statements** and to advance an alternative to standard English. Agard's poem has stanzas in which some of **the senses are alluded to**. Leonard's poem is plainer, using a single stanza or verse paragraph to refer to speech and Glaswegian dialect. The poets are from different parts of the world yet have similar views on language, about what should be said and how it should be expressed.

4. Both poems have an ironic tone intended to startle their audiences into accepting the truth of the arguments that they advance.

Quick Test

1. What is the term for words that make the sound they are describing?

2. 'Winter spread its icy grip across the land' – What type of figurative language is demonstrated here?

3. What do we call a poem that is written for a person who is dead?

4. What is the main unit of English poetry?

5. How many lines does a sonnet contain?

Answers 1. Onomatopoeia. **2.** Personification. **3.** Elegy. **4.** Quatrain. **5.** 14

Test your progress

Use the questions to test your progress.
Check your answers at the back of the book on page 95.

1. How many critical essays on poetry may you include in your folio?

   ....

2. Are you being tested on your reading or your writing?

   ....

3. Name two forms for poems.

   ....

4. What is tone?

   ....

5. What are the main forms of narration?

   ....

6. Diction is another word for the word choices that poets make for their poems. True or false?

   ....

7. What is a theme?

   ....

8. Part of a poem is a verse. True or false?

   ....

9. The classroom 'glowed like a sweet shop' is a metaphor. True or false?

   ....

10. What is 'enjambment'?

   ....

11. What does it mean to 'compare and contrast' when writing about poetry?

   ....

12. What is an oxymoron?

   ....

13. What can an oxymoron suggest?

   ....

14. Quatrains are the main units of English poetry. True or false?

   ....

15. What is free verse?

   ....

16. Why is free verse appropriate for certain poems?

....

17. What is assonance?

....

18. Where should you give your personal view of the poems that you write about?

....

19. Once you identify a figure of speech or some other poetic technique, what must you do afterwards?

....

20. What is imagery in a poem?

....

How did you do?

1–9	correct	....	start again
10–15	correct	....	getting there
16–20	correct	....	excellent

A critical essay task for you to tackle

Write a critical essay comparing 'Half-Caste' by John Agard and 'Six O'Clock News' by Tom Leonard. Consider in particular the importance of language and form in the poems and how they help to convey the essential message of both texts.

Talking and listening

What you are expected to do

You will need to do a range of targeted assessments in class for the talking component of the course covering individual and group situations.

Individual talk

When you are doing a solo talk, be clear as to the purpose of the talk. Is it:

- to convey information?
- to present an opinion or explore a topic?
- to describe a personal experience?

If you are given a free choice for an individual talk, try to pick a subject that only you could talk about. Choose something that you know really well and would enjoy talking about. Research and preparation are important aspects of an individual talk.

Group talk

There are two main types of assignment used for group talks:

1. **A task related to a text you are reading**. It might be to discuss a particular character or theme from the text, and much of your basic knowledge will come from how well you have studied the text in class. Note that in a discussion you are exchanging opinions – there is not necessarily a 'correct' answer. The key point is that you attempt to support your views with evidence.

2. **You are given a topic**, usually with some degree of topicality and even controversy. For example, you may have studied *Of Mice and Men* and your teacher sets you the task of discussing euthanasia, arising out of the book's ending. Do some **research** and **form opinions** on the topic before your assessment, as this will make it easier for you to contribute.

Top Tip

In group situations it is important that you take turns in speaking and show that you can listen! Do not talk over people.

How you will be graded

Show that you are listening by taking account of what others are saying through a variety of responses: expanding their comments, arguing against them, supporting them with additional examples.

Make a good number of relevant contributions.

Discussion
To achieve a Grade 1–3, you will need to:

Allow others to have their say.

Be consistently audible and make use of varied intonation to support meaning.

Express high quality ideas in a well-structured talk.

Be able to highlight the key points.

Be consistently audible, clear and fluent.

Individual talk
To achieve a Grade 1–3, you will need to:

Speak for a sustained length of time.

Make good use of body language and maintain appropriate eye-contact with your audience.

Hints for talking and listening

- Can you **speak with purpose in a structured way**? You need to **signpost your points** when you speak so that others can follow what you are saying and do not get bored.

- Are you able to **speak with fluency and confidence** on your chosen topic with minimal notes? **Do not make the mistake of reading your notes**.

- Do you **vary the sound of your voice to interest your audience**? Do you **use eye contact** and other **body language** to interest your listener? Sixty per cent of any communication is non-verbal! Use body language such as posture, hand gestures and eye contact, and vary the **tone and pitch of your voice**.

- Can you adapt the **register of your speech** to the task and your audience? You would hardly speak to your head teacher using the same tone of voice as you would to your best friends. You need to be conscious of how people adapt their speech to those they are talking to.

- Are you able to **use language with confidence** in a range of situations? How fluent and clear is your English?

- Can you **initiate speech**, **sustain a point of view** or **manage the contributions of others**? If you can, you would make a great host of a discussion panel.

- Can you **listen with sensitivity** and **respond accordingly**? Are you able to carry forward and further the arguments of others and follow a complex conversation?

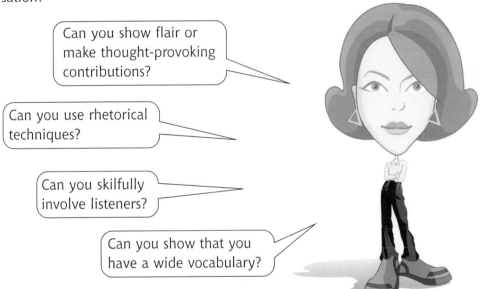

Can you show flair or make thought-provoking contributions?

Can you use rhetorical techniques?

Can you skilfully involve listeners?

Can you show that you have a wide vocabulary?

Quick Test

1. Why should you 'signpost' your talk?

2. What two ingredients are essential before you attempt an individual talk?

3. Who is in charge of a group talk?

4. Why must you speak clearly in a talk situation?

Answers 1. So that the audience can follow your argument. **2.** Research and preparation. **3.** The appointed Chairperson. **4.** So that others can understand you.

Giving a talk

Preparing your talk

1: Topic

Think of a suitable title for your talk – this will help you to focus on your topic.

Research your topic – talk to experts, do some research on the Internet, look in encyclopedias, check out your library, write to agencies, companies or embassies.

Gather resources to help you with the details, points and arguments of your talk. Find and prepare any props that you need; they will be useful for focusing and keeping your audience's attention on what you are saying.

2: Structure

Think about the structure of your talk: introduction, body and conclusion. Summarise the talk in a few paragraphs. Keep them brief. Brainstorm your talk into a flow chart.

3: Prompts

Cut up several square pieces of card just smaller than a postcard.

Write down your main ideas in words or phrases as memory prompts. Resist the temptation to write too much. Keep them brief.

Write the words or phrases twice the size of your normal writing. If you forget your next point, just glance at your card. Turn over the cards as you speak.

Number the cards in the right order. The structure of your talk will then be clear for you as well as for your audience.

4: Practice

- Practise your talk to get the structure and any specialised or unusual vocabulary clear in your mind.
- Practise speaking clearly and consider any places in your talk where you might pause and welcome questions. Questions could act as ice-breakers and help you to relax. You will also be able to gauge the impact of the early parts of your talk.
- **Practise any unusual or specialised vocabulary** so that you appear confident and do not stumble over topic-specific terms.
- Remember to get props or handouts ready if you need them.

Top Tip

Make sure that you practise your talk before you have to deliver it. Use your parents, your cat or even the mirror, but ensure that you have heard yourself before you attempt to speak to others.

Giving the talk

- Try to appear relaxed and confident. (Check the list of hints for talking and listening on page 71.)

- Stand up and try to appear lively by modulating your voice. Remember to match your talk to your audience.

- Speak as fluently and confidently as you can.

- Be prepared to field questions and show your understanding of your topic by answering them. Prepare beforehand by thinking about the kind of questions that you could be asked.

- Show that you can listen carefully and respond in a sympathetic manner to questions asked.

Self-evaluation

Evaluate your performance afterwards. What did you do well? What could you have done better? You should write down all the relevant details:

1. The date of your talk and its title.
2. Specify what type of talk it was.
3. Self-assess how your talk went. What did you do well? How did the audience respond to your talk?
4. Keep a written record of the teacher's feedback on your talk to help you improve your next one. Complete your record by identifying two or three areas for improvement (you should get these from your teacher's feedback). However, you may also be aware of these areas yourself once you have given your talk.

Top Tip

Do not just read your notes aloud – you are not being tested on your ability to read. A major aim is to talk in the most fluent and confident manner that you can.

Quick Test

1. Why would you use body language?
2. Why is it important to listen?
3. Why is it important to plan your talk?
4. Towards the end of your talk, what might you do to involve your audience?

Answers 1. It helps people to understand you and makes your speech more interesting. **2.** Conversations need listeners too; by listening, you can make better points. **3.** It helps to give a more coherent structure and improve the detail. **4.** Ask questions or show them props.

Test your progress

Use the questions to test your progress.
Check your answers at the back of the book on page 95.

1. What are the two modes of talk that are assessed?

   ....

2. How is listening assessed?

   ....

3. State three potential purposes for a solo talk?

   ....

4. Briefly explain what is meant by 'body language'.

   ....

5. What is 'register' in speech?

   ....

6. Explain what is meant by 'irony'.

   ....

7. Why is it important to listen?

   ....

8. What kinds of assignments are suitable for discussing, arguing and persuading?

   ....

9. Why is it important that you do not write out long passages for your talk?

   ....

10. What is meant by 'structure' in a talk?

    ....

11. Why is it important to self-assess after your talk?

    ....

12. A good talk is almost always:
    a) about an interesting subject
    b) well-structured and prepared
    c) funny
    d) informative.

13. Brainstorming is:
    a) a good method of structuring your talk
    b) a good way of planning your talk
    c) a good way of discussing a topic
    d) a good way of producing ideas for your talk.

14. A good way to give a fluent talk is:
   a) to write it out completely and learn it off by heart
   b) to make sure it has a beginning, middle and end
   c) to write key phrases on pieces of cards as prompts
   d) to choose a subject you know really well.

15. Which of the following is the most important factor when delivering a successful talk?
   a) Matching the subject of your talk with your audience.
   b) Providing opportunities for audience interaction.
   c) Standing up straight.
   d) Appearing relaxed and confident.

Well … the … the island in 'Lord of the Flies' is a sort of laboratory that William Golding has set up. It's like he said, 'What would happen if a group of boys was … were stranded on a desert island. He couldn't find out by putting a group of real boys on a real island so he wrote the novel as a … thought experiment. He decided on that … and he let things take their course as any scientist would. Once the boys were up and running – or not as the case may be – he introduced new elements to the basic formula to see what would happen.

So … the biggest challenge he gave the kids was the beast. It's interesting, innit, that the beast appeared in the boys' heads before it was given form by the dead parachutist. What I'm saying is that the beast is really the boys' fear an all … all the things that go wrong on the island are 'cause of fear.

This … is bad news for the rest of us. Golding reckons that fear is what makes any group of people hostile and aggressive. Just as the boys on the island can't get on because of fear … peoples in the world can't get on because of fear. It's no coincidence, is it, that the boys are stranded on the island because the adults are having a nuclear war. Er … that's it.

Question 16.

Here is a transcript of part of a talk given by a student. Read it carefully and then make five suggestions that would improve the speech.

How did you do?

1–5	correct	.... start again
6–10	correct	.... getting there
11–16	correct	.... excellent

Exam technique

The importance of the exam

Although two-thirds of you final grade is already decided, and hopefully you will have worked hard on your folio and talk assessments, the examination is still very important. This is especially true because of the way that **your folio grade and your exam grade are combined**. In effect, the two are 'rounded-up' when they don't average out to a full number. For example, a Grade 3 in your Reading folio and a Grade 2 in your Reading exam would combine to give you an overall Grade 2 for Reading. The same rule applies to the Writing exam.

It is possible, therefore, to **significantly boost your coursework grades by good examination performance**.

Managing your time

- The secret of success is to **do a little and often every day**. Assign yourself set times to do your revision. Why not stick to the times you would have used to attend your English lessons in school?
- Get together with a friend – you will help to motivate each other.
- Improve your proof-reading skills by marking the work of friends.
- Managing your time is crucial in exams. Allow yourself **five to ten minutes to check your work through for errors** of sense, spelling and punctuation. Ask yourself, 'What errors do I usually make?'

Top Tip

Use your time effectively.

Close reading exams

- Do not panic! Channel all your nervous energy and adrenaline into your exam.
- Do not be late. Each paper lasts for 50 minutes so if you are even five minutes late you will have lost 10 per cent of your time.
- Read through Close Reading passages twice: firstly to get the gist of the meaning and then for deeper understanding. Carefully read the passages and note the development of arguments and ideas as well as how they are expressed by underlining words, using a highlighter, or by making short, phrase-like notes.
- Use the paragraph references given to save wasting time.
- Do not give up! The questions do not get harder as you work through them, so even if you have found one section difficult, you may find the next page less so.

Top Tip

Read page 79 for more pointers about Close Reading.

Read carefully

Everyone tends to rush the Close Reading paper. At 50 minutes it is a tight exam, but you have enough time to tackle the task thoroughly. The key to success is not getting the questions answered – it's getting them correct! And this will not happen unless the passage has been understood. This will require **careful reading of the passage**. Pay particular attention to the topic sentences as these will form the backbone of the text.

Remember to scan through the questions between your first and second reading of the passage, as they will indicate the key areas of the passage.

Warning!

You will come across questions that offer either zero marks or two marks: 0 2. It is vital that you do enough to earn both marks in your answer as there is no half-way house. Many candidates get half the answer correct for this type of question but end up with no mark as the marker can only award zero or full marks. You will need to make two points in your answer or to make a point and then explain it more fully.

Quick Test

Here is an example from a recent General Paper:

'On the twenty-fourth of June, in the year 1914, a young man went into a house, and never came out again. His name was William Walter Gordon Maitland, aged twenty-two, of 14, Elliesland Street, Milhall, in the county of Lanarkshire and one summer afternoon he vanished from the face of the earth. It was as simple, and as complicated as that.'

1. What happened to William Maitland on 24 June, 1914? (0 2)

2. The writer describes the event as being 'as simple, and as complicated as that'.
   a) Why do you think the writer calls it 'simple'? (0 2)
   b) Why do you think the writer calls it 'complicated'? (0 2)

These questions are all 'two marks or zero' type questions. It is important not to simply write down the most obvious part of the answer and then leave it at that, as this would result in zero marks.

For example, if your answer to Question 1 was 'He disappeared', you would score no marks. Similarly, if you said, 'He went into a house', you would score zero marks. If you realised that to gain two marks you need to make two points and you wrote, 'He went into a house and disappeared', you would gain the full two marks.

Now try Question 2 for yourself.

Answers 2. a) It was simple because the facts are straightforward and going into a house is an ordinary thing to do.
b) It was complicated because there is no obvious explanation for what had happened and the whole incident is very mysterious.

Close reading

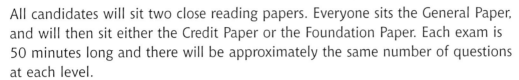

What you have to do

All candidates will sit two close reading papers. Everyone sits the General Paper, and will then sit either the Credit Paper or the Foundation Paper. Each exam is 50 minutes long and there will be approximately the same number of questions at each level.

The reading passages are designed to test your **close reading skills**; that is, **your ability to understand the writer's meaning and purpose and the way that he or she uses language**. They may be any type of writing (newspaper article, prose extract, advertising, etc.).

Foundation

The Foundation Paper covers Grades 5 and 6. At this level you can expect to read texts that are relatively **straightforward** in content and which relate to personal interests and experience. The presentation of ideas will be clear and the language uncomplicated. Many of the questions will focus on basic understanding and the retrieval of information.

General

The General Paper will contain a **greater degree of difficulty** than the Foundation Paper, but will still be accessible, on the whole, to a competent reader. Some questions on how the writer has used language are likely to feature at this level.

Credit

The Credit Paper contains **content that is challenging** and which goes beyond what would be regarded as immediately accessible. This means that you will have to work to understand the full meaning of the passage. The language is liable to be **complex** and ideas may be **more abstract** than in the other levels. Accordingly, the questions themselves will be of a **more sophisticated** nature.

What the questions are testing

It will help if you understand what the questions are designed to do. Questions are constructed to test your abilities in the following areas:

- **Reading to gain an overall impression or gist of a text** – questions here will test your general understanding of a passage.

- **Reading to obtain particular information from a text** – here you will be looking for specific bits of information such as facts.

- **Reading to grasp ideas and feelings** – this area is more difficult because it is more abstract; however, it is essentially testing your understanding of how language is used.

- **Reading to evaluate the writer's attitudes, assumptions and arguments** – perhaps the most difficult area; clearly you have to understand the passage thoroughly in order to make judgement on its effectiveness and arguments.

- **Reading to appreciate the writer's craft** – this area deals with how the writer has used language, e.g. structure, vocabulary, figurative language, punctuation (all the techniques we suggested you should use in your own writing!).

Some suggestions for tackling close reading

- At a minimum, **read the passage carefully** and then **scan through the questions**. Re-read the passage before tackling any answers.

- **Pay attention to the marks on offer** as this will indicate the number of points required in your answer. Generally speaking, one mark will require one point to be made so if there is a 2-mark answer, make sure that you are either making two points or making one point and then explaining it.

- As with the marks, **the space provided in the answer booklet is a guide as to the length** of answer required. If there is a single line and you find yourself writing a paragraph, you are probably saying too much. However, if there are three lines provided and your answer only fills half of one line, you are not answering fully enough.

- The words '**write down**' or '**quote**' in the question mean that you can lift your answer straight from the passage.

- **Answer clearly and concisely**. You are not required to write in sentences unless you have been asked to 'explain' or 'describe' something.

- '**Explain fully**' indicates that you should be using your own words.

- **Consider the context** of any words or phrases where you are unsure of the meaning. Context simply means the sentences around a particular word and it will often help you to work out the meaning.

- If searching a particular paragraph for a word or phrase, **eliminate the obvious** and then **consider the remainder** – it may be the answer!

- **Do not leave blank spaces**. Wrong answers do not lose marks.

Hunter of Dryburn

Brian McCabe

Close reading test paper

The following passage is an extract from Sean Coughlan's article, The Inside Story, Climate Change – Global Warming (The Times, 13th February).

A passage of this complexity would appear in a Credit level exam.

Read through the whole passage first, to get the gist of its main ideas. Then go back and try the questions on each section.

An explanation of the answers follows each mini-section.

Top Tip

Remember that in the exam, all the questions will follow the passage, although they will be organised to focus on sections at a time.

Global warning

Why are governments so paralysed in the face of catastrophic climate change? Sean Coughlan examines the facts and the arguments.

1. When an international team of researchers announced that climate change could kill a quarter of the species of plants and creatures currently sharing the planet with us, it was a figure so stark that the issue of global warming made headlines around the world.

2. Scientists had studied six different regions and had constructed computer models to investigate how more than 1,100 different species would survive the temperature changes that will accompany global warming. 'If the projections can be extrapolated globally, and to other groups of land animals and plants, our analyses suggest that well over a million species could be threatened with extinction as a result of climate change,' said the lead author of the research, Chris Thomas.

Climate change is triggered by the emission of 'greenhouse gases' into the environment.

3. Variety of flowers in Africa, lizards in Australia and birds in Scotland could be swept away by a climate change triggered by the emission of 'greenhouse gases' into the atmosphere. And the timescale is not a distant point on the horizon; we could have extinguished many types of life on Earth by 2050.

4. As a mid-range forecast, researchers found that the effect of climate changes would spell the end for 25 per cent of species – rising to 37 per cent on a more pessimistic projection – and the damage already in progress would lead to the extinction of 18 per cent of species.

5. Is this apocalyptic vision really going to happen? Is there a scientific consensus? And even if we wanted to limit global warming, is there any realistic chance of international cooperation?

Questions

Look at paragraphs 1–5.

1. Why did the issue of global warming make headlines around the world?   *(2 marks)*

....

....

....

....

2. Explain how the writer conveys the global nature and scale of the
danger posed.   *(2 marks)*

....

....

....

....

3. How does the use of statistics in paragraph 4 help you to understand the
meaning of 'pessimistic'?   *(2 marks)*

....

....

....

....

4. What does the phrase 'apocalyptic vision' suggest?   *(2 marks)*

....

....

....

....

Answers

4. A view of the future that suggests destruction and death.

ii) The statistics suggest the worst case scenario, 'rising to 37 per cent', indicating an even worse position than might be the case. This suggests the meaning of taking a negative view.

3. i) One mark for explaining that 'pessimistic' means to take a negative view of things.

ii) Reference in paragraph 3 to different countries to suggest global nature of the problem.

2. i) 'over a million species' – candidate should really suggest the vast scale suggested by this figure.

ii) One mark for gloss on 'stark' suggesting that the danger was a very real threat.

1. i) One mark for explaining that the research suggested a major problem – statistic 'a quarter of the species'.

Close reading passage continued ...

6. Environmental campaigners in Greenpeace are in no doubt about the extent of the danger, identifying climate change as the biggest single environmental threat to the planet. But spokesperson Ben Stewart says that the scale of the problem is such that people can feel overwhelmed – frozen in the headlights as we watch the juggernaut hurtling nearer. 'It seems as though, even when people accept that there is a huge problem, we don't feel we have the ability to do anything.'

7. But Ben Stewart believes that the message is getting through – and that the international decision taken at the Kyoto conference in 1992 to cut emissions was a cause for optimism, even though the US Government has not ratified the deal. If action is taken to ratify greenhouse emissions, he says, it won't be a moment too soon. He quotes research from the World Health Organisation which claimed that global warming was already causing the deaths of tens of thousands of people, through destruction of agriculture and the spread of diseases. He also raised the spectre of 'climate refugees', where large numbers of people will be pushed out of their own land because of global warming and will have to look for asylum elsewhere.

8. But if we are looking for a reason why there has not been urgent and immediate action to stop such a nightmare vision of the future, then we have to take a step back and see that the arguments on global warming are not cast in black and white. Scientists are far from unanimous about the cause or ultimate effect of global warming. There are also more immediate economic arguments over cutting emissions that are being held in the balance against scientific forecasts. And if it's a question of losing jobs tomorrow, or worrying about something that might happen in fifty years, then politicians are under pressure to act in the short-term.

Questions continued ...

Look at paragraphs 6–8.

5. 'frozen in the headlights as we watch the juggernaut hurtling nearer'.

   a) Explain fully the image being used here. *(2 marks)*

   ....
   ....
   ....
   ....

   b) How does it relate to the rest of the paragraph? *(2 marks)*

   ....
   ....
   ....
   ....

6. What reservation is expressed about the decision taken at the Kyoto conference to cut emissions? *(1 mark)*

....

....

7. a) Using your own words, explain how global warming is causing death. *(2 marks)*

....

....

....

....

....

b) What other 'problem' is likely to be caused by global warming? *(2 marks)*

....

....

....

....

8. Explain clearly the situation that politicians find themselves in. *(2 marks)*

....

....

....

....

Answers

5. a) The image is that of an animal mesmerised by the headlamps of an approaching lorry and unable to escape as a result.

b) It links with the final sentence which indicates that even though we know that there is a big issue about global warming to be tackled, we don't feel able to actually do anything about it.

6. The reservation is that the US has not signed up to the agreement – 'even though the US Government has not ratified the deal'.

7. a) The answer lies in the phrase 'through the destruction of agriculture and the spread of diseases', but this has to be put into the candidate's own words, i.e. through plants and crops being ruined, causing hunger, and through illnesses being passed on.

b) Global warming is likely to force people to abandon their homes because of the changed climate, and they will then have to find somewhere else to live – 'climate refugees'.

8. Politicians are forced by their voters to act on problems now rather than ones that will only have an impact in the future.

Inverted commas – speech

Inverted commas are used to **mark off direct speech**, where they are placed around the actual words spoken: for example in paragraph 6 'It seems as though, even when people accept that there is a huge problem, we don't feel we have the ability to do anything.'

Close reading passage continued ...

9. In Britain, Joe Buchdahl, coordinator of the Atmosphere, Climate and Environment Information Programme, puts forward the mainstream 'official' view. The project is supported by the Department for Environment, Food and Rural Affairs (DEFRA) to present unbiased and balanced information about global warming.

10. Buchdahl says that there is now a 'balance of evidence' which confirms the climate is changing – and that, increasingly, it is believed that there is a 'human fingerprint' on these changes.

11. The British Government reported its belief that global temperature rises 'cannot be explained by natural factors' and the evidence suggests that 'increasing greenhouse gas levels due to human activities are largely responsible'. As a result, it concluded that Britain in the short term is likely to face hotter, drier summers and warmer wetter winters. In the long term (perhaps within 200 years) it is predicted the effect will be quite the opposite – global warming may prematurely usher in a new ice age for the UK.

12. The British Isles draws its geographically misplaced warmth from the Gulf Stream, a 'conveyor belt' for warm water and consequently humid air, which originates in the Gulf of Mexico and passes through the North Atlantic. The Gulf Stream relies on a strong undercurrent of cold water, cooled by the polar ice cap.

13. Global warming is causing this 'continent-size' body of ice to melt, pouring massive amounts of fresh water into the North Atlantic. This weakens the Gulf Stream and, some scientists predict, will push it south and out of Britain's waters. No warm water would mean, while the rest of the world bakes, the region around the British Isles will literally freeze.

Inverted commas – quotations

Inverted commas are used to indicate when a quotation is being used: in paragraph 11, for example, it talks about the British Government reporting its belief that global temperature rises 'cannot be explained by natural factors'. As the British Government cannot actually speak, as such, this is a quotation either from a written report or from a speech by a spokesperson.

Questions continued ...

Look at paragraphs 9–13.

9. Using your own words, explain the key function of the Atmosphere, Climate, and Environment Information Group. *(2 marks)*

....

....

....

....

10. What does the phrase 'balance of evidence' mean? *(2 marks)*

....

....

....

....

11. What impact does the 'Gulf Stream' have on Britain's climate? *(1 mark)*

....

....

12. What long term consequence does Britain face as a result of global warming? *(1 mark)*

....

....

Answers

9. The answer lies in the phrase 'to present unbiased and balanced information', but this must be put into the candidate's own words; i.e. to provide opinion-free information from both sides of the argument.

10. It means an overall judgement based on considering the evidence from both sides of the debate.

11. It heats it up.

12. We might return to the ice age.

Close reading passage continued ...

14. But all of this doesn't necessarily mean that global warming will have the cataclysmic consequences that some scientists have suggested, says Joe Buchdahl. And he says that best-guesses should not be confused with something that will definitely happen. 'We don't know how well or badly humans and other species would adapt to changed climates and there are too many unpredictable factors to be certain about where global warming might lead.'

15. This is an international argument – and he says that we have to take seriously how the debate is perceived from other countries. If global emissions are to be cut, then the role of the US as the world's biggest economy will be vital. And in the US there are powerful lobbyists such as within the oil industry, who suggest that threats of global warning are overstated and that any hurried action could damage the economy without delivering any proven benefit.

16. There are also lobbyists in the US who argue that, rather than cutting emission, the answer lies in developing cleaner technology.

Questions continued ...

Look at paragraphs 14–16.

13. Which phrase in paragraph 8 suggests a similar meaning to cataclysmic? *(2 marks)*

....

....

....

....

14. Using your own words, explain why we cannot be certain as to what will happen in the future. *(2 marks)*

....

....

....

....

15. a) Why is the position of the US so vital to the international debate about what should happen? *(1 marks)*

....

....

b) What reservations do some US commentators have? *(2 marks)*

....

....

....

....

c) What alternative strategy to cutting emissions is suggested? *(1 marks)*

....

....

d) What might you infer about the role of 'lobbyists' from the oil industry? *(2 marks)*

....

....

....

....

Inverted commas – titles

Inverted commas can be used to **indicate the title** of something, such as a book: 'Stone Cold'. Increasingly, however, titles are being indicated by the use of italics: *Stone Cold*.

Answers

13. A nightmare vision of the future.

14. We don't know how animals and humans might change owing to climate changes. There are too many uncertainties involved to be certain what might happen.

15. a) It is the world's biggest economy.

b) That the threat has been exaggerated and that quick solutions might do more damage without actually working.

c) Cleaner technology

d) That they have a powerful voice and may have a vested interest because oil is one of the main sources of gas emissions.

Close reading passage continued ...

17. But if there is growing agreement that the climate is changing, the next big question is how we should respond. What action should we take to either delay or offset the effects? This is the challenge being taken up by a network of 200 scientists who are working on scientific responses to global warming.

18. Asher Minns, speaking on behalf of the group, says that as well as trying to cut emissions, we should be looking at how we are going to adapt to a different type of climate. For instance, if the sea level is going to rise, which parts of the coastline do we want to protect, and which will we abandon? In a relatively affluent country such as Britain, such adaptations can be made and cities beside the sea protected. But he says there needs to be advanced planning for countries such as Bangladesh, where vast numbers of people will be susceptible to sea-level changes.

19. If there are going to be more violent storms, what will it mean for developed and non-developed countries? Who will pick up the bill for the damage? Who will look after the homeless? What will happen to people living on low-lying islands which become uninhabitable?

20. There will also be adaptations to be made by agriculture, he says. A warmer climate in Britain could mean a longer growing season and for some produce, the prospect of two crops a year instead of one. But on the downside, milder weather will mean that pests and diseases are not killed off by the frost in winter.

Melting of the polar ice-caps and resulting rise in sea level will threaten many coastal cities.

Varying sentence structure

Sentences normally **begin with a subject** (the person or thing doing whatever action is being described) **followed by a verb, predicate** (the action being done). When this order is changed the writer is usually trying to create a particular effect.

Look back to the last sentence in paragraph 11, for example. This would normally be written 'It is predicted the effect will be quite the opposite in the long term (perhaps within 200 years)...

By placing the phrase 'In the long term' at the beginning of the sentence the writer is drawing attention to the timescale we are dealing with, emphasising the potentially serious consequences. (In this case it also links effectively with the previous sentence, which dealt with the 'short term' issues.)

Recognising when a sentence is structured differently from the normal pattern can assist with understanding the writer's craft and purpose.

Questions continued ...

Look at paragraphs 17–20.

16. Using your own words, explain fully the three examples used to illustrate the need to adapt to climate change.

a) ....

....

....

.... *(2 marks)*

b) ....

....

....

.... *(2 marks)*

c) ....

....

....

.... *(2 marks)*

Repetition

Repetition is a technique used by writers often to create a sense of **emphasis**. In paragraph 19 we see a series of questions being posed to create a dramatic impact and to suggest the large number of issues that require to be addressed.

Answers

16. a) From paragraph 18: The sea is getting higher because of global warming and this will mean that some seaside areas, including towns, will be under threat. In rich countries it might be possible to protect some areas but poorer countries will be badly affected without some help.

b) From paragraph 19: Changes to the weather will mean more damage being done and this will create problems such as people losing their homes.

c) Farming will change with some good effects, such as more harvests, but the lack of a cold winter will mean that insects will survive and possibly cause problems.

Close reading passage continued ...

21. But Asher Minns is in no doubt that such climate change is taking place – and that we need to face up to making a decision about making a response.

22. So where has the argument over global warming reached? In a relatively short space of time, it has become an internationally recognised issue.

23. But a consensus on the extent of the likely impact or causes of global warming remains elusive. The US, the biggest producer of greenhouse gases, remains the strongest sceptic when it comes to adopting an internationally-enforced process for reducing emissions. What is certain is that, whatever happens, the heat won't be going out of this argument for many years to come.

Inverted commas – non-literal meanings

Often when a word is used in a non-literal fashion, it is marked off by inverted commas. This is to indicate to the reader that the writer is aware of the non-conventional use of the word and wants you to understand its purpose.

Look back to paragraph 12, for example. Here, 'conveyor-belt' is in inverted commas because we are not meant to think that there is an actual conveyor belt operating. They are used to indicate that the Gulf Stream acts like a conveyor belt, carrying the warm water along its predetermined course like a conveyor belt in a factory carrying goods or parts.

Parenthesis

Parenthesis is where additional information is provided in a sentence which tells us more but which is not essential to the main point of the sentence. It can be indicated by brackets, dashes, or by a pair of commas.

In paragraph 23, for example, parenthesis is used to indicate that the US is 'the biggest producer of greenhouse gases'. This is an important fact, but if we took it out of the sentence we would still be left with the main point – that 'the US remains the strongest sceptic when it come to adopting an internationally enforced process for reducing emissions.'

Parenthesis is often used to allow the writer to add a personal comment while still presenting the facts.

Questions continued ...

Look at paragraphs 21–23.

17. 'But a consensus ...' Why has the writer chosen to begin a new paragraph with the above phrase, rather than using 'but' to join the new sentence to the preceding one?

....

....

....

.... (2 marks)

18. How effective do you consider the final paragraph to be in summing up the article?

....

....

....

.... (2 marks)

Statistics

It is important to remember that statistics are primarily numbers. The **context** in which they are used **is crucial** as to how we should interpret them.

For example if we said that 'one hundred people turned up at the meeting' – we have a bald statistic. Is that a high number or a low one? If, however, we said. 'As many as one hundred people attended the meeting', we are indicating that this is a significant figure by our use of the phrase 'as many as'. On the other hand, 'Only one hundred people turned up at the meeting', would downplay the level of the problem.

Context is key to understanding statistics.

Literal and non-literal meanings

Words have literal and non-literal meanings and it is important to recognise the difference.

When a word is used **literally** it **means exactly what it says**: 'The knife was very sharp' – 'sharp' means, here, that it has an edge to it that might cut you.

If we said, 'The teacher has a very sharp brain', we are not suggesting that the physical brain is honed to an edge but simply that the teacher is clever and quick witted. 'Sharp' is being used in a non-literal sense here to make an association that we can understand.

Answers

18. It is effective because it highlights the main difficulty outlined in the passage and it also has a play-on-words – 'the heat won't be going out of this argument' – which links with the passage's topic of global warming.

17. If he hadn't used 'but' it would have made sense, but by separating it off and making it the start of a new paragraph, he has emphasised the difficulty of getting agreement.

Writing

Choosing a task

In the exam you will have a wide choice of topics to choose from. It is important that you **make your choice quickly and appropriately**.

Try to have a **clear idea of the type of task that you are looking for**. If you are good at personal experience essays and not so good at short stories, for example, this should guide your choice of question.

Ask yourself the following questions as you consider the options:

1: Am I interested in this subject?

You will produce better work if you are writing about something in which you have a real interest as the **genuine** nature of your response will shine through.

2: Do I know enough about it?

Remember that being interested in something is not the same as knowing about it. You will find it difficult to write enough to justify a good grade if your **basic knowledge** is inadequate.

3: Can I write in the style required?

Be clear about the style of essay being asked for: **personal experience**, **argumentative**, **descriptive** or **short story**. Be especially careful about special registers such as a speech or radio script – if you are not experienced in the style being asked for it would be better to make another choice. **Writing in the wrong genre may be heavily punished**.

If the answer is 'Yes' to all three of the above questions, you can tackle the task with confidence.

Attaining a high grade

You will need to do the following to produce a good answer.

Plan your writing – at a minimum use a mind-map to generate some ideas.

Show **accuracy** in your spelling and punctuation.

Have a sound structure to your work, using **well-constructed paragraphs** with topic sentences.

Use **varied sentence structure** and **punctuation**, as well as showing **clarity** of thought.

Focus on your purpose.

Proof-read your work and **correct it where necessary**. Teachers and examiners love to see evidence of proof-reading because it shows that pupils have attained a level of maturity as independent learners.

Relevance

A **common mistake** made in the exam is for the candidate to **write the wrong type of essay**. This will almost always lead to a poorer grade and in some instances could result in a Grade 7 being awarded.

Consider the following example:

> Young people like to assert their independence from parents through their sense of fashion, their taste in music, their choice of friends. Discuss the relevance of this statement to today's youth.

The word '**discuss**' tells you that this is a **discursive essay**. However, the temptation might be to treat it as a personal experience type essay and this would lead to a poorer grade.

You must read the task carefully.

If you are invited to write in any way you choose about a topic – make sure that you <u>do</u> choose and that you have a particular style of essay in mind. The marker should be able to see clearly, for example, where an essay is about a personal experience as opposed to being a creative short story.

Where you are given a title to use, make sure that **the idea suggested by the title is central to your essay** and not simply an awkward twist at the end, as this would not justify its relevance.

Caution!

One major difference between the folio and the exam is that **in the exam you do not have the opportunity to re-draft your work**.

However, **the same standard of marking applies with regard to punctuation, paragraphing and spelling**. Take extra care, therefore, to punctuate and paragraph accurately. A significant number of missing full stops, for example, will pull an otherwise good essay down to a Grade 4 or less. And if you fail to structure your essay effectively with good paragraphing, you will again be looking at Grade 4 as your maximum.

Check over your work carefully. If you realise that you should have started a new paragraph use the symbols NP in the margin to indicate this to the marker.

Top Tip

Use Past Papers for exam practice to get a feel for how they are laid out and for the type of questions you may be asked.

> This book will have helped you maximise your folio and talk grades and prepared you well for the examination. Now go to the Leckie and Leckie Past Papers for more exam practice. Good luck!

Answers

Writing skills (pages 24–25)

Punctuation and sentences

1. You need to punctuate your work so that your readers will fully understand your meaning.
2. Check your answer against page 7. (Award yourself a mark if you got all five.)
3. Jemma, *Great Expectations*, English, the first She, Charles Dickens and Easter.
4. Full stop, semi-colon, colon, exclamation mark and question mark.
5. They join closely-related sentences; they separate sets of items in lists when there are commas within the sets or lists.
6. A question to which you do not expect a direct answer; you expect instead that your listener will agree with you.
7. Colons can introduce a list; they can introduce a sentence which expands upon the meaning of the first sentence; they can also introduce long quotations that are separated from the writer's prose.
8. Inverted commas are needed for words spoken; the speech needs to be separated from the rest of the writing by a punctuation mark; it is introduced with a capital letter; you need a new line for each speaker; and each new line should be indented three spaces from the margin.
9. Apostrophes can indicate possession or an abbreviated word or phrase.
10. Before the 's' as with the firemen's equipment.
11. Statements, exclamations, instructions or commands and questions.
12. The main clause is 'I will go to the cinema'. The dependent clause is 'as soon as I have done the washing up'.

Spelling and expression

13. Spelling phonetically sounding out each syllable:
    - Look–Say–Cover–Write–Check
    - Use a dictionary; produce a mnemonic.
14. It is 'i' before 'e' except after 'c'.
15. There is a consonant before the 'y' as with 'city'; so it is 'cities'.
16. There is a vowel before the 'y' as with 'monkey'; so it is 'monkeys'.
17. They are all to do with place.
18. Beginning, appearance, interested, grammar, tongue, definitely, necessity, rhythm, sentence.
19. Synonyms are words that mean the same.
20. Homophones are words that are different yet sound the same. For instance, 'whether' and 'weather'.
21. Connective words link phrases, sentences and paragraphs together.
22. To help signpost ideas and arguments so that readers can follow what you mean.
23. Paragraphs break up forbidding chunks of text and make meaning clear. Writers need them to organise their main points and ideas.
24. The topic sentence is the main sentence in a paragraph. The remaining sentences expand on its meaning.
25. 'Control' is the ability to write sentences and paragraphs of appropriate length with control over expression. Word choices and punctuation will also be appropriate and accurate.
26. Because.
27. The opening line of Tennyson's poem 'The Eagle' is very striking.
    'He clasps the crag with crooked hands.'
    The most noticeable thing about it is the use of the word 'hands' where the reader might have expected something like 'talons' or 'claws'. The second thing that makes the line striking is the alliteration on the letter 'c'. The repeated 'c's give the line a harsh sound which is in keeping with the eagle's harsh environment.

Writing (pages 34–35)

1. Two
2. As appropriate to task but usually between 600–800 words.
3. Functional style writing.
4. Personal writing.
5. Creative writing, e.g. short story, poetry, drama.
6. Informative piece; biography; opinion type essay; discursive.
7. A personal experience; a short story; a poem.
8. To allow your personality to shine through.
9. Revealing what you have learned or gained from a situation.
10. Your writing may become clichéd.
11. Your writing will be more genuine and therefore more effective.
12. Use statistics; compare and contrast; use an anecdote; give an example.
13. The use of 'as' or 'like' in the comparison.
14. To make your writing more descriptive and interesting.
15. An interesting beginning which draws the reader in.
16. The setting is where the story is supposed to be in time and place.
17. First and third person.
18. Third person.
19. The plan or outline of the story.
20. Notes, brainstorm or spidergram.
21. Fluency of expression and punctuation
22. Linear is a 'straight line'. There is no going backwards or forwards as the story unfolds. For example, *Romeo and Juliet* is a linear play because the action takes place over four days.
23. So that you are looking from at least two sides of a topic.
24. You can get information from knowledgeable people, libraries, the Internet, encyclopedias, companies, embassies, etc.
25. No.
26. Poetry, dramascript.
27. Yes.
28. To read over your work, checking for and correcting mistakes.
29. In the writing exam.

Reading: Responding to Literature (pages 40–41)

Question A

1. c
2. b
3. c
4. a

Question B

Sailor speech shows that they can't directly change fate

Temptation – Use the truth against him, Thane of Cawdor greeting is true when they utter it

Conclusion

Witches diagram

Temptation 2 – All three warnings are true. Just not what Macbeth expected

Effect on Lady Macbeth – Letter describes meeting – she persuades Macbeth

Effect on Macbeth – Witches not present at murder – his decision

Question C

Give yourself marks out of 10 – one mark for each point you have made. Have someone check your work.

Reading: Prose (pages 48–49)

1. The outline or structure of a piece of writing.
2. To explain what is different.
3. This refers to the kind or type of writing; for example: romance, adventure, detective, horror, etc.
4. How the writer creates effects through emotive or figurative writing.
5. Saying one thing while meaning another, or speaking the truth without knowing it.
6. Connectives which allow you to move from one argument or point to another in a fluent manner. They are often key words or phrases that are needed at the beginning of paragraphs, such as 'similarly' or 'on the other hand'.
7. First and third person.
8. He or she uses 'I' because they are in the story.
9. Not necessarily – do not confuse author with narrator.
10. Usually the third person. You can have a third-person omniscient all-seeing narrator.
11. Any of the ways set out on 'What to look for in characters' on page 43 will do for this answer.
12. An all-knowing author, usually in third-person stories.
13. Round characters develop because they change in the course of the novel. Flat characters do not change, thus they do not develop.
14. 'Conversation' – two people speaking.
15. Dialogue makes characters vivid and lifelike. What characters say reveals their motives and personality traits; readers can learn about characters from what other characters say about them.
16. New speaker, new line and indent; begin with a capital letter; introduce with a punctuation mark and use inverted commas.
17. A character speaking alone.
18. The answer is similar to that for question 15.
19. Both have: plots, stories, dialogue, characters, themes and ideas.
20. Short stories tend to concentrate on one incident, with one plot and fewer themes and a shorter time-span for the action; there are also fewer characters with less detail; the dialogue is more fragmented; description in short stories is more economical.
21. There is not enough space to do otherwise.
22. Through description; the use of imagery; variety in language and sentences; the tone of the narrator and his or her closeness to the action.
23. The choice of words chosen by the author.
24. True.
25. True.
26. False.
27. Alliteration is the repetition of initial consonants in words for an effect; assonance is the repetition of similar vowel sounds in words for an effect.
28. The main idea or message of a story.

Reading: drama (pages 58–59)

Structure and theme

1. Check your answers against page 52.
2. Comment on them.
3. History, Tragedy and Comedy. There is a sub-genre: Tragicomedy.
4. Poetic verse, blank verse and prose.
5. For the end of scenes and scenes of dramatic intensity.
6. To show dignified speech; speech that helps convey feeling and mood.
7. A sense of normality and order. 'All is well with the world'.
8. Problems are introduced and order begins to break down.
9. The point of highest dramatic intensity before the protagonist's fall.
10. Battles, unmasking, deaths, marriages, etc.
11. Order is restored and the right people are back in control.
12. A central idea or ideas.
13. Check your answers with those in 'Themes' on page 53. There are also other themes.
14. Love, appearance and reality, good and evil, identity and disguise, etc.
15. A comic scene is followed by a serious scene.
16. This makes a scene appear even more intense or light-hearted because of the contrasting emotions of the previous scene.
17. Self-knowledge is the ability to learn from your faults when others point them out to you. Characters who do so 'develop'.
18. Order – problems – chaos – climax – resolution with new order.

Imagery

19. Any kind of imagery or decorative language with alliteration, etc.
20. A comparison using 'as' or 'like'; for example, 'Clare is like a flower'.
21. It is a comparison which implies or states that something is something else: 'Clare is a flower'.
22. A metaphor that runs or is 'extended' over several lines or a scene.
23. It means 'person-making'. It is powerful metaphor in which things or ideas are given human traits for an enhanced literary effect.
24. Two opposite terms yoked together for effect; for example, 'A Hard Day's Night'.
25. A character, theme or image that recurs.
26. Imagery helps to say more about points made in dialogue and action. It reinforces and enhances the audience's ideas of the characters. It can magnify or draw attention to themes or issues in the text.
27. Characters speak with irony when they say something that is truer than they realise.
28. It is dramatically ironic when the audience knows something important that characters do not. Sometimes this is complicated by one character knowing what another does with the audience sharing their knowledge.
29. Passages and scenes of dramatic intensity. An example is where Romeo first speaks with Juliet.
30. It includes figurative language, including word-pictures like similes and metaphors.

Reading: poetry (pages 68–69)

1. Maximum of two.
2. Reading.
3. Free-verse, quatrains, couplets, sonnets, etc.
4. The attitude of the narrator to his or her topic and to the reader.
5. First and third person.
6. True.
7. A key message or idea.
8. False – it is a stanza.
9. False – it is a simile.
10. A run-on line. Poets use them for effect.
11. To 'compare' is to note what is similar; to 'contrast' is to explain what is different.
12. A figure of speech and a paradox in which two contradictory terms are brought together for an effect: 'awfully nice' and 'alone together'.
13. Usually mixed feelings or a paradox.
14. True – they are composed of two couplets.
15. Stanzas of irregular length and number.
16. It is an ideal form for conversation and argument.
17. Repetition of vowel sounds for an effect.
18. At the end of your essay. Do give your views because examiners are interested in what you think.
19. Comment on it.
20. A picture created by the poet's use of language, which may suggest associations to the reader.

Talking (pages 74–75)

1. Individual and group.
2. Through your ability to respond to comments and questions from others.
3. Convey information; express ideas and opinions; relate a personal experience.
4. Non-verbal language such as eye contact, hand gestures, etc.
5. Register is the tone you adopt when addressing various audiences; for example, you should speak to a judge differently than you would speak to a friend.
6. We are being ironic if the tone of voice we use implies the opposite meaning of the words we use.
7. Good listeners have better, more complex conversations and good turn-taking skills.
8. Debates and topical issues in the news or an issue that came out of a class text.
9. You are assessed on your ability to talk, not to read. Long, written passages prevent fluency in speech because of the temptation to look at them for reassurance.
10. The 'structure' of your talk is the clarity and order of its presentation.
11. Self-assessment is crucial for setting new targets for improvement and achieving them.
12. b
13. d
14. c
15. a
16. Various answers: avoid hesitation suggested by the various ellipsis; don't use colloquialisms or slang, e.g. 'innit'; link points more effectively, e.g. 'So...'; avoid contractions, e.g. 'cause; conclude positively rather than trailing off, e.g. 'Er... that's it.'

Index

Text Credits

Leckie & Leckie is grateful to the copyright holders, as credited, for permission to use their material. Every effort has been made to trace the copyright holders and to obtain their permission for the use of copyright material. Leckie & Leckie will gladly receive information enabling them to rectify any error or omission in subsequent editions.

Page 45: 'Flight' from The Habit of Loving © 1957 Doris Lessing. Reprinted by kind permission of Jonathan Clowes Ltd., London, on behalf of Doris Lessing.

Page 45: extract from Superman and Paula Brown's New Snowsuit, Sylvia Plath © Faber and Faber.

Page 66: 'Six o'clock News' © Tom Leonard from Intimate Voices, Etruscan Books.

Page 66: by kind permission of John Agard c/o Caroline Sheldon Literary Agency 'Half Caste' from Get Back Pimple published by Puffin (1997).

Page 80: 'The Inside Story, Climate Change - Global Warning' from the Times Educational Supplement (Scotland), © Sean Coughlan.

Photo Credits

Page 80: 'Sugar beet refining factory' © Chris Knapton/Alamy

Page 84: 'Car exhaustion' © Bjorn Andren/Alamy

Page 88: 'Icebergs in an ice floe' © image100/Alamy

Pages 11, 13, 45, 50: images reproduced by kind permission of Topham Picture Point.

4

THE BIG DOORS OF THE COUNTRY-BARN
STAND OPEN AND READY,
THE DRIED GRASS OF THE HARVEST-TIME
LOADS THE SLOW-DRAWN WAGON,
THE CLEAR LIGHT PLAYS ON THE BROWN GRAY
AND GREEN INTERTINGED,
THE ARMFULS ARE PACKED
TO THE SAGGING MOW.

WITHIN THEIR WALLS
SHALL ALL THAT FORWARDS PERFECT HUMAN
LIFE BE STARTED,
TRIED, TAUGHT, ADVANCED, VISIBLY EXHIBITED.

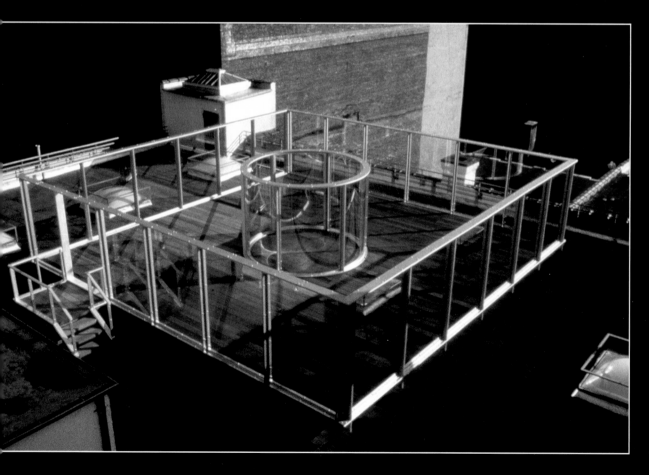

8

BLE HAPPENS PEOPLE WAKE UP
N DISCOVER ANY TRUTH
A VICTIM OF THE RULES YOU LIVE BY
WORDS TEND TO

14

Plate 1 | Jonathan Borofsky
Installation detail: Paula Cooper Gallery,
New York, 1980.

Plate 2 | Robert Gober. Installation detail:
Dia Center for the Arts, New York, 1992.

Plate 3 | Ilya Kabakov, *10 Characters:
The Man who Flew into Space from His
Apartment*, 1988.
Installation detail: Ron Feldman Gallery,
New York.

Plate 4 | Rirkrit Tiravanija, *Untitled (Still)*, 1995.
Installation detail: Carnegie Museum,
Pittsburgh.

Plate 5 | Scott Burton. Installation detail:
Equitable Center, South Plaza, New York, 1986.

Plate 6 | Siah Armajani. Hirshhorn Museum
Employees Lounge, 1982.
Installation detail: Washington D.C.

Plate 7 | Jorge Pardo, in collaboration
with The Fabric Workshop and Museum
Untitled, 1999. Installation detail: Fabric
Workshop and Museum, Philadelphia.

Plate 8 | Dan Graham, *Two Way Mirror Cylinder
Inside Cube and a Video Salon* or *Rooftop Urban
Park Project*, 1981–91. Two-way mirror, glass,
steel, wood, rubber. 274.3 × 1097.3 × 1097.3 cm.
Installation: Dia Art Center, New York.

Plate 9 | Walter De Maria, *The Lightning
Field*, 1977.
Installation: Quemado, New Mexico.

Plates 10 and 11 | James Turrell, *Sky Piece*, 2000.
Installation: Live Oak Friends Meeting
House, Houston.

Plate 12 | Jenny Holzer, *Untitled (Selections
from Truisms, Inflammatory Essays, The
Living Series, The Survival Series, Under a Rock,
Laments and Child Text)*, 1989. Extended helical
tricolor L.E.D. electronic-display signboard.
Installation detail: Solomon R. Guggenheim
Museum, New York, 1998–99.

Plate 13 | Christo and Jeanne-Claude
Wrapped Reichstag, Berlin, 1977–95.

Plate 14 | Vanessa Beecroft
Installation detail: The Solomon R.
Guggenheim Museum, New York, 1998.

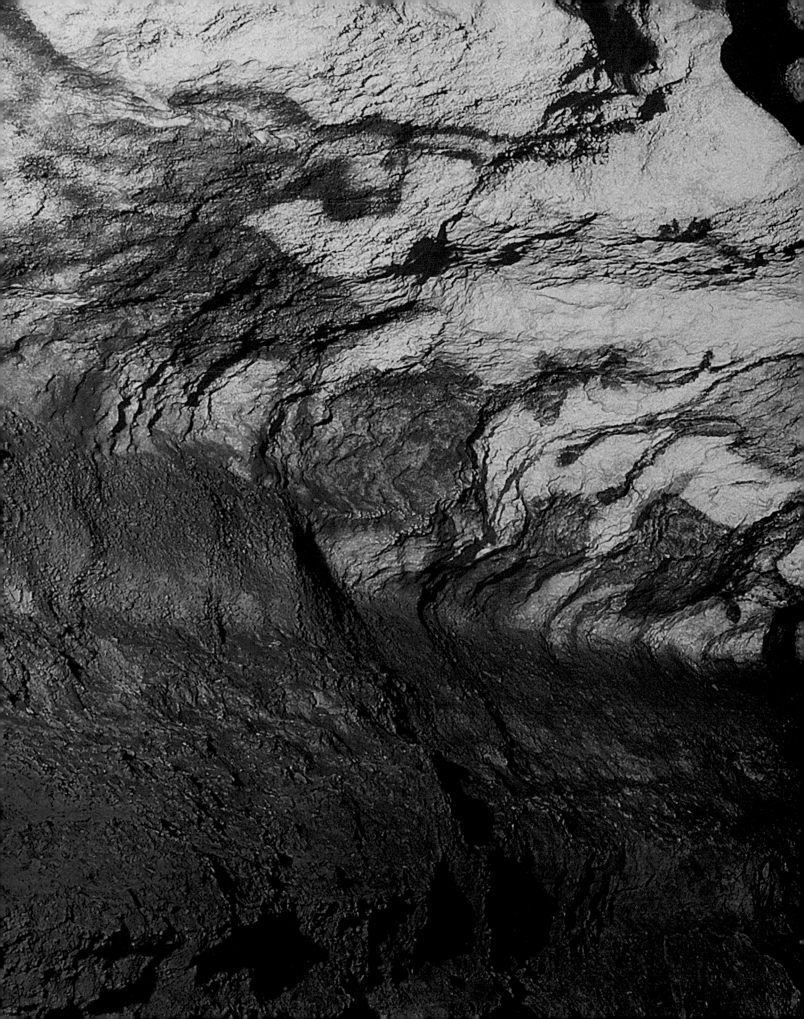

MARK ROSENTHAL

Understanding
Installation Art

From Duchamp
to Holzer

Prestel

Munich · Berlin · London · New York

Front cover: Ilya Kabakov, *10 Characters: The Man who Flew into Space
from His Apartment*, 1988 (detail). See p. 42
Back cover: Walter De Maria, *The Lightning Field*, 1977 (detail). See p. 85

Prestel Verlag
Königinstrasse 9, D-80539 Munich
Tel. +49 (89) 381709-0
Fax +49 (89) 381709-35
www.prestel.de

Prestel Publishing Ltd.
4, Bloomsbury Place, London WC1A 2QA
Tel. +44 (020) 7323-5004
Fax +44 (020) 7636-8004

Prestel Publishing
175 Fifth Avenue, Suite 402,
New York, N.Y. 10010
Tel. +1 (212) 995-2720
Fax +1 (212) 995-2733
www.prestel.com

Library of Congress Control Number: 2003107833

The Deutsche Bibliothek holds a record of this publication
in the Deutsche Nationalbibliographie; detailed bibliographical
data can be found under: http://dnb.dde.de

Prestel books are available worldwide. Please contact your nearest
bookseller or one of the above addresses for information concerning
your local distributor.

Editorial direction: Philippa Hurd
Proof-reading: Lisa Garland
Design and layout: Matthias Hauer
Typeface: ›TheSans‹ by Luc(as) de Groot
Origination: ReproLine, Munich
Printing: Sellier, Freising
Binding: Conzella, Pfarrkirchen

Printed in Germany on acid-free paper.

ISBN 3-7913-2984-7

CONTENTS

1 | Lascaux cave, detail.

Understanding Installation Art

We live in an era of contemporary art exhibitions consisting of galleries filled with objects and images spread on all surfaces. The denizen of this art world can go whole days without standing before a discrete painting or sculpture: he or she must slowly circumnavigate a space to experience the artwork that is found there. While these manifestations may appear chaotic if not an assault on the viewer's senses and expectations, in contemporary parlance we are in the presence of a broad-based phenomenon known as installation art.

Though seemingly shocking in its revolutionary appearance by comparison with painting and sculpture, installation has always been with us. For instance, when artists painted on the walls of the caves in Lascaux (fig. 1), they were creating a variation of what is known as site-specific installation: art that is made for a particular place, so much so that it cannot easily be moved because the work is not an object but is attached to the surroundings. Indeed, the Lascaux artists made canny use of the undulating wall surfaces to help render the features of the animals. When painting the Sistine Chapel, Michelangelo repeated the site-specific approach; similarly, when he created the Laurentian Library foyer, he, like an architect, determined every aspect of the physical experience to be had there.

Curiously, when an artist from the past harmonized an image with a site, that aim has not always been acknowledged. For example, if one peruses the dozens of slides at the Williams College slide library of Fra Angelico's paintings for the monks' cells at San Marco in Florence (fig. 2), one would not find a single one that shows an entire room holding a painting. Yet the physical character of each space was crucial to this artist's numerous aesthetic decisions about the narrative portrayal and the viewing experience in that small room. In other words, there is a tendency to overlook the actual and unchangeable context of some works of art, even though that aspect of its creation (the site) may have been central to an understanding of it. But many modern and contemporary artists have built their endeavors on this larger view of what constitutes a work of art.

2 | Fra Angelico, *Madonna and Child*, c. 1438–45.
Museo di San Marco, Florence.

In the contemporary period, the multivalent character of installation art has yet to be fully grasped. First and foremost, it must be understood and recognized as a medium, however elastic in its material definition, offering the broadest possibilities for investigation and expression. Second, having achieved worldwide reach, this practice may enable art to actually achieve an ambition for universality. Third, because there is no frame separating this art from its viewing context, the work and the space having melded together into an approximation of a life experience, the sphere of art has effectively been compromised, even democratized. Fourth, that late nineteenth-century German art shibboleth and chimera, the *Gesamtkunstwerk*, wherein the artist has total command of a space and might use any artistic means, including architecture, music, dance, and theater, along with the visual arts, to create a synesthetic environment, has become an everyday occurrence.[1]

Installation art threatens to become the predominant mode of expression for the modern world as we know it, with its global character, desire for sensory overload, and demand for non-elitist practices. The traditional hunger for art that possesses exaltant feeling and intellectual stimulation is in no way diminished by installation. Simply put, art has redirected and expanded its borders so as to comprise new areas of content and experience. With the medium of installation, art may be said to have reinvigorated itself.

The contemporary phenomenon of installation has often been marginalized: witness Rosalind Krauss writing of "Sculpture in the Expanded Field" to suggest that the discipline of sculpture has simply seized a larger area for itself.[2] However, her neat turn of phrase minimizes the revolutionary aspect of installation *vis-à-vis* sculpture. To begin with, a sculpture is simply one object whereas an installation consists of many or none. Hence, in contrast to Krauss's assertion, installation multiplies and magnifies the medium of sculpture. When found in a museum, a contemporary installation has a particularly transgressive thrust in relation to expectations about sculpture, and art in general, for the sanctity and sublime isolation of a sculpted art object, carefully if not extravagantly framed or literally on a pedestal, is absent. In this new kind of art, the integrity of and focus on an individual work are abandoned in favor of a multiplicity of objects, images, and experiences, which spew forth without regard for isolation. The exalted status of art is undercut by the quotidian-type experience—with its sights, smells, and generally ephemeral character—that is central to installation. If art is metaphorically the province of the church (as it once in fact served), artists are declaring war, saying let everyday life into the sacred precinct. In that regard, the implicit value of an individual work of art is diminished, as cheap trinkets often substitute for oil paint and bronze.

Because the sources, motivations, and types of this approach to art have been diverse and multi-dimensional in the last eighty years or so, a definition is perhaps best left to a physical description. Installation refers to a dedicated space in which one artistic vision or aura is at work, setting forth various kinds of phenomena. An installation may be defined as anything the artist wants to do when given a room in which to work, a definition that deliberately creates a broad swath of possibilities. In an installation there is unlikely to be a single object, but an assemblage, attached or not. Conversely, an installation may consist of no objects at all but a spatial experience, not unlike an architectural manifestation. Regardless, the viewer is usually in an enclosed space, swept up in a work of art much larger in expanse than an individual object can normally create.[3] As with the term composition in the traditionally understood context of art, the artist has created an arrangement that is an integrated, cohesive, carefully contrived whole.

As with any genre or art technique having a range of qualities, installation is a way of working, like painting or watercolor, chosen because of its inherent options and exploited for these effects. If installation is recognized as a long-standing technique, then it is unlikely to end soon, as if a mere moment in the passing stream of contemporary art, as one critic has implied.[4] But equally, the many aspects that compose the current ubiquity of installation make it particularly appropriate as a medium befitting contemporary society.

In what may come to be seen as the most apt and prophetic description of modern art ever uttered, Robert Rauschenberg once stated that he worked "in the gap between art and life."[5] Throughout the modern era, in ways too numerous and obvious to outline, artists have repeatedly evinced discomfort and outright dissatisfaction with the limits of art as given by historical precedents, limits which denied the material of life. Their responses have ranged from anti-art sentiments, via efforts by which the literal framing and segregating apparatus of art are removed, to the simple desire to create a more inclusive form of art, namely one that takes "life" into account. So ubiquitous is this sentiment that even abstract artists exhibit dissatisfaction with historical art's separation from reality. For modern artists, the old forms and concepts of art needed refurbishment, their premise being that the world is far more complex and rich than earlier practice had allowed. The aspiration of the modern installation artist became in large part how to reflect the experience of life—its complex issues, aspects, and appearances. The technique of installation has proved to be a useful tool by which to rhetorically speak about and investigate life. Thus, whereas Rauschenberg works in the "gap," the installation artist may attempt a rapprochement encompassing both art and life.

The lifelike qualities of installation art group themselves around two paramount matters: space and time. The viewer is asked to investigate the work of art much as he or she might explore some phenomenon in life, making one's way through actual space and time in order to gain knowledge. Just as life consists of one perception followed by another, each a fleeting, non-linear moment, an installation courts the same dense, ephemeral experience. Whereas painting and sculpture freeze time and perhaps suggest something eternal, installation abhors such an effect. The viewer is in the present, experiencing temporal flow and spatial awareness. The time and space of the viewer coincide with the art, with no separation or dichotomy between the perceiver and the object. In other words, life pervades this form of art.

With this unframed form of art sharing the space of the viewer and being as authentic as any other space in the viewer's experience, we have reached a pinnacle in art's evolution toward the accurate depiction of space, time, and the world. Cohabiting with the environment, installation thereby can *be* life in some great impersonation. Through this physical convergence and the use of commonplace materials, it can, also, potentially comment on the human condition in a way that is profoundly effective because it is replete with the substance of life. Moreover, by engaging the surrounding space in this intimate fashion, an installation can speak to and about that specific space, to ponder its physical and theoretical being—its identity.

In the last third of the twentieth century, we were presented with what Carl Andre called "sculpture as place,"[6] that is, a discrete three-dimensional work of art that establishes a sense of locale and, at the same time, promotes an interrelationship with the setting. Subsequently, as the work of art became increasingly entwined with its location in installation art, the context itself became triumphant in the field of art.[7] In fact, the context often became the subject matter and content of the installation work, so that if a museum or another purely art setting was the locale, then that place became the starting point for a discussion of the meaning of the work. And with the broad-based emergence of installation art, any number of new kinds of art locations came into use, from prisons to train stations to shop windows. With each of these, as with the art locale, there came another starting point for an investigation by the artist of some aspect of contemporary life. Hence, Robert Irwin said that "no thing [i.e. art] ever really transcends its immediate environment."[8] With the triumph of context, it might be added, comes the triumph of life, too, in the sphere of installation art.

While the diversity of installation art may appear bewildering, it is possible to propose a taxonomy, with four poles to the approach:

Enchantments   Impersonations

Interventions   Rapprochements

The top two belong to a larger genus called "filled-space installation" and the lower pair belong to a type called "site-specific installation." Filled spaces are fairly easily redone at other locations because there is coherence between the parts of each, one to the other, rather than the parts cohering with the whole space in a significant way. This type may even appear isolated from its site: to describe the composition of a filled-space installation is not likely to include the surroundings. By contrast, a site-specific installation is inextricably linked to the locale: the parts relate to one another but, more importantly, they relate to the larger space. Indeed, the site-specific artist will have spent considerable time exploring the location of the work, hence, an analysis of the composition of a site-specific installation must include its locale, because it derives its very form and perhaps physical substance, too, as well as its meaning, from the context. Moving it is impossible, since the work cannot be understood or seen except in relation to the place. The viewer witnesses a dialogue, as it were, between the artist and the space.

The filled space is usually more literary or psychologically inclined—concerned with artifice, private reality, enchantment, or idealization, even as it is experienced in real time. On the other hand, the site-specific work has a kind of hardheaded rootedness to the world, and is usually quite plastic and perceptual in character.

All this is not to say there are no crossovers between the four types, for often there are convergences. But by recognizing a taxonomy it is possible to talk literally and specifically about installation art, to chart the genealogy of a work, and to explore the meaningful implications of each type and genus. I will discuss primarily installations that have appeared in art contexts. Though that is limiting in certain ways, it allows us to see most clearly the innovative aspect of installation work to art history, and the part it plays in the changing character of museums today.

The prototypical example of an enchantment-type installation in the twentieth century is Kurt Schwitters's *Merzbau* (fig. 3). Between approximately 1919 and 1937, he built this environment within his home in Hanover, Germany. The title was based on the term he used for virtually his entire life's work—*Merz*—but it was applied here to a structure. The Dadaist Schwitters wanted to express a nuanced psychological dimension that individual works lacked, and with the installation technique he created a large-scale field of imaginary possibilities, epitomized by his subtitle, *Cathedral of Erotic Misery*. This walk-through environment comprised every surface, each of which was energized by rectilinear or biomorphic wood and plaster forms, discarded objects, and material donated by friends. Schwitters expressed his personal meaning through the iconographic use of the grottos and columnar forms that dominate the symbolic formal vocabulary. Mimicking the atmosphere of the film *The Cabinet of Dr. Caligari* in three dimensions, *Merzbau* enveloped the viewer.

In many ways partaking of the *Cathedral* connotation in the title, the architectural aspect of *Merzbau* illustrated an important aspect of installation as it would subsequently develop. Like a large cathedral, an installation can transport its viewer into a state of awe, providing also a sense of physical smallness *vis-à-vis* the all-consuming vision of the installation's artist. Some kind of transformation might even occur whereby the visitor is converted, as it were, to the vision of the creator. Schwitters wrote of a "contemplative immersion of the self in art", in which the individual would experience release from "life, from all things that disturb mankind."[9] A *Gesamtkunstwerk*, in that it synthesizes painting, sculpture, and architecture, this installation was obviously site-specific at first. In later years, however, it was reconstructed on a number of occasions, although because of its destruction in 1943 during World War II, only one of the five room installations was known in detail. That difficulty is endemic to the medium of installation, haunting its existence.

An overall environment with little or no escape route, the enchantment draws heavily on theatrical roots, the suspension of disbelief being chief among these. One witnesses an extreme vision of reality or may have the sense of being inside the artist's mind, indeed, a simulacrum of a consciousness is created. Familiar cultural referents, and literary and psychological possibilities proliferate. The installation is mentally absorbing

3 | Kurt Schwitters,
Merzbau, 1919–37 (detail).

4 | *Opening of First International Dada Fair, Berlin,* 1920.
Standing, from left to right: Raoul Hausmann, Otto
Burchard, Johannes Baader, Wieland and Margarete
Herzfelde, George Grosz, John Heartfield; seated:
Hanne Hoech, Otto Schmalhausen.

and a spectacle. Various kinds of tableaux lie in the background, too, along with a high degree of "falsity … artificiality … deceit,"[10] in the words of one of its chief practitioners, Ilya Kabakov. Beholding more than physically participating, the viewer's sense of his or her body is usually minimal, though physical circulation of the work may be involved.

Enchanted spaces, because they envelope the viewer so completely, rarely relate to the architectural settings in which they are installed, though some artists happily take advantage of unusual physical possibilities to enhance their visions. As Kabakov suggests, windows are an anathema, for they reveal the rejected world; if the ceiling or floor is emphasized, each will likely suggest the sky or the earth.[11] Even when dependent to some extent on the specific site, the artist who tends toward enchantment is often quite amenable to moving the installation or fitting it into another location if asked. Usually physically elaborate, these works may involve synesthetic and multimedia effects.

The 1920s were a particularly fertile time for installation work. There was a great deal of experimentation at the Bauhaus, among the Russian constructivists, and by the De Stijl group in Holland. Typically, their installations involved interchange and collaboration between practitioners of

5 | Marcel Duchamp, *1,200 Bags of Coal*, 1938.
Mixed media assemblage.
Installation: Charles Ratton Gallery, Paris, 1938.

various media. The First International Dada Fair in Berlin (fig. 4), 1920, consisted of a messy, floor-to-ceiling atmosphere of objects by a number of artists working in a collaborative fashion. Posters, photographs, sculptures, and paintings together replicated the effect of a collage, albeit in a three-dimensional environment. With layers and overlaps of images and meaning, the artists presented a model of the world, and how it might be dissected and understood. Typical of Berlin Dada, as opposed to Dada manifestations in other cities, this exhibition was intensely political in tone, with exhortations that were antagonistic toward the German government and that favored communism. The Dada Fair thus represented a politicized version of the Enchantment format. Although the works were arranged in accordance with the given gallery site, the concept could certainly have been applied to any variety of locations. Most important was that the installation was a violently anti-aesthetic statement, with individual works serving a larger purpose. The very sense of disorder and anarchy reiterated the expressive political message, and art assumed a new purpose.

As might be expected, Marcel Duchamp was a crucial figure for enchantments and other types of installation.[12] For the International Exposition of Surrealism, at the Galerie Charles Ratton in Paris in 1938, he made an installation that at once comprised all the paintings by other artists hung in the space, while embodying a work of art on its own. Duchamp hung twelve hundred sacks of coal from above, and placed leaves and a brazier on the ground (fig. 5). Though ceding the traditional art surface—the walls—he at once co-opted the other works within his own floor-to-ceiling grotto of transformation. His unaesthetic materials epitomize the metamorphosis inherent in an enchantment, with the quotidian world turned into art, and vice versa. There is even a deliberate confusion between the two contexts.

For this same exhibition, Salvador Dalí showed *Le Taxi Pluvieux* [*The Rainy Taxi*] (1938) which was a kind of miniature installation, just large enough for a single viewer to join the ghoulish occupants of the taxi-cab. The following year, Dalí created a full-scale, highly theatrical installation entitled *Dream of Venus* for the New York World's Fair. This phantasmagoria, along with *Merzbau*, set the stage for all subsequent enchantments, in that a surreal tinge with either bewitching, perplexing, or even frightening overtones might predominate.

Duchamp's interest in the installation approach culminated with the conception of his famed final work, *Etant donnés* (1946–66) (fig. 6). The viewer wanders into a darkened room not much larger than a broom closet where he or she is ambushed by the artist. Tempted to look through the

6 | Marcel Duchamp,
Etant donnés,
1946–66.
Mixed media
assemblage,
242.6 × 177.8 cm.
Installation:
Philadelphia
Museum of Art.

7 | *Main Street*, U.S.A.
DISNEYLAND® Park at the DISNEYLAND® Resort.

peephole of light, the viewer becomes a voyeur of a sexually provocative scene, quite unlike the many nudes to be found elsewhere in the museum setting. Here the onlooker "completes" the work of art in that classically Duchampian sense, for until the figure in the tableau is spied on, a "connection" between the work and the spectator is not completed. (Indeed, only when the viewer has stepped on a hidden switch beneath the carpet at the entry to the room is the electric light of the installation illuminated.) Though *Etant donnés* benefits especially from a museum location, both because of the subject and the expectations and attitude of a museum visitor, any museum setting would be equally productive.

Just after World War II, the next great example of an enchantment, though not found in an art context, could be said to be Disneyland, opened in Anaheim, California in 1955 (fig. 7). Perhaps it is shocking to think of Disneyland in the context of art, but within the narrower practice of installation, it offers an exceedingly apt comparison. There, the visitor is a participant in what Walt Disney, like Schwitters, described as a transforming experience: "Here you leave today and enter the world of yesterday, tomorrow and fantasy."[13] The themes found at Disneyland offered a new vision of familiar surroundings, while the perambulation of it promoted an interactive and spatial relationship. Disneyland, according to Jeffrey Saletnik, instituted environments that "work on the assumption that the participant brings with him the tools—his body and his senses —in which to experience the work on a phenomenological level. The participant need not be versed in the history of art to have a primary reaction to an installation work."[14]

Disneyland was perhaps the single most significant and influential force in shaping a large American public's expectations about similar experiences, suggesting that a total environment of sensory pleasures might be possible in a "leisure" situation.[15] In turn, one could ruminate on the extent to which this form of activity became the prototype for an expectation that art was potentially a "leisure entertainment," too, much as newspapers routinely lump the arts together in sections under this rubric. In other words, some portion of the art-going public came to expect and want to be catered to by cultural activities that offer a participatory component, and which installations are so thoroughly geared to provide. A full-body escape from reality, in which someone else's aura and world-view dominate the viewer's entire perceptual field, is the goal. This comparison shows that an apparently non-art phenomenon possesses characteristics associated with the artistic tendency of installation, and that both types of work require a very similar type of participation by the viewer.

Tableaux of all kinds have existed through many eras, indeed, the phenomenon of the period room, still found in many museums, is a variant on this. In each example a milieu is created that is observed and perhaps participated in; these are also highly movable affairs. Along with large-scale theatrical productions, such manifestations are part of the backdrop of enchantments, as is Disneyland. During the late 1950s and early 1960s, the tableau was the fundamental approach of artists such as George Segal and Edward Kienholz, and on a small scale, Joseph Cornell. All made intimate worlds that one observed in a kind of voyeuristic fashion, the viewer having the sense of being on the verge of trespassing on some private place. But in the late 1950s and early 1960s, artists began expanding on these examples, perhaps with Disneyland's all-encompassing model consciously or subconsciously in mind, to produce theatrical-cum-art events known as happenings. Pioneered by Alan Kaprow, happenings were theatrically oriented in the most fundamental sense, but offered the possibility for the viewer to walk through staging replete with sensory stimulation, unlike what occurred before the proscenium. The artificiality of the situation along with its insubstantial materials made for the perception that process and momentary experience were paramount. These were performances, so the creator's and viewer's time were the same.

The sense of a tableau is very much the situation in the installations of Joseph Beuys, Chris Burden, Robert Gober, Ann Hamilton, and Juan Muñoz among others. For instance, Beuys's *Plight* (1984) is a walk in environment, in which the felt-covered walls immediately create an other-worldly aura. The objects within, like a Symbolist dreamscape, suggest a sphere of portents. Muñoz's *Double Bind* (2001) (figs. 8a and 8b) at the Tate Gallery, London, is a highly dramatic work that tantalizes the viewer who must remain below its spaces. We spy on the activities occurring overhead, in a kind of Piranesian sphere made three-dimensional. The *Untitled* (fig. 9) installation for the Dia Art Center by Gober in 1992, is similarly surrealistic for its unexpected conjunctions, and not a little frightening in its claustrophobic setting. Though initially created specifically for their sites, each of these three works, with their hermetic and enclosed arrangements, can be retrofitted at other locations.

8a, 8b | Juan Muñoz, *Double Bind*, 2001.
Installation detail: Tate Modern, London.

9 | Robert Gober. Installation detail:
Dia Center for the Arts, New York, 1992.

Likewise, the many video installations that have populated the art world for thirty years follow the model of the Enchantment, with the viewer standing before a dream- or nightmare-like world, more often contemplating than participating. Bruce Nauman, Shirin Neshat, and Bill Viola make video installations that appear on at least two surfaces simultaneously, thereby surrounding the viewer. Though initially presented in one space, each work is easily moved to another.

Ilya Kabakov is perhaps best known for his installations of ersatz Russian tenements, in which is found an ambiguity between enchantment, re-creation, and impersonation (fig. 10). The Western viewer is immersed and engrossed in the post-World War II Soviet Union, with all its deprivations. Whereas flimsy objects may elsewhere suggest the detritus of a consumer society, similar material in a Kabakov installation has poetic implications. For him, forlorn objects help to create an atmosphere redolent of Soviet times,[16] as the aura of postwar Germany is suggested by the materials in Beuys's installations and vitrines. In keeping with the enchantment approach, Kabakov wants to create a separation, using walls and doorways, between his installation and the museum or gallery in which it is found, all the better to create for the spectator the sense of entering a world apart from the external world. Nonetheless, as with so many installation artists, placement in a museum is very desirable to Kabakov because, he says, the art context provides a "refuge."[17]

From the early 1970s through the late 1980s, Jonathan Borofsky has made a career of filling art spaces with his form of enchantment. Consisting

10 | Ilya Kabakov, *10 Characters: The Man who Flew into Space from His Apartment*, 1988. Installation detail: Ron Feldman Gallery, New York.

11 | Jonathan Borofsky. Installation detail: Paula Cooper Gallery, New York, 1980.

of paintings, sculptures, and wall drawings, as well as music on occasion, each installation is arrayed on every possible surface and space. Typically, Borofsky drew images that extended from one flat surface to another so as to reinforce the aura of an inner, free-associating landscape. Although site-specific, his wall drawings were really intended to erase any sense of the architecture at all. Closest to the ambience of cave painting, Borofsky's installations were walk-in dreams; in some cases, participation was encouraged, for example, by the presence of a ping-pong table (fig. 11).

The enchantment format is particularly the province of nomadic, global artists who enjoy international citizenship at massive biennale-type exhibitions. Their approach—reenacting or simulating a far-off locale—requires a movable endeavor, going along with the type of exhibitions in which these artists so often participate. *Explorer and Explorers Confronting the History of Exploration…! The Theater of the World* (2002) by Georges Adéagbo, a Benin artist, was created for the Documenta exhibition in Kassel, Germany. As with Borofsky, one feels as if one has entered the mind of the artist, in this case seeing the wildly diverse ideas and interests possessed by him. Indeed, it is a kind of global village of sources, from Joseph Beuys to Georges Rouault to Egypt to South America. For that same exhibition, Pascal Marthine Tayou simulated a Cameroon village with *Game Station*, and Tania Bruguera approximated a Cuban jail. All of these works demonstrate the convergence of the enchantment with the impersonation.

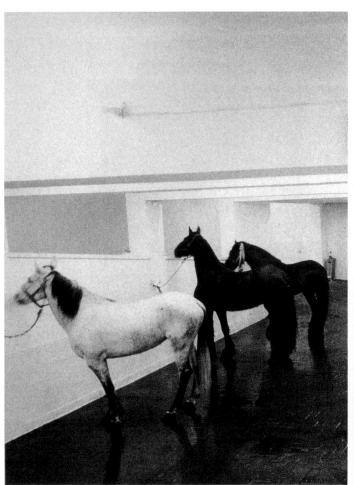

12 | Jannis Kounellis, Installation:
Galleria l'Atticco, Rome, 1969.

Instead of creating an imaginary place that is dreamlike—enchanted, or nightmarish—some artists present either an impersonation of a life situation or one that subtly elaborates upon that condition. When Jannis Kounellis filled Galleria l'Attico in Rome with twelve horses in 1969, he duplicated a situation from life in the context of art (fig. 12). Is this an impersonation of a stable, or a parody of the traditional verities of art, with that discipline corrected as it were? Of course, there are innumerable examples of artists who approximate the appearances of life in art, but with the impersonation type of installation artists may have reached a penultimate stage, actually cohabiting with life in the most fundamental way.

Depending on the location, an impersonation may or may not be site-specific. If the installation literally replaces a normally functioning space in the world beyond art, the artwork is certainly site-specific. Residing in an art context, on the other hand, these works are more easily movable. The capitalistic consumer society, replete with throwaway objects and commonplace media techniques, usually informs the impersonation, adding to its verity and establishing the primary context by which to interpret it. The concept of art as something exalted is thereby questioned or diminished, because the visitor may use the space very much as if it is a life situation. As with Disneyland, no art background is needed to recognize and take part in these simulations, hence the artist attains a wide audience even as he or she still holds onto avant-garde status. This installation artist has the best of two worlds, being potentially a social engineer with esteemed motives while retaining a bit of bohemian status.[18]

With enchantments, the boundary between art and the quotidian world is guarded and maintained, as is the viewer's sense of being before art. By contrast, impersonations often cross that divide, so that the viewer may not even recognize the presence of a work of art. Also, an enchantment projects the aura of the artist/auteur, who imbues the atmosphere with an individual imagination; by contrast, an impersonation renders the artist a rather self-effacing, even anti-elitist being. All that said, impersonations are finally tableaux, too, and may have a dreamy aspect to the extent that they are removed from the real world. Nevertheless, by their impersonating pose, these suggest that the artists want their dreams to be rooted in a sense of the everyday.

Another way to understand an impersonation is against the backdrop of tribal practices wherein art as we know it does not exist. Rather, tribal objects—now so revered in art museums—were practically and ritualistically used, and were totally integrated with their societies in ways that our works of art are usually denied. By simulating life situations, impersonations approach this model, and reinforce an intention on the part of these artists *vis-à-vis* life.

By way of introducing the variety and possibilities of the impersonation, it is useful to quote Jean Baudrillard on the topic of the image, for in each example of this type of installation an image is projected:

> Such would be the successive phases of the image:
>> it is the reflection of a profound reality;
>> it masks and denatures a profound reality;
>> it masks the *absence* of a profound reality;
>> it has no relation to reality whatsoever:
>> it is its own pure simulacrum.
>
> In the first case, the image is a *good* appearance—representation is of the sacramental order. In the second, it is an evil appearance—it is of the order of maleficence. In the third, it plays at being an appearance—it is of the order of sorcery. In the fourth, it is no longer of the order of appearances, but of simulation.[19]

An impersonation crisscrosses these definitions, always questioning whether a profound reality exists, and offering meta-realities as substitutes for contemplation.

Marcel Duchamp's *Fountain* (1917) (fig. 13), though not an installation, could be seen as the starting point for the impersonation-type work, representing an example of art that maliciously mimics life or offers up life as art. With both Duchamp and later, Kounellis, the viewer may be confused about the nature of art, and its separation or convergence with life experience. Similarly, how does one distinguish between the sensual experience of looking at art and at commercial goods, or at a stable? Baudrillard's distinctions offer a worthy starting point.

As the aforementioned artistic collaborations in Russia, Germany, and Holland gathered steam, artists attempted to put their talents in the service of larger societal goals, making everyday objects. Though doomed to disappointment and disparagement, these artists' goal

13 | Marcel Duchamp, *Fountain* (second version), 1950.
Readymade: glazed sanitary china with black paint,
30.5 × 38.1 × 45.7 cm.

14 | Street Scene
Colonial Williamsburg Foundation.

effectively reduced the exalted status of art. In the case of the De Stijl group, the artists Theo van Doesburg, Sophie Taeuber-Arp, and Hans Arp were commissioned to redesign the interior of a Strasbourg restaurant called the *Café Aubette*. Between 1926 and 1928, the trio designed every aspect of the three-story building; what ensued was a public space that benefited from the artistic skills of its creators. Unlike Duchamp's ironical gesture, this endeavor was an ardent attempt to improve the everyday world. It also introduced the idea of art (an art installation) that effectively functioned in the world, an art that lived in the time of the everyday, too, (this as opposed to the way art normally acts and where it typically lives).

Another type of impersonation can be seen at Colonial Williamsburg, Virginia, opened in 1927–28 (fig. 14). Whereas Disneyland presents itself only as a fantasy, Williamsburg, though also an imaginary invention, pretends to be an architectural preservation project. Notwithstanding that its pretensions to correct restoration have been skewered by architectural historians, Williamsburg impersonates an historic locale. It is simply a hoax, made more believable by the apparatus of museum-education methods.

When, in his 1961 book *Silence*, John Cage recommended: "We must bring about a music which is like furniture,"[20] he set the stage for the impersonation of life by an installation in the post-World War II period, and the desire of the artist to instill prosaic experience into aesthetic form. In this regard, one recalls a famous story told by the sculptor Tony Smith, of the night in the early 1950s when he drove on the unfinished New Jersey Turnpike. The experience was profound for him:

> I thought to myself … that's the end of art. Most painting
> looks pretty pictorial after that. There is no way you can
> frame it [the road], you just have to experience it.[21]

In other words, for Smith as well as for Cage, art could not compete with a lived experience. It is a short jump to Claes Oldenburg's famed *The Store* (1961) (fig. 15),[22] in which the artist rented a storefront on the lower East Side of New York City, and installed papier-mâché simulations of various objects that might be found in a commercial establishment. These objects would hardly be construed as real but, rather, as freehand renderings of how life might look if an artist got hold of it. Following the example of Oldenburg, Martin Kippenberger impersonated and parodied an office setting in *The Happy End of Kafka's "Amerika,"* 1994. Similarly Andrea Zittel makes camper vans which, though one can climb in, are

15 | Claes Oldenburg
The Store, 1961.
Installation detail:
New York.

16 | Sam Taylor-Wood, *Third Party*, 1999.
Seven 16-mm film projections with sound,
transferred to DVD.
Installation detail: Mathew Marks Gallery,
New York, 2000.

small, movable installations that suggest how life might be lived if an artist were to elaborate on its appurtenances. More straightforward is Sam Taylor-Wood's video installation of a cocktail party, *Third Party* (fig. 16), shown at the Matthew Marks Gallery in New York, in 2000. Among eight video projection screens, the visitor is given the sense of being present at a certain soirée, albeit as a fly-on-the-wall. With sights as well as sounds, it was an all-over, surround-sound experience, effectively a simulation.

When asked to create a work for the 1997 Documenta exhibition, Christine Hill took over a storefront in a pedestrian arcade, some distance from the exhibition halls, and opened a working thrift store, *Volksboutique* (fig. 17). While recollecting Oldenburg, this installation carried the idea of an impersonation to its utmost conclusion. So, too, Rirkrit Tiravanija , who created an Indian restaurant within the Carnegie International Exhibition in Pittsburgh in 1995 (fig. 18). Both of these installations are a functioning space, thus completely dissolving the usual boundary between art and life. One might even question whether impersonation is an issue here or whether the artists simply want to abandon art in favor of commerce. If the answer is positive, Hill and Tiravanija could be described, following Baudrillard's model, as masking "the absence of a profound reality," the latter defined as the normally seen contents of an art museum if not the museum itself.

Though the installations by Kounellis, Hill, and Tiravanija could easily be recreated, the one essential constant is an art context, by which the artist contrasts conventional expectations with the newly found possibilities presented with installation. In a remarkable, though hardly surprising reversal, the designers of the Comme des Garçons clothing store in the gallery-filled district of Chelsea, in New York City, built an environment in 1999 that seems quite intentionally to approximate the sensory experience of being within a *Torqued Ellipse* sculpture by Richard Serra. The store, in Chelsea no less, makes life (that is, commerce) into art; perhaps the intention reflects the merchant's supposition that the store "is the reflection of a profound reality" (Baudrillard). Though Serra would complain, the Comme des Garçons architecture should hardly be surprising in an era in which installation art seems ubiquitous even beyond art spaces.

One type of recent impersonation is particularly involved with the idealistic notions of the 1920s' Europeans. Scott Burton was often commissioned to make furniture for public spaces, as at the Equitable Center, New York City in 1986 (fig. 19). By producing variations on well-known designs, often in different materials, he enhanced life a bit more than if a

17 | Christine Hill, *Volksboutique*, 1997.
Installation:, Documenta, Kassel.

18 | Rirkrit Tiravanija, *Untitled (Still),* 1995.
Installation detail: Carnegie Museum, Pittsburgh.

19 | Scott Burton. Installation detail: Equitable Center,
South Plaza, New York, 1986.

20 | Siah Armajani, Hirshhorn Museum Employees
Lounge, 1982. Installation detail: Washington D.C.

21 | Jorge Pardo, in collaboration with The Fabric
Workshop and Museum, *Untitled*, 1999.
Installation detail: Fabric Workshop and Museum,
Philadelphia.

department store had been asked to do the furnishings. Commenting on his type of work, Burton said:

> I want to get some social meaning back into art. And I'd like to help change art into some kind of design. I think that the moral, the ethical dimension of art is mostly gone, and only in a newly significant relationship with a nonart audience can any ethical dimension come back to art…. I feel that the autonomy of the studio artist is a trivial thing by now in our society. Who cares if you paint it blue instead of red?[23]

While Burton's furniture-cum-art is quite camouflaged, Siah Armajani's work usually announces itself. Armajani has built a career of making bridges, reading rooms, and other more-or-less functioning architectural situations; his commissions have even included an employees lounge for the Hirshhorn Museum and Sculpture Garden in Washington, D.C. (fig. 20). Upon coming upon one of Armajani's works, the viewer knows life has been significantly changed and, depending on the perspective of the beholder, possibly improved and made more vital. We are presented with a meta-reality wherein we know a commonplace function is still present, but its appearance has been transformed. The Fabric Workshop and Museum in Philadelphia has been devoted to such an outlook for twenty-five years, so that its intent was clear when it commissioned Jorge Pardo to reinvent its lobby and video-viewing room in 1999 (fig. 21). But like an ironist, Pardo does not always allow the parts to function as life demands, witness a glass bathroom door that is only partially sandblasted. With Burton, Armajani, and Pardo, art improved, indeed, made wondrous fairly conventional situations.

All of these installations are site-specific, with each intended to fit its location like a glove, forming a rapprochement between art and life, and disguising the former in order to perform the functions of the latter. Oddly, there is a reversal in these examples between traditional notions of art versus design: whereas in the past designers might have wanted to be called artists, here artists are happily embracing the identity of designer/architects, much as was the case in Europe in the 1920s. As Baudrillard said about images, installations that function as impersonations raise questions about the everyday world, about art, and about the presence or absence of a "profound reality."

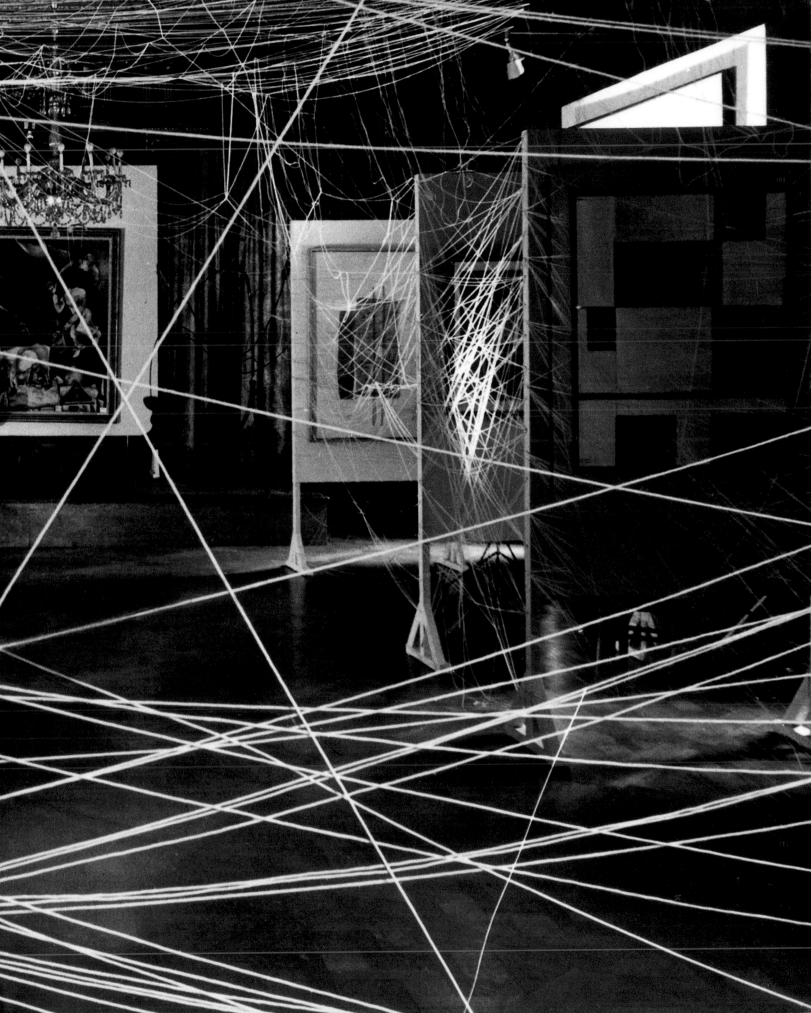

22a, 22b | Daniel Buren
Within and Beyond the Frame,
work in situ, October 1973.
Installation detail:
John Weber Gallery, New York.

Some artists have made a practice of employing the medium of installation to investigate the physical, functional, intellectual, cultural, or institutional character of the locales at which they are asked to produce works. For these artists the site of the work of art is neither neutral nor without inflection, and installation's role becomes a critique and perhaps even transgression on the site. (Certainly Pardo's work at the Fabric Workshop is a crossover between an impersonation and an intervention.) With this approach, installation moves away from the conventional themes of art and addresses its literal surrounding spaces. Daniel Buren, a pioneer in this mode, rhetorically pleads: "Can art get down from its pedestal and rise to street level?"[24] Hence, in a work for the John Weber Gallery in New York, *Within and Beyond the Frame* (1973) (figs. 22a and 22b) Buren successfully invited the street into the gallery by extending his signature, striped sheets through the open window onto West Broadway. In so doing, Buren intended to undo the idea that art-viewing was a quasi-spiritual activity which occurred in a space isolated from life. Buren wanted to compromise the identity of the art space by having street life intrude into it.

Museums, in particular,—and not just art museums—offer fertile territory because historical tradition makes a good foil for the inquiring, even liberating power of the intervention. According to Buren: "The questioning work has an obligation … to reveal the false discretion of these depersonalized architectures and to make them emerge from their false neutrality."[25] The museum and art become empty ideals in need of renovation if not outright destruction, as it were; but at the same time the opponent is the larger framework of society in which the museum and art are simply two of its respected totems. This type of installation is thus a tool of inquiry and even attack.

Interventions are an outgrowth of art that refuses to abide by conventional practices, art that makes for an unwelcome houseguest, as it were. They recall the aforementioned works by Duchamp: not only did he create confusion about the nature of a space, he played a behavioral game with the viewer's physical movements. Duchamp created a similar problem in his *Mile of String* (1942) (fig. 23) installation, for it would have been quite difficult for a viewer to maneuver around and through the string to see the more conventional works of art on the walls.

23 | Marcel Duchamp, *Mile of String*, 1942.
Gelatin silver print, 19.4 × 25.4 cm.
Installation: First Papers of Surrealism
exhibition, New York.

Starting in the early 1960s, there were many assaults on conventional thinking about the previously decorous nature of a work of art. Frank Stella's shaped canvases suggested extension beyond the painting (forget a frame, for there was none) to the wall itself and the room. This strategy was quickly picked up by the many strands of sculpture that are loosely known as minimalist, post-minimalist, earth, and conceptual art, in all of which the sculptural objects spread out aggressively into the spaces of exhibition. Rather than existing as self-contained structures in which the only spatial concerns were illusory or internal, these works engaged with real places, at times intervening in the physical space.[26] The viewer co-habits with these works of art and the spaces holding them.

24 | Carl Andre
Foreground: *100 Pieces of Copper*, 1968.
Background: *100 Lead Square*, 1968.
Installation: Wide White Space Gallery,
Antwerp, 1968.
© Carl Andre / Licensed by VAGA,
New York, NY

A floor-bound work by Carl Andre creates a complex situation for the viewer, especially those who saw these sculptures for the first time alone in a gallery. Initially the work seems virtually unnoticeable in a space, so that the room itself assumes great prominence and fills the vision of the viewer (fig. 24). Banal in character, the machine-made, modular components seem to possess scant aesthetic interest, their very anonymity speaking to the apparent objectivity of the dialogue with space. Robert Morris described the onlooker of Andre's sculpture observing "two domains simultaneously: that of the work's shallow blanket of space, and those upper regions free of art from which he commands a viewpoint outside the work."[27] The beholder even engaged Andre's work physically —by walking on it—an unimaginable transgression in the history of sculpture, a transgression with many implications to do with the viewer's role and the artist's own conception of himself *vis-à-vis* the beholder. The viewer experiences or consumes the art with his or her feet.

In Andre's extended lines on the floor, he led the viewer through the gallery, meanwhile calling attention to various prosaic aspects of the room-as-undistinguished-room, rather than as art gallery.[28] In effect, the work of art frames the space,[29] a fascinating reversal of fortunes, and emphasizes its physical dimension instead of its aesthetic function. Numerous writers have noted the theatrical aspect of such encounters, in which one becomes aware of one's own experience of such objects.[30] That quality of beholding oneself beholding is often a crucial behavior associated with much installation art, especially of the site-specific variety.

Though minimal art was rarely site-specific in the sense discussed here, these sculptures work in tandem with and even embrace literal space, if only in a generic sense—wall, floor, ceiling, corner. On reflection, one often thinks of these works in relation to their surroundings, the sculptures depending on the environment and being so much about space. But most minimal works are in fact quite movable, with each simply forming a new, still pointed, relationship with the next set of surroundings.

Just after the first burst of minimalism, a number of artists rebelled against the predictable regularity of its structures and grids, though they were strongly influenced by the spatial explorations of this breakthrough movement. With wall drawings, which came early in his career, Richard Serra expressed the wish to displace architecture,[31] an aspiration much in keeping with the spirit of intervention. He wanted to "establish and structure disjunctive, contradictory spaces," and to "engage … attack and restructure" a given space,[32] this an implicit goal of much minimalist sculpture. In effect, the medium of installation is an ideal technique for this type of investigation because it can go outside itself literally and figuratively, and can, in effect, be anything. In his sculpture Serra tended to create an internal, hermetic composition of parts, which must be circumnavigated to be appreciated. But with *Delineator* (1974–75) (fig. 25), the spectator is surrounded in a highly threatening manner, an experience that is rarely found in the art context.

Serra's *Delineator* as well as Bruce Nauman's *Double Steel Cage* (1974), and *Clown Torture* (1987) (fig. 26), indicate the confluence of a filled-space-type installation (one that could fairly easily be moved) with a site-specific intervention. These are deliberately aggressive toward the viewer, insisting on an uncomfortable and unwanted participation, and are transgressive with regard to the particular art sites at which each is installed at any one time. Whereas with Andre, the viewer might have a kind of walk in the park (or a museum), with Nauman and Serra there could be an assault. Movable in the same way that minimalist works were, these

25 | Richard Serra, *Delineator*, 1974–75.
Steel, two plates, each 2.5 × 30.5 × 66 cm.
Installation: Ace Gallery, Los Angeles.

26 | Bruce Nauman, *Clown Torture*, 1987.
Four color video monitors, four speakers,
four laserdisc players, two video projectors,
four laser discs (color, sound).
Installation: Lannan Foundation, Los Angeles.

sculptures are composed of a freestanding arrangement of parts that form an enclosure. Though seen within a larger space, each has its own internal logic and formal integrity. Again, the viewer has a real time and space experience of that location in particular.

Beside the physical aspects of a museum building, its sociological character offers a highly fertile area of exploration. Within the field known as conceptualism, beginning in the mid 1960s, numerous individuals questioned the exalted contexts of art, and in their questioning, the art object itself became incidental to the larger field of interest. In effect, the context had supplanted the primacy of the art object. Whereas for many earlier artists, the museum had been a grand goal ("the museum as muse," as a recent exhibition proclaimed), now it became the object of criticism and even anger. Artists felt their art institutions had stood too far apart from issues present in daily life. To redress what was at times seen as "wrong," certain installation artists sought to intervene in the sacred precinct of the art space. Their works were absolutely site specific; indeed, the site was more than an accomplice to the work, it was the subject itself.

Buren was among the first artists to examine this content in Europe: "The questioning work has an obligation ... to reveal the false discretion of these depersonalized architectures and to make them emerge from their false neutrality."[33] In the United States, Michael Asher shared this subversive ambition; in fact, he was even more diabolical about the art scene and desirous of undercutting its pretensions. Asked to participate in a 1977 exhibition of large-scale sculpture in Münster, Germany, Asher hired a camper van and relocated it on a weekly basis, nineteen times in all, on the perimeter of the city. Here was literally the largest sculpture one might imagine, making scale and interest in it a kind of perverse preoccupation of the organizing curator and the art audience. For an exhibition in Los Angeles at the Claire Copley Gallery in 1974, Asher emptied the gallery of all internal walls separating the front viewing area from the rear offices for gallery business (fig. 27). Upon entering, the unsuspecting visitor simply found a group of people engaged in conversation and coffee drinking. Asher's installation brilliantly critiqued both functions that occurred in the gallery: the clandestine activity in back was brought forward for exposure, and the usual public activity was circumvented. Instead of beholding a transcendent object, the viewer beheld merchandizing practice in an empty storefront. Rather than an enchantment, we have the actual space, warts and all.[34]

Other manifestations of this kind of approach occurred throughout the 1970s. For instance, at an exhibition at the Sonnabend Gallery, New

27 | Michael Asher
Installation detail: Claire Copley Gallery, Los Angeles, 1974.

28 a, 28 b | Vito Acconci, *Seedbed*, January 1972.
Wooden ramp: 76.2 × 670.56 × 914.4 cm.
Installation detail: Sonnabend Gallery, New York.
Performance / Installation 9 days, 8 hours a day
during a 3-week exhibition.

York, in 1972, Vito Acconci hid beneath the floorboards of a ramp that visitors crossed (figs. 28a and 28b). Otherwise empty, the gallery was enlivened by Acconci's groans as he masturbated. Called *Seedbed*, this installation included the sphere of performance art,[35] all for the purpose of subverting "the 'innocence' of space."[36] Hans Haacke has often investigated what lay behind the impassive face of the museum institution. In 1971, he created an uproar at the Guggenheim Museum with his proposal to show photographs of the slum dwellings owned by a member of the Board of Trustees of that institution in order to air the dirty laundry of the Museum and its financing. Not surprisingly, this impolite work was rejected by the Museum staff.

The impetus toward intervention has continued with enthusiasm in recent years. For instance, Vanessa Beecroft made the infamous "male gaze"—the viewer examining the female body—the subject at a variety of art venues. At the Guggenheim Museum, 1998, women in Gucci bikinis and panty hose paraded before an audience made to feel voyeuristic rather than aesthetically minded, all this on Fifth Avenue no less (fig. 29). Here the nude in Duchamp's *Etant Donnés* has stepped out into the viewer's space.

There are also freestanding, albeit interventionist installations. For example Alfredo Jaar juxtaposed photographs of Brazilian mine workers and nineteenth-century paintings of Indians in landscapes in a work entitled *Spheres of Influence* (fig. 30), made in 1989 for the 1990 Sydney Biennale. Martha Rosler unexpectedly brought images of homeless people into the hallowed halls of an art space, with *Home Front*, at the Dia Center

29 | Vanessa Beecroft. Installation detail: The Solomon R. Guggenheim Museum, New York, 1998.

30 | Alfredo Jaar, *Spheres of Influence*, 1989.
Set of six lightboxes with color transparencies,
each 30.5 × 182.9 × 17.8 cm.
Installation: Sydney Biennale, 1990.

in 1989. Similar to the effect Minimalist sculptures have on their environs, these works engage each art context, and, likewise, any space will do for these movable installations. Most important is that installation serves a fascinating and far-reaching purpose: to provide a "lingua franca" of the nomadic art scene, whereby itinerant artists, many from non-Western cultures, participate on world stages and effectively "communicate interculturally."[37] Thomas McEvilley has noted that installation is ideally suited to this role "because it does not unambiguously proclaim any particular cultural hegemony." "Much of it is rooted in the ritualistic environments of cultures outside the industrialized West."[38] Given the increasing occurrence of transcultural experiences, the art technique of installation can effectively investigate the multiple realities and points of view common to one's experiences of life.

When Rebecca Horn was asked to participate in the sculpture exhibition for Münster in 1987, she made *Concert in Reverse* (figs. 31a, b, c) for an

31a, 31b, 31c | Rebecca Horn, *Concert in Reverse*, 1987.
Installation detail: Münster.

32 | Fred Wilson, *Mining the Museum-Metal Works*, 1992.
Installation detail, showing slave shackles with nine-
teenth-century American silver objects: Maryland
Historical Society, Baltimore.

METALWORK
1793-1880

old prison that had been reused in the Nazi years. Her installation consisted of improbable objects and somber lighting to bring the macabre site back to the present for viewers. Similarly sociological in ambition, Fred Wilson organized a landmark, site-specific exhibition called *Mining the Museum* (fig. 32). Asked to create an installation for the Maryland Historical Society in 1992, he, like an archaeologist of mores, found in the storerooms of this institution a wealth of material showing the lives of African Americans in United States history. These works were introduced into the usual displays of the Baltimore Historical Society to riveting effect; it was as if the other side of the coin had been revealed for the first time in that museum's history.[39]

There is a quasi-analytical, cultural, and impersonal character to many interventions. Such works seem to possess a moral integrity, too, that is reinforced by the fact that often they cannot be bought or sold, if only because each is utterly rooted to one place. Compared to the commodity status of so many other objects within a museum (and in life), this type of installation is an obdurate entity, with elusive physical borders, that is unlikely to be co-opted by the marketplace.

Deeply subversive, the intervention often upsets the bourgeois expectations of the audience, who might seek solace in art-viewing spaces and in the potential for works of art to offer escape. These artists do not want to cooperate in satisfying such expectations, and are anti-elitist in the extreme, both about art and the audience for it. All connotations toward timelessness and privilege—for art and its history, for the sites of art, and for its audience—are under attack, as the social spheres of life are introduced into these areas by the technique of installation.

33 | Robert Irwin, *Scrim Veil-Black Rectangle-Natural Light*, 1977. Cloth, metal, wood, 365 × 3.5 × 124 cm. Installation detail: The Whitney Museum of American Art, New York.

The other side of the coin within the area of site-specific installation is the Rapprochement wherein the artist sees the site as an accomplice, not an enemy of the work of art. Walking off the elevator onto the fourth floor of the Whitney Museum in 1977, the viewer was at first disoriented and then enveloped by the space created by Robert Irwin (fig. 33). He had simply hung a single sheet of scrim across the room, dividing the entire space, and turned off the lights, (the "Cyclops" window provided the only illumination in the gallery). At once reticent, this work of art, nonetheless, turned the space into an otherworldly environment.

The context of this type of installation is the subject, content, and shaping influence of the work of art, as it had been with the intervention, but it is the physical context that is preeminent. With a rapprochement, the work of art often has a more formal than cultural character. So site specific is this installation, and so at one with its locale, that this kind of work may on occasion appear invisible. Such a work is simply there and present, seemingly made anonymously and without the sign of an artist's hand. If objects, *per se*, play a role, it is a minor and fully integrated part, or the objects may seem to dissolve in the space, for the art manifestation is space itself. This is the un/non-work of art: unpretentious, unobtrusive, unframed/non-iconic, non-narrative, non-allusive, non-didactic, non-objective.

There is a kind of natural quality about the viewer's experience of the rapprochement, for he or she physically cohabits with the art, living in the present and a real time and place, not in an historical, analytical, or imaginative realm. The perceptual perambulation is paramount. Along with the eye, the body is involved; physical and sensory recognitions add to our understanding of the space. One's experience of the place is joined with the aforementioned sense of oneself: Goldberg says the viewer "experiences experience,"[40] and O'Doherty describes "looking at ourselves looking."[41] Because this art is so interactive, Roald Nasgaard could claim it as part of the humanist tradition: "It places man at the very center of itself."[42] It is the ultimate in figurative art, with the human being present not by depiction or implication but by actual presence, and necessary for the completion of the work.

If enchantments are best compared to theater, rapprochements should be related to architecture. In the former, a suspension of disbelief is necessary, whereas in the latter, there is an everyday quality about the sensation.

Both architecture and site-specific installation require an unequivocally physical and perceptual engagement to achieve some degree of knowledge about the surroundings. By contrast, in theater there is a boundary separating the viewer and the art, inducing a comparatively passive response. Architecture and the site-specific installation establish a powerful sense of place—place that is large and complicated. In both, the creators formulate spatial composition by the placement of walls, doors, ceilings, and other elements. Rather than a room full of things, the room, or a larger spatial complex, is the *sine qua non* of the work. Coincidentally, throughout the history of art, artists have attempted to depict space in pictorial works, but with site-specific installation and architecture, space that is real and encompassing is the departure point.

Great architectural environments, replete with perambulatory possibilities, come to mind as the first important exemplars of the rapprochement installation. In the Temple Precinct of Queen Hatshepsut in Egypt, the visitor moved from one extraordinary situation to the next, along a ramp, through large courtyards, past vistas, and stopping places, finally concluding the journey in a small chamber in the hillside. All movement is determined by the architect, whose genius is demonstrated by the formation and manipulation of space. The viewer is the center of the creator's interest, his or her perceptual journey through space the focus of all artistic decisions. In effect, the viewer's passage is an interactive experience. That it was a sculptor/painter, Michelangelo, who created the Laurentian Library and Capitoline Hill, only reinforces the idea of a unifying vision necessary to make space a living organism for artistic exploration. Robert Morris aptly celebrated Bernini's achievement in the Piazza of Saint Peter's in Rome, saying he had turned "architecture into sculpture."[43] One might well add the corollary to this statement, that Bernini had turned sculpture into architecture, thus making an installation.

In Art Nouveau architecture, the effect of a rapprochement between all the arts in one seamless ensemble was extravagantly explored. A veritable *Gesamtkunstwerk*, the radiant Villa Solvay (1893) by Victor Horta, evinces an indoor–outdoor synthesis. This effect is reinforced by the fact that the walls are often broken and corners eliminated, making the interior spaces merge as well. Paintings and sculptures complete this remarkably theatrical ensemble that verges on sensory overload. It is an example of a rapprochement that is an enchanted space, too.[44]

A more modernist rapprochement in architecture is Mies van der Rohe's *Barcelona Pavilion*, 1929, about which Philip Johnson said it is a place where "space is channeled rather than confined—it is never stopped but is allowed to flow constantly."[45] That channeling, as in Hatshepsut, makes the experience of it extraordinary; it is a space in which the viewer has the self-conscious sense of him or herself experiencing the creative aura made by van der Rohe.

El Lissitzky's *Proun Room* (1923), is an interesting cross between an enchantment and rapprochement. This was an attempt to create a united environment in which the wall paintings carried the eye around the space as if no architectural elements were present at all. [46] The viewer could easily become disoriented and engulfed by the abstract forms.[47] In this and other examples, the works of art are subservient to larger concerns regarding space, with a new kind of decorative impulse ascendant. Indeed, at this time, décor was not a pejorative idea; rather, the overall *Gesamtkunstwerk* was the ambition.

In 1958 Yves Klein entitled his exhibition—an empty room at the Gallery Clert—*Le Vide* (*The Void*) (fig. 34 a, b, c, d) (unlike Michael Asher's empty room, Klein did mask the backroom). Here was not only a synthesis of space and object, of which there was none, but a declaration of content, Klein proposing that the *Void* could be experienced in a prosaic empty room. Two years later, the artist Arman cunningly filled the same space to overflowing, and called the exhibition *Le Plein*—that is, the plenitude of life. For our purposes, he, too, had made a rapprochement, taking full account of the space's physical dimensions along with its recent history. (It is interesting, too, to see two very different responses to the same space.[48]) Some years later, Mark Rothko made paintings to fill a chapel designed by Philip Johnson in Houston, Texas, which opened in 1971. This assemblage of canvases might be said to have an effect similar to Klein's, namely to evoke the void, and likewise, each artist was responsible for creating an aura that totally unites all within. Yet another, more literal, void was also created in Houston, by James Turrell. His *Sky Piece* (2000) (fig. 35) at the Live Oak Friends Meeting House, is a simple rectangular opening in the curved ceiling, which introduces all that is above into the space of worship. This remarkable example of a rapprochement at once replaces the ceiling paintings of the past with a very literal, yet equally spiritual rendering.

The desire for an elevated state, which is the provenance of many abstract artists of the twentieth century, echoes in the work of certain installation artists who create a rapprochement with their surroundings. Emanations of light and presentiments of a void are the chief experiences of their purified spaces. Nevertheless, since the viewer simply experiences all this in a physically real space, much as one lives in a nonlinear fashion

34a, 34b, 34c, 34d | Yves Klein, *The Void*, 1958.
Installation detail: Iris Clert Gallery, Paris.

35 | James Turrell, *Sky Piece*, 2000.
Installation: Live Oak Friends Meeting House, Houston.

36 | Dan Graham, *Two Way Mirror Cylinder Inside Cube
and a Video Salon* or *Rooftop Urban Park Project*, 1981–91.
Two-way mirror, glass, steel, wood, rubber,
274.3 × 1097.3 × 1097.3 cm.
Installation: Dia Art Center, New York.

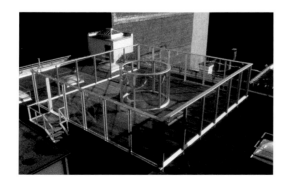

in life, with the senses piqued in all kinds of ways, there is a parallel with other life phenomena. That is, the artists do not at all seek to carry the viewer elsewhere, but to suggest that the ineffable exists in the present and the prosaic.

Along with its role in relation to the intervention, minimal art and its immediate successors should be seen in the context of the rapprochement. For example, each of Robert Smithson's portable *Corner Piece* (fig. 37) series (1968) at once takes into account the surrounding. Like Duchamp's *Large Glass* (1915–23), a photograph of one of these works will literally include a room, hence a *Corner Piece* effectively merges with its environment. Similarly, Dan Graham's enclosure on the roof of the Dia Foundation, New York, entitled *Rooftop Urban Park Project* (1991) (fig. 36), speaks directly to the surrounding space, though it, too, could be moved to a new locale.[49]

In Smithson's earth works, particularly the famed *Spiral Jetty* (1970) (fig. 38), he combined interventionist and rapprochement attitudes. On the one hand, he marked the space of the lake in a dramatic, even transgressive way. On the other hand, the work is certainly integrated there, indeed, could hardly be seen or imagined anywhere else. In the second generation of earth artists, Alan Sonfist produced an installation entitled *Time Landscape* (1965) (fig. 39). Given a busy corner of Manhattan at which to make a work of art, Sonfist simply returned the northeast corner of the intersection of Houston and West Broadway to the vegetal state that had existed there thousands of years ago. The seamless aspect of this rapprochement is so perfect that few who pass realize a work of art is there, let alone grasp its ingenious and unpretentious premise.

37 | Robert Smithson, *Red Sandstone and Corner Piece*,
1968. Sandstone from Sandy Hook Quarry, New Jersey,
mirrors, each 10.2 × 10.2 cm.
© Estate of Robert Smithson / Licensed by VAGA,
New York, NY

38 | Robert Smithson, *Spiral Jetty*, 1970.
Black rock, salt crystals, earth, red water (algae),
7.6 × 38.1 × 3810 × 1.3 cm.
Installation: Great Salt Lake, Utah.
© Estate of Robert Smithson / Licensed by VAGA,
New York, NY

39 | Alan Sonfist, *Time Landscape*, 1965.
Installation detail: New York.

In the career of Christo and Jeanne-Claude, these artists have drawn attention to their chosen sites in an enchanting yet detailed fashion. For instance, *Wrapped Reichstag, Berlin* (1977–95) (fig. 40), triggered close attention to every aspect of the building features; at the same time, the Reichstag gained an extraordinarily haunting character by the artists' handling of it. Their utterly deft rapprochement can be compared to the approach of Walter De Maria in *The Lightning Field* (1970–77) (fig. 41), in which a grid structure seems at first glance to have simply landed on the New Mexico desert. But upon actual inspection, the viewer detects all manner of calls and responses: between the physical site and its history for Native Americans, and the artist's formal decisions. Yet another approach can be seen in the installations of Patrick Ireland, whose rope drawings are initially a response to a given site. However, each becomes a *tour de force* of internal relationships that finally turns the viewer in on his or her own experience of the space created by the artist's ropes.

Another kind of rapprochement exists in the work of Jenny Holzer. Her installation for the Guggenheim Museum in Bilbao is a wondrous and brilliant use of the space as was her earlier installation for the Guggenheim Museum in New York City (1998–99) (fig. 43). In these, her formal gestures in the spaces are profoundly at one with the architectural surrounding, but as is her custom she also offers a plethora of content in the form of her words. The result is a synthesis of the rapprochement and intervention approaches.

Janet Cardiff created an altogether different sort of traversal in her work entitled *Real Time* (fig. 42) for the Carnegie International exhibition in 1997. To start with, she spent a good deal of time investigating the site for ideas, as all site-specific artists do. Then, utilizing the technique of the handheld, digital camera, she accompanied the viewer on a walk through the entire Carnegie Institute complex in Pittsburgh. The experience was physical, of the space, of sound,[50] and of one's perambulation. Cardiff's script was at once eerie and immediate in the headset, as one explored this fascinating complex of buildings. Though time and space were real, and this installation perfectly melded with the site, enhancing it and making it all the more fascinating, even gripping, an added, enchanted reality pertained by virtue of her soliloquy. Indeed, with sound and sight so piqued, the viewer gained a highly synesthetic experience. Cardiff suggests an interesting parallel when she observes: "Kids today can read books, watch TV and listen to a CD at the same time and get meaning out of all of them."[51] Similarly, her highly layered works appeal in particular to a youthful audience or to those open to this type of contemporary experience.

41 | Walter De Maria, *The Lightning Field*, 1977.
Installation: Quemado, New Mexico.

When Germano Celant wrote his important narrative of installation in 1982, he declared that the main distinction imparted from the early part of the century was between the surrealist and constructivist type of work.[52] But with the onrush of interest in installation in the last forty years or so, there has been a great expansion and evolution, with installation being propelled into a new stage of its development. The influence of installation is apparent everywhere. No longer content to simply install a group of discrete objects, painters and sculptors as diverse as Ellsworth Kelly and Gerhard Richter, and Matthew Barney (see fig. 44) and Damien Hirst, are making installations of their discrete works.

Andreas Huyssens described culture as always seeking a "genuine encounter with the real ... to hide the fact that the real is in agony due to the spread of simulation."[53] In artists' eternal quest toward greater realism, installation becomes the latest manifestation and achievement in that quest, offering the most profound contact yet with the real. Though it is among the oldest of art practices, recent incarnations of installation typify contemporary thinking. Many artists are demonstrating that for them discrete works of art are not adequate to express the complexities of this age, nor is the traditional, exalted object appropriate for the present time. This is not to say, yet again, that painting is dead, only that it will often be subsumed into larger contexts. And with the use of popular media, for example video and photography, and unpretentious materials, installation projects a more immediate impact on contemporary audiences than conventional media. Installation therefore represents a radical edge, blandly subsuming when not critiquing all that is conventional.

In a fascinating declaration about the current state of music, the composer Philip Glass could have been speaking to the situation in the visual arts:

> For me the great event of the 20th century was not the
> continuation of the central European avant-garde to the last
> gasp. I see the great musical adventure of our time as the
> emergence of a world-music culture, which crosses lines of
> geography, race and music.[54]

As with music, the practice of installation throughout the world creates an artistic cross-fertilization, one that minimizes the effect of the early twentieth-century European avant-garde on current developments and, instead, promotes hybridization of every imaginable kind. The very nature of an installation gives the artist an extraordinary opportunity by which

42 | Janet Cardiff, *In Real Time,* 1997. Audio, video walk.
Installation detail: Carnegie Library, Pittsburgh.

43 | Jenny Holzer
Untitled (Selections from Truisms, Inflammatory Essays, The Living Series, The Survival Series, Under a Rock, Laments and Child Text), 1989.
Extended helical tricolor L.E.D. electronic-display signboard. Installation detail: Solomon R. Guggenheim Museum, New York, 1998–99.

44 | Matthew Barney, *The Cremaster Cycle*, 1994–2002. Installation detail: The Solomon R. Guggenheim Museum, New York, 2003.

to accommodate complex views of time, space, cultural diversity, philosophy, imagination, and cultural criticism. That Rauschenbergian interest in the gap between art and life has been replaced by an artistic statement that contains both poles within itself. And at a time when the abstruse mysteries of some contemporary art leave general audiences uninterested if not hostile, installation art gives the opportunity for a broader sweep into the public sector, through its subjects, techniques, and effects that are completely available to the uninitiated.[55] Whereas the art of the 1960s and 1970s failed in gathering a large public, and failed in putting its arms around the cultural concerns of that period, the burgeoning and developing medium of installation goes a long way toward satisfying those goals.

A fascinating and still perhaps unanswerable question given that we do not yet have sufficient distance is what makes a successful installation? One might speak of an advance in the practice's technique by claiming an important achievement, for example, the capacity of installation to subsume more complex thematic material. But if the familiar old shibboleth called wonder is engendered in an audience still seeking such experiences, is that not a sign, too? If so engendered, perhaps artists will have taken wonder back from the lords of Disney, and reclaimed it for the art.

1 Ilya Kabakov calls his activity "'total' installation" in the title of his book *On the Total Installation*, trans. Gabriele Leupold, Cindy Martin, Bonn: Cantz Verlag, 1995; and in 1958 Allan Kaprow wrote an essay entitled "Notes on the Creation of a Total Art," in *Essays on the Blurring of Art and Life*, Berkeley: University of California Press, 1993.

2 Rosalind Krauss, "Sculpture in the Expanded Field," in *The Anti-Aesthetic: Post Modern Culture*, ed. Hal Foster, London and Sydney: Pluto Press, 1983, 31–42.

3 Kabakov says that the "viewer … finds himself inside of it, engrossed in it." Walls are required, Kabakov says, to separate the viewer from the external world, much as the picture frame operates at the edge of a painting. (Kabakov, 243, 256.) However, as described in this volume, this requirement only refers to some installations.

4 Michael Kimmelman attacked installation as "spectacle [that] may be allowed to supersede content," as if the former is by its very nature dangerous in art and the latter, whether spurious or not, is a prerequisite in and of itself. Michael Kimmelman, "Installation Art Moves In, Moves On," *New York Times*, Arts & Leisure, section 2, August 9, 1998, 1, 32. However, few art experiences can rival brilliant spectacle joined with content worth contemplating.

5 Robert Rauschenberg quoted in *Sixteen Americans*, (exh. cat.), ed. Dorothy C. Miller, New York: Museum of Modern Art, 1959, 58.

6 Quoted in David Bourdon, "The Razed Sites of Carl Andre," in *Artforum*, vol.5, no.2 (October 1966), 14–17.

7 Brian O'Doherty went further to announce that the "context devours the object, becoming it." *Inside the White Cube: The Ideology of the Gallery Space*, Santa Monica and San Francisco: The Lapis Press, 1986, 7. I have benefited enormously from O'Doherty's brilliant and still quite pertinent analysis.

8 *Robert Irwin*, New York: Whitney Museum of American Art, 1977, 23.

9 Kurt Schwitters, "Ich und meine Ziele," in *Das literarische Werke*, vol 5: *Manifeste und kritische Prose*, Cologne: DuMont, 1981.

10 Kabakov, 246.

11 Ibid., 257.

12 Duchamp's role in relation to installation has lately been explored in some depth. See Lewis Kachur, *Displaying the Marvelous: Marcel Duchamp, Salvador Dalí, and Surrealist Exhibition Installation*, Cambridge: MIT Press, 2001.

13 Quoted in an unpublished paper for a seminar at William College, fall 1999, Jeffrey T. Saletnik, "Installed Environments as Sensory Experience: Phenomenology and Walt Disney's World(s)," 3. Saletnik notes that Disney collaborated with Salvador Dalí on a film entitled *Destino* in 1946.

14 Ibid., 7.

15 Ibid., 1.

16 Kabakov, 244, 268–69.

17 Ibid., 272–3.

18 Pointed out in an unpublished paper for a seminar at Williams College, fall 1999, Jennie King, "Installation in Disguise: Finding Art in the Form of the Functional," 7.

19 Jean Baudrillard, *Simulacra and Simulation*, trans. Sheila Faria Glaser, Ann Arbor: University of Michigan Press, 1994, 6.

20 John Cage, *Silence*, Cambridge, Mass. and London: MIT Press, 1961, 76.

21 Quoted in Michael Fried, "Art and Objecthood," in *Minimal Art: A Critical Anthology*, ed. Gregory Battcock, New York: E.F. Dutton & Co., Inc., 1968, 131.

22 There are numerous other, similar works, including Edward Kienholz, *Barney's Beanery* (1965), Ben Vautrier, *Store Front* (1967), and Red Grooms, *The Bookstore* (1978).

23 Quoted in *Artists and Architects Collaborate: Designing the Wiesner Building*, Cambridge, Mass. and London: MIT Press, 1985, 62, 66.

24 Quoted in *Munster Sculpture Projects*, 1997, 491.

25 Daniel Buren, "Notes on Work in Connection with the Places Where It is Installed. Taken Between 1967 and 1975, Some of Which Are Specially Summarized Here for the September/October 1975 Edition of Studio International," *Studio International*, 190 (Sept. – Oct., 1975), 125.

26 The Corner Reliefs by Vladimir Tatlin, (1914–15), are certainly a major precedent for sculptures that take into account their surrounding spaces.

27 Robert Morris, "The Present Tense of Space," in *Art in America*, 66, no.1 (Jan. – Feb., 1978), 76.

28 Donald Judd's sculptures could be cited in this regard, too, for these address real spaces. For instance, his stacked units create a connection between the floor and ceiling of a room.

29 For more on this aspect, see O'Doherty, 13.

30 See, for instance, Roselee Goldberg, "Space as Praxis," in *Studio International*, 190 (Sept. – Oct. 1975), 134; and Nicholas Oliveira, Nicola Oxley, Michael Petry, *Installation Art*, Washington, D.C.: Smithsonian Institution Press, 1994, 29.

31 Serra discusses this in Michael Auping, *Drawing Rooms*, Fort Worth: Modern Art Museum of Fort Worth, 1994, 108.

32 Ibid., 107.

33 Buren, *Studio International*, p.125.

34 William Anastasi incised cuts into the walls of galleries and museum spaces, this to literally "undercut" the ostensible neutrality of the art environment. Like the destructive effect of graffiti, Anastasi's actions despoiled the place where one might expect to see art. Likewise, Gordon Matta-Clark cut large, often nicely geometrical holes in the sides of buildings.

35 The root in a performance for an installation is also the technique of Joseph Beuys, as well as Jonathan Borofsky's wall drawings within installations, and, on occasion, Joan Jonas, among others.

36 Miwon Kwon, "One Place After Another: Notes on Site Specificity," in *October*, 80 (Spring 1997), 87.

37 Discussed in an unpublished paper for a seminar at Williams College, fall 1999, Lisa Dorin, "Installation as a Transcultural Language," 3–4.

38 Thomas McEvilley, "Tracking the Indian Diaspora," in *Art in America*, 86, no. 10 (Oct. 1998), 75.

39 There is a more benign version of artists' participation at museums, with the practice of museums engaging them to make installations of their collections, as at MAK, Vienna, and the Artists Choice series at the Museum of Modern Art. Also, Robert Wilson's installations at the Stuck Villa, Munich, and in Copenhagen.

40 Goldberg, 134.

41 O'Doherty, 55.

42 Roald Naasgard, *Structures for Behaviour: New Sculptures by Robert Morris, David Rabinovitch, Richard Serra and George Trakas*, Toronto: Art Gallery of Ontario, 1978, 4.

43 Morris, 78.

44 See also *Casa Balla* (1925) by Giacomo Balla, where all surfaces are made into one, with walls flowing into paintings.

45 Cited in Mary Anne Staniszewski, *The Power of Display*, Cambridge Mass., and London: MIT Press, 1999, 37.

46 Theo van Doesburg and the De Stijl group, though mostly painters, experimented uniting their medium with architecture; surprisingly, they made the former serve the latter. As their paintings were completely abstract, the resulting structures had a remarkable purity about them, with a freshness of materials, colors, and forms. Few objects were to be found there, and everything was seamlessly united.

47 Subsequently, Lissitsky's *Abstract Cabinet* (1925), "improved" the way museums exhibit by making certain the walls and works of art formed a harmonious environment.

48 Another experiment in this regard is the present author's *Andre, Buren, Irwin, Nordman: Space as Support*, Berkeley: University Art Museum, 1979.

49 In this regard, compare Moholy-Nagy's Light-Space Modulator (1922–30), in which the sculpture calls attention to the surroundings; Michael Snow's oeuvre; and, more recently, Olafur Eliasson's *Your Now is my Surroundings* (2000), at Bonakdar Jancou Gallery, New York. All of these examples are movable.

50 A major figure in the area of sound installation is Max Neuhaus; cf. his *Final Source Search* (1977), in Times Square, New York City.

51 Meeka Walsh, intro., and Robert Enright, interview, "Pleasure Principals: The Art of Janel Cardiff and George Bures Miller," in *Border Crossings*, 20, no.2 (Summer 2001), 33.

52 Germano Celant, "A Visual Machine: Art Installation and its Modern Archetypes," (exh. cat.) in Documenta 7, vol.2, Kassel, 1982, XVII.

53 Andreas Huyssens, *Twilight Memories, Marking Time in a Culture of Amnesia*, New York: Routledge, 1995, 30.

54 Philip Glass, "George Harrison, World-Music Catalyst and Great-Souled Man," *New York Times*, Arts & Leisure, part 2, December 9, 2001, 33.

55 Oliveira describes the evolution that "extend[s] the area of practice from the studio to the public space," 7.

PHOTOGRAPHIC ACKNOWLEDGMENTS

Fig. 1   Photo: Hans Hinz.

Fig. 2   Photo: Nicolò Orsi Battaglini

Fig. 3   Photo courtesy Sprengel Museum, Hannover. © 2003 Artists Rights Society (ARS), New York / VG Bild-Kunst, Bonn.

Fig. 4   Photo courtesy Bildarchiv Preussischer Kulturbesitz, Berlin.

Fig. 5   Photo: Joan Broderick, Courtesy Philadelphia Museum of Art. © 2003 Artists Rights Society (ARS), New York / ADAGP, Paris / Succession Marcel Duchamp.

Fig. 6   Photo: Graydon Wood, Courtesy Philadelphia Museum of Art. © 2003 Artists Rights Society (ARS), New York / ADAGP, Paris / Succession Marcel Duchamp.

Fig. 7   © Disney Enterprises, Inc.

Figs. 8a and 8b   Photo courtesy of the estate of Juan Munoz and Marian Goodman Gallery, New York.

Fig. 9 and pl. 2   Photo courtesy the artist and Matthew Marks Gallery, New York. Photo: Bill Jacobson.

Fig. 10 and pl. 3   Photo courtesy Ilya and Emila Kabakov. © Ilya Kabakov.

Fig. 11 and pl. 1   Photo: eeva-inkeri, courtesy Paula Cooper Gallery, New York. © Jonathan Borofsky.

Fig. 12   © Claudio Abate.

Fig. 13   Philadelphia Museum of Art: Gift (by exchange) of Mrs. Herbert Cameron Morris. Photo: Graydon Wood, courtesy Philadelphia Museum of Art. © Artists Rights Society (ARS), New York / ADAGP, Paris / Succession Marcel Duchamp.

Fig. 14   Abby Aldrich Rockefeller Folk Art Museum, Williamsburg, VA.

Fig. 15   Photo: Robert McElroy, Licensed by VAGA. © Claes Oldenburg and Coosje van Bruggen.

Fig. 16   Photo courtesy Matthew Marks Gallery, New York.

Fig. 17   Photo: Uwe Walter; courtesy Ronald Feldman Fine Arts, New York.

Fig. 18 and pl. 4   Photo courtesy Gavin Brown's enterprise, New York.

Fig. 19 and pl. 5   Photo courtesy Max Protetch Gallery, New York. © 2003 Estate of Scott Burton / Artists Rights Society (ARS), New York.

Fig. 20 and pl. 6   Photo courtesy the artist and Senior & Shopmaker Gallery, New York.

Fig. 21 and pl. 7   © Jorge Pardo and The Fabric Workshop and Museum, Philadelphia.

Figs. 22a and 22b   © Daniel Buren.

Fig. 23   Photo: John Schiff, Philadelphia Museum of Art, lent by Mme. Marcel Duchamp. © 2003 Artists Rights Society (ARS), New York / ADAGP, Paris / Succession Marcel Duchamp.

Fig. 24   Photo courtesy Paula Cooper Gallery, New York. © Carl Andre / Licensed by VAGA, New York.

Fig. 25   Installation: Los Angeles, Ace Gallery. © Richard Serra.

Fig. 26   Watson F. Blair Prize Fund; W.L. Mead Endowment; Twentieth-Century Purchase Fund; Through prior gift of Joseph Winterbotham; Gift of Lannan Foundation, 1997.162. Photograph by Susan Einstein. Photograph © 2001, The Art Institute of Chicago. © 2003 Bruce Nauman / Artists Rights Society (ARS), New York.

Fig. 27   Photo: Gary Kruger, courtesy the artist.

Figs. 28a and 28b   Photo: Kathy Dillon; courtesy Barbara Gladstone Gallery, New York.

Fig. 29 and pl. 14   Photo courtesy Deitch Projects, New York. © Vanessa Beecroft.

Fig. 30   Photo courtesy the artist and Galerie Lelong, New York.